God
at
Ground
Zero

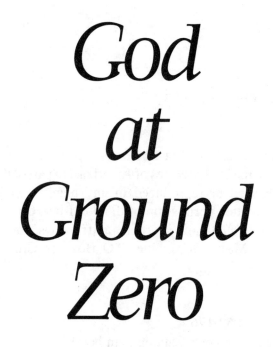

God
at
Ground
Zero

*The Manhattan Project and a Scientist's
Discovery of Christ, the Creator*

Curt Sewell

Master
Books

First printing: July 1997

ISBN: 0-89052-176-4
Library of Congress Catalog Number: 97-70170

Cover design by Steve Diggs & Friends, Nashville, TN

DEDICATION

This book is dedicated to my Lord and Saviour Jesus Christ, and to the edification and growth of His people, especially to students and their parents.

ACKNOWLEDGMENTS

I'd like to thank my wife, Wanda B. Sewell, for all that she has done to make this book possible. Without her help and encouragement, her patience in assisting with the proof-reading and constructive proof-listening, this could never have been completed.

I'm also thankful to critical reviewers, physicist Dr. Richard Beeler, geologist Mr. Bruce Kososki, biologist and dentist Dr. Peter Rashe. In part, they showed some disagreement with some of my concepts, but that disagreement led to improvements in the text and a better presentation. Any errors in the text are my own.

Contents

PREFACE

For years I felt as if I were sitting on a fence, wavering between two semi-firm beliefs. This was an uncomfortable position, because both sets of doctrines were important to me, and they each seemed to possess good foundational reason.

As a child, I had been taught that humankind had descended via an evolutionary route from the apes. For proof, I was told about fossils of early humans, such as the "Piltdown man," widely acclaimed as the "missing link."

But as a young adult, I had accepted Jesus Christ as my Saviour, and had learned to believe that the Bible was true. A simple reading of the Bible seemed to teach conclusively that God had created the world and all of its contents in six days, thousands of years ago.

In college, my belief in evolution became stronger, because I learned more details, such as the phylogenetic relationships between all of the various creatures around us. I was taught about radioactive dating methods (still in early stages), and how they "proved" that the earth was many hundreds of millions of years old.

In my first professional job, in an early atomic weapons lab of World War II, I became acquainted with several world-famous physicists. Although my own work in electronics had nothing to do with evolution, a number of conversations with these "experts" involved cosmology and age-of-the-earth topics. Surely all these great scientists must know the truth.

In the late 1950s, I became chief engineer of a company whose business was radiochemical analyses and radio-dating measurements. Part of my duties involved designing better instruments to perform these measurements. Of course, I had to learn more about radioactivity and the theory of geochronology, as well as the importance of various foundational assumptions. I was soon beginning to feel like an expert in some phases of this work.

But I was also active in Christianity, and there was definitely a conflict. On Sundays, I could believe the Bible, but on workdays I had to disregard important biblical sections. There seemed to be no easy reconciliation.

I tried a number of compromises, such as the "six-long-day theory," then the idea of "progressive creation." I even tried to digest the idea of a gap between Genesis 1:1 and 1:2, which involved a former creation. None of these seemed to make sense, from either point of view. I finally settled into my own version of "theistic evolution," but there were obvious problems. It was discouraging; was real truth non-existent?

Then, in the late 1960s, a friend loaned me a copy of a paper called the *Bible-Science NewsLetter*. I found that there were actually some real scientists who believed the literal truth of the biblical account of creation. I was surprised, but also dubious. These people must not understand the real facts of either position; they must be fanciful dreamers. So I began to search for more study materials.

I found a book by Morris and Whitcomb, *The Genesis Flood*, that discussed actual scientific evidence, showing that maybe the Great Flood was real.[1] I learned of the *Creation Research Society Quarterly*, published by a group which required an advanced scientific degree plus a commitment to the principles of a sudden six-day creation. Their technical papers were well-written. But I was still stubborn;

belief in science and evolution was ego-satisfying, and I wanted to maintain the respect of scientific friends.

I read as much about creationism as I could get my hands on, but I also studied many polemics against creationism written by evolutionists. I was surprised that most of their diatribes were not factual; their criticisms showed religious prejudice, and their defenses only sounded like speculations.

I read books and articles written by evolutionists, looking for solid facts that could act as some sort of proof that evolution was true. But I didn't find many real evidences that could serve this function. Instead, each speculative theory served as a steppingstone for the next idea. It was mostly a paper chain.

Finally I realized that a choice between the two positions was not dictated by the facts or evidences; it was basically a question of one's philosophy — in effect, his religion! This realization took me about five years to reach and, when it finally became clear in my mind, left me no choice. Jesus said, "You can't serve God and Mammon" (Matt. 6:24). I had been vainly trying to serve both. My full commitment to God and His magnificent creation was slow in coming, but finally became complete. Now I've spent the last 20-some years in more study, and in trying to spread the news that creation is a better explanation than is evolution.

Now, after discussing these issues with many other people, I've found that deception is widespread. The opposition to creationism is led by powerful forces. In the fall of 1981 the National Academy of Sciences and the National Association of Biology Teachers met for the purpose of "evolving a coordinated response to the so-called scientific creationists. . . ."

One outcome of this meeting was the formation of Committees of Correspondence to work at the grassroots level. Then in 1983 an umbrella group, the National Center for Science Education, was formed to support and coordinate their activities. Their booklet, *Voices for Evolution*, was published in 1989. This is a collection of political statements from a wide variety of scientific, religious, and educational organizations, denouncing creationism. These statements do not speak of factual evidence, but of philosophy and political action. Many of these use almost identical phraseology, showing that a common author had distributed sample papers that were adopted by each of the participating groups, possibly without full discussion. These groups, formed for the purpose of combating belief in creation, have prestigious-sounding names and are financed by grants from several foundations and by taxpayer-supported government sources. No wonder they're powerful and have been so effective; they've helped to mandate the teaching that "evolution is a fact" in the public schools of many states.

Of course, there are also several creationist groups trying to influence public opinion. A few try to get creationism included in public schools, but most realize that the legal process has all but precluded that. These all operate "on a shoestring," financed by contributions from supporters. None have the backing of rich foundations or grants from government. Some are forced to spend precious resources defending themselves against attacks from evolutionist forces.

There have been a number of creationist books published; these range in quality from "pretty good" to "excellent." A few of the most striking books, in terms of describing the weakness and deception of evolutionist ideas, come from good scientists who are not creationists. Most of the creationist authors write from a religious perspective; most of these include scientific material, but often those parts are not as well-documented as they could be.

That leads to the reason I felt driven to write this book. Students need a source that is easy to read, while at the same time one that offers accurate, well-documented information to counter the misinformation that's often taught in schools and the entertainment media. Their parents need a source they can use to assist these students in evaluating the religious and scientific truth of those who are molding their future.

Belief in either creation or evolution does not just bear on one's scientific outlook. It affects a person's view toward many social issues such as the abortion controversy, medical advances, public health, environmental issues that affect regulating processes, the proper role of government and how it interacts with personal rights, etc.

One's belief about origins also has a profound effect on his religious outlook. A belief that we owe our existence to blind chance, acting in a purely materialistic way, is not likely to lead us to a strong belief in a personal God; it's quite likely to put us in the scoffer's camp. From either viewpoint, this is an important aspect of life — one that affects our spiritual outlook.

The world has recently been amazed at the transformation that has begun in the lands that used to be the Union of Soviet Socialist Republics. Since 1917 this vast domain was locked into a harsh dictatorship, and the world has suffered because of it. Two key factors of their communistic doctrine were their official insistence on atheism and evolution.

Near the end of 1992 Evgeniy Kurkin, deputy minister of education for the Republic of Russia, was quoted (by Dr. Charles Stanley) as saying:

> It is true that our country has many problems. However the greatest problem we have is that God does not live in our land any longer. Seventy years ago we closed Him out of our country, and it has caused so many problems in our society we cannot count them. It has undermined and caused great caverns to run beneath our society, and

made it collapse. We must put God back into our country, and we must begin with our children.[2]

There were many factors that led to this tremendous change in their governmental system. Economics is touted as the major cause. Yet we can't discount that in the early 1980s one of Russia's top scientists, biologist Dr. Dmitri A. Kuznetsov, converted from evolutionism to scientific creationism after reading material from Dr. Henry Morris and other Institute for Creation Research scientists. Some time later, he turned from atheism to a strong belief in God. He helped to organize a group of several hundred Russian Christian creationist scientists, and opened the door to several world conferences on creationism.

Since then, Russia has enthusiastically opened its doors to the Christian gospel, and is incorporating biblical material into its public education system. These people, after years of having been deprived of a knowledge of God, now recognize that their problems were caused by "closing God out of our country."

It's ironic and frightening that just as Russia is opening its doors to godly teaching, America is closing hers. Russian Deputy Education Minister Kurkin went on to say, "Worldwide educational reform may actually spread from Russia, which is setting the stage and pattern for return to moral Bible values in the schools."[3]

Surely, one of the most important problems that America faces is its decline in godly morals, and the sad fact is that our educational system is leading us in this downhill plunge.

The teaching in our school systems that we owe our existence only to materialistic evolution is the scientific core, or foundation, on which our slide to disaster is based. If America is to survive, we must recognize the fallacy of this godless foundation, we must rise up and insist that our younger generation realize the truth — that our reason for being and our source of blessing is the Almighty Creator God.

It is my prayer that this book may help to make students and parents aware of the actual truth of how our world and its inhabitants came into existence.

About This Book Title

My original "working title" was much too prosaic (*Compare: Creation vs. Evolution*), so my publisher suggested changing it. At first I was shocked, but I've come to like it. Let me explain.

When I was 20 years old and an army technician, I was assigned to Los Alamos — the secret laboratory of the World War II Manhattan Project. Our job was to develop an atomic weapon, and I was a witness to the world's first atomic explosion.

That moment had a strong impact on my life, as well as on the world. I was blessed to have been one of the few people who actually saw that world-changing blast. That was over 50 years ago, and most of the others who were there are now gone.

The term "ground zero" can have several meanings — the spot directly under the tower on which that bomb exploded, but also it's a synonym for "epicenter," "a point of origin," "the aiming point," and others — all related to the central point of action. At the time of that test, I wasn't thinking of God, but just the fact that the bomb actually worked in spite of its preliminary structure and a myriad of primitive connections, showed that many people must have been praying. God was there! In less than a month, this device was directly responsible for the ending of that terrible war.

Now I know that God was actually the one who was at the first "Ground Zero," at the instant that Genesis describes as "In the beginning, God created the heavens and the earth." He was the Great Creator, and was certainly at the central point of action. After realizing the literal truth of those opening chapters of Genesis, I've come to recognize that

God is at the "ground zero" of my own life. He is the reason I exist, and the one for whom I try to live. And I'm looking forward to some day being at His final "ground zero" in heaven.

Curt Sewell
Livermore, CA

Endnotes

[1]John C. Whitcomb and Henry M. Morris, *The Genesis Flood* (Phillipsburg, NJ: P & R Publishing, 1961).
[2]Dr. Charles Stanley, Atlanta, GA, "In Touch" sermon, 1993.
[3]Ibid.

Chapter 1

HOW I GOT
TO WHERE I AM

... VIA THE WORLD'S
FIRST ATOMIC BOMB

I was lying face down in the damp sand, peering through the pre-dawn darkness. Around me I could barely detect the dark hulks of other men, each lying prone with an olive green army raincoat clutched in a hand. Although we'd had some rain a couple of hours earlier, the sky was now almost clear and I could even see a few stars. I shivered. Even in mid-July, this southern New Mexico desert got cold at night.

We all waited expectantly, in fearful eagerness, and finally heard an officer's shout, "Okay, men, cover up — it should be in less than a minute, now." Each of us pulled a raincoat open, awkwardly tugging it over our heads and backs, while still lying prone. We had been told to be sure that the raincoat completely covered our heads and blocked our eyes, then to lie face down with our eyes clamped shut. No one knew what that blinding flash would really be like, but no one wanted his eyes to be damaged.

Some of us knew that the name of these hills — *Jornada del Muerte* (Journey of Death) had originated with the Spanish conquistadors some 300 years earlier. They had been ambushed by Apache Indians who were furious that these foreigners were invading their lands. Most of us simply called the place by its code name, "the Trinity site."

It was July 16, 1945. I was 21 years old, a young sergeant in the U.S. Army's Special Engineer Detachment. For most of the past year, I had worked between 18 and 22 hours a day, seven days a week. Now the moment of truth was almost on us — the day we had been working toward. Would the gadget work?

Our laboratories were 200 miles from here, high on the eastern slope of the Jemez Mountains of northern New Mexico. They occupied a series of finger mesas and canyons, accessible only by a narrow, winding road that snaked upward along a shelf that had been carved into the sides of steep cliffs. In some spots, one could see downward several hundred feet to the canyon floor, dotted with dusty pine trees. At the same time, on the other side of the car, the cliff was almost straight up to a mesa that was out of sight. The main set of log buildings had at one time been the Los Alamos Ranch School, a place where rich men could send their sons to absorb some scholarship while at the same time learning to ride horses and explore the rugged mountains. Now the land had been taken over by the U.S. Army, to serve as the secret laboratories that would bring an end to this terrible World War II.

My thoughts had been wandering as I lay in the dark, damp sand. Suddenly, I saw, *but also felt,* an intense flash of light, even penetrating the coat over my head, and with my eyes clamped shut. It was eerie because it was so intense, and yet absolutely silent. I waited a few seconds, then cautiously looked out. The entire southern sky was brilliant, then gradually the edges faded, to frame an almost spherical cloud of colored light. It was boiling with shifting colors —

red, blue, purple, and green. It reminded me of a bucket of oily soup bubbling slowly as it boiled. A few seconds later a column of smoke seemed to rise from the ground and meet the cloud, forming the well-known mushroom shape.

I'm not sure how long we stood, mesmerized by this eerie light. Awed whispers could be heard in the silent dawn. Then suddenly the ground shook, and a sharp boom and a tremendous tumbling sound began — reverberating back and forth as the shockwave bounced from one hill to another. Even from 18 miles distant, the sound seemed deafening.

✳ ✳ ✳

Some 30 years later, in about 1975, a co-worker said to me, "Curt, I want to thank you for saving my life." He went on to explain that he had been raised in Hong Kong, had been captured by the Japanese in early 1942 as a young American boy, and had been kept in several Japanese prison camps. Their treatment kept getting worse, until in the spring of 1945 fellow prisoners had been killed to conserve food. His group was scheduled to be next. Then, with no explanation, all the guards disappeared and the gates were forced open. He learned later that the atomic bomb had just been dropped on Hiroshima and the guards had deserted.

There have also been others who thanked me for my part in making those atomic bombs that ended the worst war in world history, and saved hundreds of thousands of lives that otherwise would have been lost in a last desperate invasion of Japan.

✳ ✳ ✳

How does one describe the journey from Point A to Point B? Sometimes that answer is simple, but if the journey traverses thousands of miles, over 50 years, and involves blind alleys and forks in the road, the description becomes a biographical travelogue.

In this case, Point A involved this writer as a young man just out of college, with an intense interest in science and a naive acceptance of all that "science" proclaimed, and a dream of a career in either a laboratory or a university. That dream was first interrupted, then enhanced, by my enlistment in the U.S. Army during World War II, and my participation in the development and testing of the world's first atomic bomb at the army's secret laboratory at Los Alamos, New Mexico.

Point B shows that same man, much older and more mature, having realized most of those early dreams, but now having a much different outlook. I now realize that my early eager acceptance of all that science proclaimed was just a belief in a facade — a materialistic smoke screen whose foundation was shifting sand. This change in outlook — the realization that "science" was not really the ultimate truth it claims to be — didn't take place overnight. It took some 20 years for me to finally realize that God and His Bible take precedence. For me, this wasn't an easy transition — it involved much study and soul-searching. Many of the steps I went through involved things we read about in history books today, and many people find a fresh perspective on some of these to be quite interesting. This book is written to describe some of these. It's been a fun trip.

I'd like to emphasize that I lay no claim to having been a prestigious scientist, although my name is listed in "Who's Who in Technology" and also in "Directory of American Men and Women of Science." I'm now retired after spending some 45 years as a professional electronics circuit-design engineer, almost always working in some field of nuclear science, and much of that time was spent on projects that were on the cutting edge of technology. I've been rather closely associated at times with men who were definitely prestigious. These associations gave me a keen awareness of scientific practices and beliefs.

WORLD WAR II

Beginning in about 1937 the world became anxious about the military activities of Germany, Italy, and Japan. But, since the U.S. wasn't directly involved in either area, most Americans that I knew were only mildly concerned. Then, about six months after I graduated from high school, on December 7, 1941, the Japanese air force unexpectedly bombed our naval and air bases at Pearl Harbor, Hawaii. Our Pacific armed forces were almost wiped out. Suddenly we were at war. A number of my friends went into the military, and several were killed. Our forces kept suffering defeats for the first year or two.

I was in college and was told that since I showed aptitude for science and mathematics, I should join a reserve unit and stay in school as long as possible, then become some sort of technical officer. But in June of 1943 I was called into active service. That summer was the most miserable of my life, going through infantry basic training in the heat of a Texas summer at Camp Fannin. Near the end of those months, officers came through and conducted batteries of IQ tests and personality tests, giving no answers to the questions we asked. At graduation, I was told that I'd been selected to attend the Army Specialized Training Program, or ASTP.

I learned that this was advanced classroom work, and was held at a number of regular colleges. I spent the next nine months at the University of New Hampshire, and learned that New Hampshire winters were just as cold and uncomfortable as Texas summers were hot and uncomfortable. But the classwork was fascinating to me. The curriculum was very similar to the technical portions of a Master of Science degree, except that there were no classes in English, economics, or other non-technical subjects. It was all solid science and engineering, which suited me just fine. Others in my classes were about like me — bright young men with some regular college behind them, but not yet having graduated. The pace was fast and heavy.

But there were occasional off-hours, and these, too, were fascinating. Since this was wartime, most of the civilian males who would normally have been in college were in the armed forces, leaving the campus filled with only female students. Our unit of a few hundred young GI's comprised about the only bunch of men available for these girls, and we had our choice of "the pick of the litter." Naturally, not many of us complained!

My final term of ASTP was at Virginia Polytechnic Institute. Then, in September 1944, teams of test-givers and interviewers arrived, with more batteries of questions. I was selected to go into something called the Manhattan Project, which I had never heard of because it was surrounded with secrecy. A number of us were sent to Oak Ridge, Tennessee, not far from Knoxville. I was there for a couple of weeks of more interviews and tests before two of my friends and I were chosen for assignment to some unnamed place in New Mexico. This turned out to be Los Alamos, but since this name was highly classified and never used in public, it was just called "the Hill."

America's transportation system during the 1940s was poor. Automobiles were well-developed, but most highways only had one lane in each direction. During the war years, tires and gasoline were severely rationed, so that no one could drive far without a good reason. The twin-engine propeller-driven DC-3 was the best airliner, and air schedules were almost nonexistent. Buses were always overcrowded, hot and slow. Trains were the most common means of long-distance travel, but they, too, were often subject to long delays. Military shipments took priority.

When three of us were selected at Oak Ridge for assignment to Los Alamos, we were handed train tickets and a sealed envelope that we were not to open until the train had been underway for at least an hour. It said to get off the train at a stop called "Lamy, New Mexico," and then to call a certain phone number for further instructions. We were given four days to report there.

We got as far as Kansas City, and were told that no more trains were scheduled to go into New Mexico for several days. This wouldn't allow enough time, so we walked through the rail yards, asking trainmen where each train was headed. Finally a brakeman pointed to a train that should go through New Mexico on its way to the West Coast, so we just got on board. It turned out that this was a troop train, packed with U.S. marines bound for the Pacific. We were three stowaways, U.S. Army soldiers, surrounded by hundreds of hostile marines. Inter-service rivalries at that time were intense, and we were afraid for our lives. Fortunately we survived the trip.

We got off, as directed, at Lamy. Our hearts sank. There was one small train station building, about six dilapidated houses, no stores that we could see, and at least a million miles of sand in every direction. There were tumbleweeds and sagebrush, but no trees. Was this where we were to spend the rest of the war?

THE LOS ALAMOS LABORATORY

It turned out that our magic phone number was in Santa Fe, about 25 miles away, and we were told to just wait — someone would come and pick us up. Five hours later, a master sergeant came in an army van, drove us through Santa Fe and on, over roads that got increasingly rougher and filled with twisting turns. We were obviously climbing. Finally, at about midnight, we passed through a guard gate, were deposited at a barracks, and slept an exhausted sleep.

Next day, I saw that the "town," if it could be called that, looked like a typical small, temporary army community. Buildings were of frame construction, painted gray or olive-drab green, or covered with asphalt siding. The roads were not paved, and during the rainy seasons became quagmires of gumbo mud. But the surrounding country was beautiful. Pine and fir forests surrounded the town. In the summer there were the most magnificent thunder and lightning storms I've ever seen, and snow in the winter was sometimes a foot deep. But it didn't last more than a week, usually. Occasional deer, bears, and mountain lions were seen or heard around the outskirts of town.

Located about 35 miles northwest of Santa Fe on the Pajarito Plateau, this was an ideal place to maintain secrecy. The country was very rugged, consisting of finger mesas cut apart by steep-walled deep canyons. Behind us, the peaks of the Jemez range topped 10,000 feet; to the east was the Rio Grande valley, at about 5,000 feet. We were about halfway between, and could see across the valley for almost 100 miles to the Sangre de Christo mountains northeast of Santa Fe. At sunset these peaks took on a rosy glow, which led to that "Blood of Christ" name. Several Indian pueblos lined the banks of the Rio Grande.

When I reported for work, I learned that this was, indeed, a unique community. Operated by the government, its population was strangely mixed. Its only purpose for existence was for research and production of an atomic bomb which would be used to end this terrible war. I didn't learn what that purpose was for several months; we were just told that everything there was top secret. Such a project had been proposed by Einstein and a few other top scientists, but no one knew whether or not such a thing was feasible. Very few people had even heard that it might be theoretically possible.

The top positions in the laboratory were held by civilian scientists. Dr. J. Robert Oppenheimer from the University of California at Berkeley was in charge. He had selected a few dozen top scientists to perform the research. The lab was divided into divisions (mine was G-Division, which stood for "Gadget," the nickname for the bomb). Below that were various groups (mine was G-4 — Electronics). There was a central technical area, but much of the experimental work took place at outlying sites, for safety and security reasons. Explosions were often heard from these sites — tests to show how materials behaved under stress.

It had soon become apparent that many more than the original few dozen people would be needed. Many medium-level scientists had been drafted, placed in a special engineer detachment of the Army Corps of Engineers, and assigned to the lab. Many college students such as myself were given specialized training in the Army, then placed in the special engineers (or S.E.D.'s). Many of the S.E.D.'s were very capable scientists, others were young men who showed promise. Another category of laboratory personnel was made up of less-skilled civilians, many of whom were wives or family members of the scientific staff.

Thus the entire laboratory staff was a mixture of famous civilian scientists, less-famous civilians, and an array of army personnel, which later included women of the WAAC's. The chain of command was just as assorted. Dr. Oppenheimer (we all called him "Oppie") was the top man of the lab, but below him were civilians and military. Below them was another level of civilians and military. The distinction between these two categories was not at all sharp.

Support for the laboratory was just as strangely organized. Again, it was a mixed bag of people. Most of the security was provided by military police, but there was also a group of FBI men. Town services such as housing, transportation, road maintenance, food supplies, water, electricity, and all the services needed by families living in a completely isolated community, were under the responsibility of the army, and performed by the Army Post Engineer Detachment and civilian contractors.

My group leader was Wm. A. (Willy) Higinbotham, a small man with thick glasses and a large forehead, who always reminded me of an owl. Friendly and unassuming, he had a knack for helping those under him to develop their own capabilities. He also was prolific in making new circuit designs which advanced the art of electronic instrumentation. Shortly after the war's end, he was one of the founders of the Association of Los Alamos Scientists, a group dedicated to non-proliferation of nuclear weapons. I also became a charter member of this group. Later he became chairman of the Federation of American Scientists, which has renamed its Washington headquarters building "Higinbotham Hall." Ironically, his obituary, in November 1994, emphasized one of Willy's minor inventions, an electronic tennis game, and referred to him as "the father of video games."

Other senior staff members in our group included Matt Sands and Bill Elmore, both of whom had been physics professors before the war; Ernie Titterton, who was a member of the British Mission; Dick Watts; and others.

More famous names included scientists and professors from various prestigious places, mostly in the U.S., but some came from foreign countries. Most of those were refugees from Germany, Austria, Hungary, and Italy. Albert Einstein was an occasional visitor, but I never saw him. The best-known man whom I knew personally was world-famous physicist Niels Bohr, the Dane whose model of the atom, having a central nucleus circled by electrons in precise orbits, is still shown in textbooks. Bohr had escaped the Nazis in October 1943 and was carried in a small fishing boat from Copenhagen to Sweden. There he was put in the bomb bay of a British Mosquito bomber and flown to England, finally arriving in the U.S. But he almost didn't make it — his head was too big for the oxygen mask, and he had lost consciousness and was almost frozen when the plane arrived in England. At Los Alamos, his very presence was highly classified. His code name there was "Nick Baker." Not many knew who he really was.

Enrico Fermi had been the co-discoverer of nuclear fission in Italy. After escaping from the Fascists, he found his way to the University of Chicago and led the effort to build an atomic pile and produce the first chain reaction. I remember his eyes more than anything else — intensely piercing.

Edward Teller had come from Hungary. He walked with a limp, and had dark, bushy eyebrows and a heavy German accent. He always reminded me of a gruff bear. It was a poorly kept secret that he and Oppenheimer had several differences of opinion — Teller pushed for concentrating on building a hydrogen weapon, and later became known as the father of the hydrogen bomb. But it wouldn't have been possible at that time, because an H-bomb required a fission explosion as a trigger.

I didn't know John von Neumann until after the war. I spent some time in the late 1940s or early 1950s working with him on one of the first digital computers, a vacuum-tube monster called "the Maniac."

Louis Alvarez, Ed McMillan, and Emilio Segre had come from the University of California at Berkeley. Alvarez later became famous for his suggestion that an asteroid impacted the earth some 65 million years ago, creating a dust cloud that led to the extinction of the dinosaurs. My only contact with him was to design and build instrumentation for an experiment he called the racetrack, to measure wave velocity in a waveguide.

Louis Slotin was a Canadian physicist who became the first fatality in a nuclear radiation accident. In early 1945 he was trying to experimentally measure the mass required for a self-sustaining chain reaction. A screwdriver slipped, a pellet fell, the open test assembly became supercritical, and flooded the room with radiation. He died a few days later. Also severely burned was Al Graves, with whom I worked on several occasions. His wife Elizabeth (Diz) Graves was also a high-level physicist there.

Richard Feynman may have been the most brilliant young man on the Hill. He was a physicist and mathematician who worked in the theoretical division, and I knew nothing about his work. But his off-hours activities were legendary. Like many others, he chafed under rules of military secrecy, and made a game of seeing how far he could bend them. All our mail, both incoming and outgoing, was censored. We mailed our letters in unsealed envelopes for the censors to read, then seal. Feynman's wife was ill with a fatal disease, and he amused her by encoding messages in his letters to her. But the censors were not amused. Another of his "games" concerned the repositories, where classified documents were kept after hours. He would come to the lab late at night, somehow figure the combination to a safe, open it and put in a message "Guess Who?" then close it. The next day its guardian would find the message and report it to the FBI. They soon knew who was doing this, but he was too valuable a scientist to suffer more than a hand-slap.

Many of us played our own variety of "beat-the-security" game. One of my friends worked in the badge office, which produced the badges used to gain access to the tech area and other classified rooms. Another friend and I borrowed his key and used the photography equipment to make badges for ourselves, except these showed a picture of Matt Sand's dog instead of our own faces. We actually used these to enter the tech area several times. One sharper-than-usual MP finally noticed, said "Okay, now let's see your own badge," but didn't report us.

The man whom I remember most clearly was at first known to me only as Oppie. He seemed to have a habit of wandering through the labs at night, stopping for "bull sessions," visiting with us as we worked in long overtime periods. We usually welcomed the break. He was always dressed in shapeless khaki pants and a hat that had taken on its own shape through use and misuse. He talked of things like horseback rides he had taken through the Jemez Mountains, but never about our atomic mission. Later I learned that he was J. Robert Oppenheimer, the director of the entire laboratory.

The whole Manhattan District atomic project was under the responsibility of General Leslie Groves of the Army's Corps of Engineers in Washington. He tried to make the place run like a military installation should. But military details frustrated most of the civilian scientists, and Oppenheimer refused to give Groves free rein. Oppie was responsible for the technical work, and he insisted that scientists can't work "according to the rule book," like Groves wanted. One point of irritation on both sides was secrecy. Groves wanted to keep all work descriptions within strict compartments, never to be discussed openly. Oppenheimer insisted on freedom to discuss problems with fellow workers, thus making it more like a campus. One outcome of this was a series of colloquia, which I remember with pleasure.

Each week a colloquium was held, at which one of the senior staff members would discuss some topic. Attendance was limited to members who held white badges — those who had been cleared by security for access to top secret information. I received my white badge several months after I arrived at Los Alamos. Some of the topics involved review of the principles on which various groups were working, some discussed problems that still existed, and sometimes there were suggestions made from the floor as to how those problems might be open to solution. Some colloquia had to do with electronic circuit design. I never spoke at these, but counted it a privilege to be able to hear famous people speak in person.

I remember one colloquium where George Gamow described a theory that he and several colleagues had proposed — the "Big Bang" as an idea about the initial formation of the universe. At that time, the accepted theory was the "Steady State" model, proposed by Sir Fred Hoyle and others. At this time, very few had even heard of the Big Bang idea, and it struck me as pretty far-out. (I still think of it this way — I now believe in the Genesis account of God's creation.) It wasn't until the mid-1960s that the Big Bang theory was commonly accepted. This is actually the only time during my wartime stay at Los Alamos that I heard any discussion that involved the differences between the two basic beliefs about the origin of our world. At that time, I was still a believer in evolution and in the ancient age of the universe, because that was all I had been taught in school, and that's what all my colleagues believed. I'd never heard of "scientific creationism."

PRIMITIVE TECHNOLOGY

Electronic technology in those days would be unrecognizable to modern technicians. There were no transistors, IC chips, printed-circuit boards, or automatic assembly methods. Vacuum tubes were the only active devices available, and instruments were built by soldering in one component at a time, by hand. My first assignment was fabricating various specially designed instruments used in nuclear measurements or in explosive tests. All of our instruments had to be designed and built in our own shops; there were almost no commercially available sources, not even for oscilloscopes or pulse generators. Much ingenuity was required, both in design and construction. If we didn't have something, which was often, we improvised or designed and built it from scratch. This was true for test instruments, components, and construction methods.

Within two weeks I was advanced to trouble-shooting and repair, and it wasn't long before I took on the responsibility for some simple designs. This was fun, because it required the mathematical skills and electronic theories I had learned in ASTP during the previous year. But, for the duration of the war, my main duties involved fabrication and supervision. I took charge of a section of the electronic fabrication shop, which employed a mixture of less-skilled army personnel and civilian women, most of whom had almost no skill in electronics or the use of tools. During the day I taught them how to use a soldering iron and do most of the construction of simple instruments. At night I did other things, such as "debugging" the just-completed projects and making them work right. I began a schedule of working 18-to-22 hour days, for 6-1/2 days a week.

Intense work schedules of this sort were not uncommon for Los Alamos during the war. Most parts of the lab were officially on an 8-hour day, six days per week, but everyone who knew what the lab was striving to accomplish was very eager to get the job done quickly. We knew that if we were successful this terrible war would soon be over.

But there was so very much that was completely unknown, that must be studied carefully under almost impossible circumstances. There were two possible metals that could be used to produce a fission explosion — Uranium-235 and Plutonium-239. But U-235 was an extremely rare natural isotope of uranium. A huge plant had been built at Oak Ridge, Tennessee, to isolate and separate this isotope. But this was tremendously complicated and expensive. By early 1944 only small quantities had been obtained, not nearly enough to make a bomb. Plutonium is not a natural element, but must be manufactured in a nuclear reactor, or "atomic pile." Such a set of reactors was built at Hanford, Washington. But the first tiny bits of plutonium didn't become available until the spring of 1944, a few months before I arrived at Los Alamos.

There were also two possible methods of detonation. The earliest was called the "gun method," and was actually used in the first atomic bomb dropped on Japan. A naval cannon formed the bomb body. About half of a critical mass of fissionable metal was fastened securely at the muzzle end of the barrel and the projectile contained the other half. When the two collided, there was more than a critical mass, and the explosion occurred. But this was an extremely heavy and inefficient device and for various technical reasons couldn't be used with plutonium. It used U-235.

The "implosion" method was cleaner, more efficient, and could use plutonium. But the technical problems seemed almost insurmountable until early in 1945. The active material here was spherical, and was surrounded by almost conventional high explosives which had to be detonated in such a way that the shockwave surrounded the core in a smooth simultaneous squeeze, all the way around. No one knew how to achieve such a result.

For these reasons, a great many practical experiments had to be performed, using techniques that were far beyond anything previously known. Actual nuclear materials weren't available in any quantity, and the exact nuclear characteristics couldn't be known until they were. And these characteristics would determine the size of sphere and the amount of high explosive required. Each of these necessary parameters depended on other factors, and the spiraling circle of interdependent bits of knowledge made progress very difficult. For these reasons, much field testing was required, and every field test required electronic measuring equipment, and that was my part of the responsibility.

Massive bombing raids had done terrible damage to Japan, but hadn't seemed to bring war's end any closer. If we couldn't get at least two atomic bombs ready, an invasion of the Japanese mainland seemed necessary. Official estimates were that this would probably kill over a million Americans and Japanese.

THE TRINITY TEST

By February 1945, top scientists became confident that the implosion method would probably work, and all efforts began to concentrate in this direction. Since this would, if successful, result in an explosion massively bigger than any in history, and at this stage no one even knew for sure that a chain reaction could even be sustained, a test explosion of an actual bomb was deemed absolutely necessary. A mid-July 1945 date was set, and the already hectic work schedule accelerated. But technical problems still were overwhelming. Only tiny quantities of plutonium had even existed until May. Even in the last days before war's end, people carefully sifted through floor sweepings in the metallurgy labs to scrape together fissionable material. If a third bomb had been required for use on Japan, it would have taken months to produce.

Oppenheimer had led the search for a suitable test location the previous summer, and the choice finally settled on a spot in the northwest corner of the Alamagordo Air Base bombing range — an 18-by-24-mile valley, named by Spanish conquistadors "Jornada del Muerte" (Journey of Death) at the end of the 16th century. A little over 200 air miles south of Los Alamos, and many miles from the nearest highway, its isolation was superb, and yet people could shuttle from "the Hill" via Carco's Beechcraft Bonanzas without much difficulty. That was an interesting scenic flight, which I made on a number of occasions.

Ken Bainbridge was named director of the test operation, and helped choose the site. He urged Oppenheimer to come up with a code name for the test operation. Oppie happened to be relaxing with a book of John Donne's poems, and read the following lines:

Batter my heart, three-person'd God; for, you
As yet but knock, breathe, shine, and seek to mend.

He was inspired from this to coin the desired code name, Trinity.

President Roosevelt died on April 12, 1945. He and England's Winston Churchill were the only top-level national leaders who even knew about the atomic bomb project. Even Vice President Harry Truman didn't know of the laboratory's existence until the day after he became president. But he picked up the leadership traces very well. Russia's Josef Stalin, an ally with the U.S. and Britain at that time, had been kept in the dark. Even though Russia was allied with us against Germany and Italy, no one at the top level trusted them fully. All felt that the Communist machine would later try to dominate the world — a feeling that proved to be true.

But Russia had underground knowledge that such a project was being undertaken. They had planted at least two spies in our midst, and learned some of the details of bomb design and construction. Yet these men couldn't learn much about the future plans for the big test.

Klaus Fuchs was a brilliant theoretical physicist, a member of the British Mission and a quiet, withdrawn man. He had left Germany for England in 1934 to escape from Hitler, and became a British citizen in 1942. He was a dedicated Communist. I knew him slightly, but never had the chance to become friends. My main contacts with him were in the classified document reading room (a highly restricted area), where I saw him on a number of occasions studying intently. I wondered why he spent so much time there. I found out later that he was learning all he could, then funneling the information to Russia through contacts in Philadelphia, Julius and Ethyl Rosenberg. They were key links to Russia and, after the war, were executed in 1953 for espionage activities. In March of 1950 Fuchs was convicted in England of "communicat[ing] . . . information relating to atomic research . . . calculated to be . . . useful to an enemy." He was sentenced to 14 years in prison, but was expelled to East Germany in June of 1959. He married and became deputy director of the Institute for Nuclear Physics at Rossendorf. He died in January of 1988. David Greenglas, Ethyl Rosenberg's brother and another spy, was an S.E.D. who lived in the same barracks that I did. I didn't especially like him, because of his gruff demeanor, and his "know-it-all" attitude of superiority. He was a machinist by trade, and had a good opportunity to make sketches of things he made, and other things he saw in the shops — things such as molds for the high-explosive lenses which fit together around the nuclear core of an implosion bomb. These sketches found their way to Rosenberg, and thence to Russia.

But despite these security leaks, developments proceeded in good speed, and by early July everything was ready for the big Trinity test. This was still a highly classified event, and most of the people on the Hill didn't know anything about it. But the air became charged with anticipation. Those of us who had white badges and had access to secret information all longed for the chance to see this climactic test, even though at this time no one knew whether or not it would be successful. I had designed and built a couple of counters to measure the radiation from this test, but they were now successfully installed and working, so I had no official need to be there.

But some of the leaders took pity on me and several dozen others about like me — hard-working GI's who had put in a lot of hard work, but had no real function at Trinity. They put together a group of us, said we would be used to evacuate the area around in case of accident, and hauled us in army trucks to the site. I'm sure this was a manufactured excuse, because we were given absolutely no training in evacuation techniques. Weather was not favorable at first, and we loafed for a couple of days. But early in the morning of July 16, 1945, the big shot was fired. It worked better than almost anyone had dreamed. My memory of that event is described as the opening in this chapter.

A DUAL BLESSING

For some time before Trinity, I had charge of an electronic fabrication shop which employed a dozen or so people. Most of these were inexperienced women, and the rest were S.E.D.'s. One of the girls in the shop had arrived a couple of months before. Her name was Wanda Beall, and she had just graduated from high school in Alpine, Texas. For several months I was too busy to have any social life, so I didn't get to know her very well.

After the war was over, we began to date, and by October our feelings for each other intensified. But there was a problem — she was a dedicated Christian, and I was not. I had been raised in a Christian home and had attended church, but for the wrong reasons — I was more interested in the girls than in the sermons, and had never acknowledged Jesus as my Saviour and Lord. Wanda wanted me to become a Christian before we made any plans for marriage.

Los Alamos (or the Hill, as it was still known) was a town without a church of any kind. There was an army chaplain, but no chapel. Wanda and some of her friends had begun a Bible study fellowship several months before, and now she took me into its midst. I was impressed with the testimonies I heard there, and now I'm sure that I had been the subject of much prayer. In any event, after just a few weeks, I realized that my spiritual life had been zero, and felt a strong need of forgiveness for my sins. I asked Jesus into my heart, and felt like a new person. Those around me noticed a change in my appearance and behavior. I had become a Christian! That was almost 50 years ago, and I'm still extremely grateful for that change. I now have the power of the universe living within me, guiding and comforting me.

Now that she and I were both Christians, "members of the same team," we planned our marriage and set the date for two days before Christmas, on Sunday just after the church service (which was held in Theater #2). But we hadn't counted on the weather, and it didn't cooperate. Los Alamos was a temporary army post, set on a hill that had no water of its own, and was almost 2,000 feet above the Rio Grande River in the valley below. Our only source of water was a pipe that had been just laid on the surface of the ground, since it was only intended to be a temporary place. But that winter was severe. The pipeline froze and burst in mid-December, and the only source of drinking water was a series of army tank trucks that laboriously hauled water from the river. People carried buckets, pots, and pans to the central area where the trucks parked, filled them and carried them back to their living quarters. There were no baths or showers for anyone for two weeks or more. In order to reduce water consumption, the army issued emergency furloughs to as many of its men as could be spared, and civilians were encouraged to take a Christmas vacation. I was considered essential to the operation of our group, so I had to stay there.

My parents were able to come to the wedding, and arrived from Iowa Park, Texas, on a Saturday afternoon, tired from a long drive, and hoping for a relaxing hot bath and soft bed, but no such luxury awaited them. There was no water except by the glassful, and no guest hotel. Wanda's sister lived in a dormitory (with her husband), and they had left the Hill on vacation. So Dora and Red graciously offered their one room and bed to my parents. But the pipes in the shower room were dry, and no bath was available. My parents were accustomed to normal civilization, and thought that we were certainly in a primitive state — and they were right! Next day's church service was sparsely attended because of the two feet of snow on the ground, and the GI organist had been furloughed to save water, but we didn't care. It was certainly not a fancy wedding, but it has been a blessed marriage. We celebrated our 50-year anniversary on December 23, 1995. We have three sons and seven grand-children who are all successful. God has been good to us, and we're grateful.

In March 1946 I was discharged from the army and was offered a job by the University of California (which employed all of the civilians in the laboratory) as an electronics engineer. My salary was the grand sum of $275 per month. We thought that was wonderful. Salaries were based on prevailing wages in similar jobs in industry, except ours were a little higher to compensate for the isolation we endured in the mountains of New Mexico. But expenses were also low — the highest rent we ever paid there was $85 per month for a small three-bedroom house, utilities included. It's easy now to see the effect that inflation has had on our economy. We stayed in Los Alamos until 1957. We were beginning to feel like we'd be there forever, and were beginning to chafe because of the "Big Brother" atmosphere; the government owned everything, and controlled almost every aspect of our lives.

Then, in the spring of 1957 I received a surprise phone call from New York, from Dr. J. Lawrence Kulp, professor of geochemistry at Columbia University, and director of geochronology at Lamont Geological Observatory. He and some colleagues had a small company, Isotopes, Inc., in New Jersey, and they needed a chief engineer. He offered a pair of plane tickets and expenses so that my wife and I could go there, be interviewed for the job, and consider a move. I'd never heard of him before, and hadn't dreamed of trying to find another job, but the timing seemed right to get out from under the government oppression we were feeling. We took the trip, liked what we saw, and made the move in mid-August 1957.

ISOTOPES, INC.

My work at Isotopes, Inc. involved designing and supervising various types of measurements of trace amounts of radioactivity. These fell into two broad applications. Both types required the development of improved methods of minimizing errors involving background radiation and low counting rates.

The first involved determining the amount of radioactive debris from atmospheric testing of nuclear bombs that had contaminated the human food chain, and thence had been ingested by people all over the world. One of our large programs involved the analysis of bone samples from hospitals and morgues that were sent to us from many different countries. At that time no one knew how much radiation a person could tolerate without damage. This was considered to be a vital piece of information, and many different approaches were taken, by many government and private agencies, so as to intelligently plan public health strategies.

The prevailing opinion of most experts at that time was that there was a "threshold" amount of radiation a person could tolerate without damage, and we tried to find that threshold. It turned out that this concept was mistaken — most scientists now agree that any amount of radiation is damaging. Small doses just take longer for their effects to be realized. Today we often see newspaper reports that criticize some of those early experiments. We often forget that hindsight gives a clearer insight than was known by those with the immediate need at that time. The nuclear age was just beginning, and effects of small amounts of radiation were completely unknown. Scientists were scrambling to learn as much as possible, as soon as possible, so that they might be somewhat ready to deal with some possible emergency. After all, a nuclear attack from the USSR was considered quite likely in those days. During the late 1950s Russia did violate a test moratorium that was in place, with a series of massive hydrogen bomb blasts, some more powerful than any that we had ever exploded. The high altitude sampling program at Isotopes, Inc. was the first to detect particles from those tests.

The second broad range of measurements involved Carbon-14 dating. Many of these were for industrial customers, who were interested in establishing legal ownership questions. In others, the samples were archaeological artifacts — items found in excavations. Some of our customers were government agencies, some were other laboratories, others were legal firms.

The company's leaders also had strong ties with the nearby Lamont Geological Observatory, one of whose primary concerns involved the world's oceans, their bottoms, and how they got there. They studied currents, their patterns, and also studied core samples of the ocean floor. Age determinations and chemical analyses played strong parts in these studies.

Many of our lunchtime conversations revolved around these subjects, and the current theories of terrestrial evolution. Everyone there, including myself, believed in evolution and in the ancient age of the universe, because that's what we'd all been taught. This was an era when science was considered the king of knowledge, and the modern ideas of scientific creationism hadn't been proposed at that time.

But a few of our people were also Christians. The relationship between biblical truth and long-age geochronology was a question that kept coming up. Everyone seemed able to resolve this question in ways that offered temporary satisfaction for each one — but always sacrificing literal interpretations of the Bible's teachings about thousands of years. The millions and billions of years of earth-age, as taught by science, always was considered to be of primary truth; the Bible was secondary. Yet the fact that the subject was discussed so often shows that this solution wasn't truly satisfying.

Circular logic played a strong role in these discussions. No one can read the mind of God, or describe why He did this or that. But we all tried to outguess Him, and figure out how or why He did things the way the Bible says He did.

Dr. Kulp was often one of the participants. He was a world-famous geochronologist, a well-known professor, and also a Christian who followed the "progressive creationist" concept. He was a good friend who loved to talk about ideas, and to share his knowledge with others. These discussions usually began by talking about new discoveries, such as "sea-floor spreading," that led to the concept now known as "tectonic plate movements." Then they moved on to speculation on how these measurements could be enhanced for better accuracy or to minimize errors. They quickly got into the underlying assumptions that were fundamental to any dating process, and then often also involved the conflicts that came from reading biblical descriptions. Some of the participants were Christians and nominal Bible-believers who used some sort of rationalization schemes, such as progressive creation, theistic evolution, or the gap theory. It was fairly easy to say that early Genesis used figurative language, and wasn't intended to be taken literally. But when those chapters are read they don't sound like figurative language. Hebrew scholars agree that they are written in a way that seems intended to sound literally true.

Here is an extreme over-simplification of many of our lunchtime discussions. This pattern, of course, doesn't represent direct questions and answers between two people — it illustrates the general flow of discussion among a group of participants. We often digressed into much more detailed technical subjects, not shown here.

Question: How do we know the earth is actually extremely old?

Answer: Well, originally this knowledge came from the necessity of the long time required for evolution to have occurred. Also, just look around and see that the ground surface looks old. Uplifts and erosion must have taken place to make mountains look like they do, and those things take time. And now, of course, we have dating methods using radioactive decay to prove that the earth is old.

Question: But these dating methods rely on a prior knowledge of initial conditions. How do we know how much "mother isotope" and "daughter isotope" was present initially?

Answer: One of the best methods is to look at the composition of meteorites, which were formed at the same time as the earth, and have very little Pb-206. We can also calculate a lot from mathematical models.

Question: But you say that meteorites were formed at the same time and in the same way as the earth, slowly, a long time ago? Isn't that relying on an assumption that contains the subject we're trying to prove?

Answer: Well, sure, there is some circular logic there, but all modern scientists agree now that that's the way it all started. It must be true.

Question: But just for the sake of argument, suppose the Bible is really true after all, and that God actually did create it all quickly, and just made it look like a mature world? After all, it says God made Adam and Eve as grown-ups, not as little babies. Why couldn't He do the same with rocks?

Answer: Well, what kind of a God would do that? That would say that God is trying to deceive us, by making it look older than the Bible says it is. Surely God expects us to use common sense.

Question: But doesn't the Bible sound like God's telling us the earth is really young? If it's actually ancient, then aren't you saying that God deceives us with the biblical account?

Answer: Well, I don't think that Genesis is supposed to be taken literally. It's an allegory, to show religious values (who and why), not scientific facts (how and when).

This shows some of the typical sorts of reasoning often used in such debates, and this kind of discussion is endless. None of us seemed to realize there are many evidences of a young earth and a sudden mature creation. There's no logical stopping point, unless someone simply says, "Well, I believe the Bible is true." But at that time, I didn't know any scientists who would do that. Today's scientific creationism movement didn't begin for another decade. Particularly in those days, it was a hard thing for a scientist to swallow. He had to forsake almost all that he'd been taught in school, and all that most of his colleagues believed. He had to take a lot of scorn from his fellows.

Today, 1990s, I sometimes forget those early discussions, and tend to be annoyed at fellow Christians, scientists, who have difficulty in accepting the scientific truth of early Genesis. This is a mistake — I forget that once I was in that same situation. It took me several years to make that break, even after I had become aware of many scientific evidences that proclaim the truth of a sudden creation, just a few thousand years ago. That's part of the reason I'm writing this book.

My work at Isotopes, Inc. stopped suddenly in the spring of 1962, when financial reverses in the company forced a restructure that closed the instrumentation section. For the first time in my life, I was without a job. But, for some reason, I wasn't worried; my wife and I had faith that God had something in mind for us. I found a temporary "summer replacement" job at WABC-TV network headquarters in New York City, an easy commute and a really fun position. This lasted for 2-1/2 months, long enough for me to send out resumes and find another job. That job turned out to be as an electronics design engineer at Lawrence Livermore Laboratory, in Livermore, California. We made that move in mid-October 1962.

LAWRENCE LIVERMORE LAB

Prior to the establishment of this laboratory in the early 1950s, all of the U.S. atomic weapons work was done at Los Alamos lab, in New Mexico. The U.S. was locked in the "Cold War" with Russia during those years, and the political decision was made to establish another lab, not so much in competition with Los Alamos as to not "put all our eggs in one basket," in case of a nuclear attack on Los Alamos. In general terms, the work at Livermore roughly paralleled that at Los Alamos, although there was also a competitive spirit, and somewhat different emphases. At first my own work involved the design of instruments for the measurement of nuclear reactions.

None of this work was related to any sort of geochronology or evolution, and I had no reason to think too much about the conflict between modern science and the Bible. Most of the time I was able to separate the two, except during some Bible studies with other Christians. I wanted to believe the Bible, but I was still convinced that scientific explanations must outweigh the Genesis description in those cases where there appeared to be a conflict. Yet I considered (and hoped) it to be one of those things that would some day be resolved, but maybe only after I got to heaven and could ask God himself to explain it all.

MY "CONVERSION" TO CREATIONISM

Then one day, a friend, Bob Gest, loaned me a copy of the *Bible-Science Newsletter,* a tabloid-sized monthly publication. This contained articles that described several evidences showing that the biblical story might be true after all! It referred to a number of real scientists who actually believed that Genesis was true! This surprised me, and piqued my interest, and I quickly subscribed to it. Some of the articles referred to a book *The Genesis Flood*, by John Whitcomb and Henry Morris, which I purchased and read. This was amazing — it made the entire Genesis account reasonable, in terms that were compatible with my knowledge of science. (Years later, it's become common to refer to this book as the one that began the modern scientific creationist movement.)[1] I saw that the problem wasn't with any kind of scientific measurement; the basic problem was the set of assumptions behind the theories.

The first major error I became aware of was the "Theory of Uniformitarianism." This is a foundationstone of modern science. It proclaims that everything in nature has always followed the laws of nature, and that these laws have always behaved in the same ways they do now, and that earth processes follow about the same rates as at present. Implicit in this theory, but often not stated, is the idea that a supernatural intervention (such as the sudden miraculous creation or the major worldwide flood of Noah) never took place. Any such supernatural action would have been a "singular event" that obviously couldn't be repeated in a scientific experiment, so it must have been outside of the domain of science. In this way, the Genesis account was put aside as a non-scientific story, and was automatically ruled out of any scientific explanation. In other words, materialism became the only permissible mode for our origin to have occurred, and "the beginning" must have been according to the laws of nature, controlled by the uniformitarian principle.

I began to look at many of the scientific evidences — such things as fossils, rock structures, and radiogenic dating — to see how forcefully they fit into scientific theories. I realized that they could all fit into the creationist story just as well, if not better, than they fit the evolution idea. At first, this was surprising to me, and it took a few years of puzzlement before I could reject all of the teachings and indoctrinations of my previous years of experience. Most Christians who haven't had scientific training don't realize the difficulty that scientists have in accepting the literal truth of Genesis; it violates the very foundation of all they've been taught in science.

I read popular science magazines such as *Scientific American*, journals such as *Science*, and also textbooks by well-known scientists. I was struck by how many tentative words such as "probably," "may have been," and "very likely" were included in their descriptions of how evolution progressed. I was also impressed by how many real evidences were ignored. For example, I haven't found a single explanation of pleochroic halos of primordial polonium, other than by creationists such as Robert Gentry.[2] I also found that scientists disagreed on many subjects because the only reasonable one (God's miraculous creation) is rejected, and there's no other that fits all the evidences. For example, even though the moon is by far the closest heavenly body and has been extensively studied, there are four different theories as to how it may have formed, none of them agree, and every one of them has been found to violate fundamental laws of physics.[3]

I finally understood that evidences (rocks, fossils, etc.) don't prove either position, but that they can be fitted into either theory. Creation versus evolution is not equivalent to a fight between science and religion — these are both religious belief-systems. I summarized this into two statements:

> • Neither creation nor evolution is a truly scientific theory, because neither can be proved by the evidences, nor can either one be disproved, and
>
> • Both creation and evolution are religious beliefs, because both require a faith to believe. One faith is theistic, the other atheistic or materialistic.

Since I finally got this settled in my own mind, I've tried to help others to realize this truth. I've found there's a great deal of misinformation and propaganda out there. Our public school system, public media, and most government-funded grants are strongly slanted toward the materialist interpretations, and heap scorn on religious beliefs that "in the beginning God created the heavens and the earth." This is really a battle of Satan versus God.

RETIREMENT

In January of 1988 the lab's budget was cut and they had to reduce their manpower. Many employees became frightened about the chance of losing their jobs, but lab management arranged for voluntary early retirements, by offering a financial incentive. I hadn't intended to stop work that early (I wasn't quite 64), but a couple of days later I realized that this was the best thing to do, and that this was the right time. I put a sign on my office door saying, *"I quit the rat race — the rats won."* Now I have the chance to stay busy doing the things I want, instead of what some manager decides needs to be done. I've never regretted it.

During my retirement years so far, I've intensified my studies of creation vs. evolution, and have also increased my Bible studies. I've taken courses in geology and astronomy at the local community college, so that I would know some of the latest ideas of evolutionist science. These just reinforced my conviction that God's miraculous creation was the best explanation for our origin. I've spent time writing on these subjects, and this present book is one result. Now I'm eager to see what the Lord has for my next step.

Looking back, I see a number of points in my life where God has obviously intervened, so as to change the normal course of events and thus guide me along. My selection for ASTP and the Manhattan Project was certainly an improbable thing, and Dr. Kulp's phone call offering a job at Isotopes, Inc. was totally unexpected and life-changing. I hadn't applied for, or even known about, either of these positions, yet they put me in spots that I'm sure fit God's life-plan perfectly. I got the chance to spend many years working with famous scientists, and learning the methods of science. When I had to leave Isotopes, Inc., I sent out a dozen job applications, and thought my qualifications would surely bring me several offers, so my prayer at that time was, "Lord, please show me which one you want me to take. Please open the one door that you want me to go through." I was surprised to receive only the one offer from Lawrence Livermore Lab, until I remembered that prayer. Even during the time that I had no job, each time an expense came along, an unexpected check came also; we never did without.

These "coincidences" have convinced me that, if we just yield ourselves to God's guidance, and try to obey His commands, He'll put us in the right spots at the right time. There is a Bible verse that my wife and I adopted as "our verse," many years ago. It is Romans 8:26–28, and it says:

> In the same way, the Spirit helps us in our weakness. We do not know what we ought to pray for, but the Spirit himself intercedes for us with groans that words cannot express. And he who searches our hearts knows the mind of the Spirit, because the Spirit intercedes for the saints in accordance with God's will. And we know that in all things God works for the good of those who love him, who have been called according to his purpose.

This Scripture has certainly been proven true in our lives.

✳ ✳ ✳

This has been the story of how a young man, just out of college and fascinated with all that science offered, and who, for years naively accepted science as the "ultimate truth," spent his lifetime working in scientific laboratories, and finally realized that many of his original beliefs were wrong. Now he's older and wiser, having studied the scientific evidences and theories from both sides of the fence. Now he has his faith firmly centered on the one true God, the Creator and maintainer of the earth and all of its creatures, primarily its humans. God is not just a creative force, but actually loves us, and gave us the Bible so that we can understand Him. A key verse in that book says:

> For God so loved the world, that He gave His only begotten Son, that whosoever believeth in Him should not perish, but have everlasting life (John 3:16).

Life so far has been fascinating and rewarding; I'm looking forward to that everlasting life with Him in heaven.

SOME BOOKS ABOUT WARTIME LOS ALAMOS

A number of books have been written that tell different portions of the Los Alamos story. The ones in my own library include:

Eleanor Jette, *Inside Box 1663* (Los Alamos, NM: Los Alamos Historical Society, 1977). A personal account of life as the wife of a Los Alamos scientist during the war years at Los Alamos. Not technical.

James W. Kunetka, *City of Fire: Los Alamos and the Atomic Age*, 1943–1945 (Albuquerque, NM: University of New Mexico Press, 1978). A well-documented history describing the development work of the wartime Manhattan Project, leading to the world's first atomic bombs.

Lansing Lamont, *Day of Trinity* (New York, NY: Atheneum, 1965). A well-documented history describing the development work of the war-time Manhattan Project, leading to the world's first atomic bombs. Quite a bit of material is included about the political discussions in Washington, debating several aspects of how to use the atomic bomb(s) to end World War II.

Richard Rhodes, *The Making of the Atomic Bomb* (New York, NY, Touchstone, Simon & Schuster, 1986). A Pulitzer prizewinning account, this is one of the most complete and descriptive stories about this subject. Nobel Laureate Dr. I.I. Rabi said of this book, "An epic worthy of Milton."

Robert Serber, *The Los Alamos Primer* (Berkeley, CA: University of California Press, 1992). A fascinating document, this contains the five lectures given by Serber to the newly assembled scientists at Los Alamos in April 1943. These contain the gist of all the technical knowledge about nuclear reactions that was known at that time. For several years this was classified Top Secret, and was given to newly arrived scientists to bring them up to date on what Los Alamos was all about.

Robert Chadwell Williams, *Klaus Fuchs, Atom Spy*, (Cambridge, MA: Harvard University Press, 1987). A detailed biography of Klaus Fuchs, and a good description of how he became a spy for the Soviet Union.

Endnotes

[1] John C. Whitcomb and Henry M. Morris, *The Genesis Flood* (Phillipsburg, NJ: P & R Publishing, 1961).

[2] Robert V. Gentry, *Creation's Tiny Mystery*, (Knoxville, TN: Earth Science Associates, 1986).

[3] J.C. Whitcomb and D.B. DeYoung, *The Moon: Its Creation, Form and Significance*, (Winona Lake, IN: BMH Books, 1978), p. 35–51.

Chapter 2

DEFINING SOME TERMS

The world embarrasses me, and I cannot dream that this watch exists and has no watch-maker.   (Voltaire)

There's no more reason to believe that man descended from some inferior animal than there is to believe that a stately mansion has descended from a small cottage.
(William Jennings Bryan)

WHY THIS BOOK?

The question of "How did this world and all of its inhabitants get here?" is one that has always stirred debate, and the past few decades have done little to quell the disagreement. We all have our opinions, and most of them are not without some basis, but are they based on facts or dogma? In this book we'll try to shed some factual light, so that our opinions can be shaped more intelligently, less emotionally.

THE ORIGINS QUESTION —
SCIENTIFIC or RELIGIOUS?

The answers to that question can almost always be put into one of two broad categories:

> 1. They were deliberately created by some supernatural force, along with the laws of nature that govern the universe, or
> 2. They happened spontaneously — the natural result of the "laws of nature," operating in a random manner. It's obvious that this must involve some sort of evolution.

Which of these two conclusions one reaches is determined primarily by one's answer to this question — "Is there a God who can and will intervene miraculously in the affairs of this world?" This is often, but not always, closely linked with whether or not one wishes to believe in the literal truth of the Bible.

It's likely, therefore, that one's opinions about origins are often formed by one's answer to a religious question. If we believe strongly in God, then we'll probably choose answer number one above; but if we doubt the existence of a God who can and does intervene, our choice will probably be number two. Conversely, if a person is taught to believe that evolution is true, the natural result is often to doubt the biblical account of God's creation.

Notice that this foundation for our origins viewpoint is primarily a philosophical choice; physical evidences are only peripheral to the argument. Both sides agree that the earth is a marvelous and exotic place, and contains a wealth of complicated things — rocks, plants, animals, etc. But all the evidences can be fitted into either viewpoint. Thus, the choice of creation or evolution is not one of science vs. religion, in spite of what many people have tried to make it appear.

Well-known evolutionist Professor Douglas Futuyma,

in a book praised by Ernst Mayr as "a masterly summation of the evidence for evolution," said essentially the same thing except from the opposite viewpoint.

> Anyone who believes in Genesis as a literal description of history must hold a world view that is entirely incompatible with the idea of evolution, not to speak of science itself. . . . Where science insists on material, mechanistic causes that can be understood by physics and chemistry, the literal believer in Genesis invokes unknowable supernatural forces.
>
> Perhaps more importantly, if the world and its creatures developed purely by material, physical forces, it could not have been designed and has no purpose or goal. The fundamentalist, in contrast, believes that everything in the world, every species and every characteristic of every species, was designed by an intelligent, purposeful artificer, and that it was made for a purpose.[1]

You may say, don't the "facts of science" prove the truth of evolution? Most scientists honestly believe this because that's what their leading writers in scientific journals say, but an examination of the facts shows that the opposite is true. Examined objectively, I think the true "facts" of science (as opposed to the "beliefs" of evolutionary activists) show the truth of God's miraculous creation.

University of California Professor of Law Phillip Johnson examined the validity and logic of evolutionist doctrines in his book *Darwin on Trial*. Johnson explains his own religious views about origins as follows:

> I am not interested in any claims that are based upon a literal reading of the Bible, nor do I understand the concept of creation as narrowly as Duane Gish does. If an omnipotent Creator exists He might have created things instantaneously in a

single week or through gradual evolution over billions of years. He might have employed means wholly inaccessible to science, or mechanisms that are at least in part understandable through scientific investigation.[2]

So we see that Johnson is not "grinding an axe" in favor of creationism. He simply examined all the evidences for Darwinism and the logic behind them to see if they might be able to stand up in a court of law. He concluded that natural selection is nothing more than a tautology, that the evidence for Darwinism is based on unprovable assumptions, and that, in effect, Darwinists have a religious outlook and feeling:

> The continual efforts to base a religion or ethical system upon evolution are not an aberration, and practically all the most prominent Darwinist writers have tried their hand at it. Darwinist evolution is an imaginative story about who we are and where we came from, which is to say it is a creation myth. As such it is an obvious starting point for speculation about how we ought to live and what we ought to value. A creationist appropriately starts with God's creation and God's will for man. A scientific naturalist just as appropriately starts with evolution and with man as a product of nature.[3]

In this book we'll look at several of the oft-quoted "evidences" of evolution, and find that either they are based on assumptions that can't be proven or that they misrepresent the true facts. We'll also see that there are a number of good evidences showing that a better explanation is God's creation. This book is written for the purpose of showing the truth of the following comparative statements:

1. Both creationism and evolutionism are

religious in nature, because they both require some sort of faith to believe.

2. Neither evolution nor creation is truly scientific, because neither one can be proven or disproven. Neither is adaptable to the scientific method, since "the beginning" is beyond experimental reach.

3. The actual scientific evidence favors the creation belief more than it does the idea of evolution.

From this we can see that, since neither of these basic belief systems is truly scientific, then all of the logic involved in trying to "prove" either one is basically a process of circular reasoning. That is, before evidences mean much, they must be "fitted into" a foundational hypothesis.

1. If one accepts the reality of a God who is capable of miraculous intervention, then it's easy enough to fit the evidences observed in geological strata into the concept of the biblical flood. From that, one can build a hypothesis that demonstrates how such a flood caused the physical features that we see on earth today.

2. But if one rejects the idea of such a God, one must begin with the assumption that these strata must be viewed in a naturalistic manner. This naturally leads to a hypothesis that describes how, over very long periods of time, natural processes caused the features that we see around us.

No matter which of these two frameworks we choose as a starting point, all further theories must be "fitted into" that foundational initial assumption. All of the arguments rely on that starting point, and reinforce that starting point. So, as far as logical positive proof is concerned, both are classical examples of circular reasoning.

FOUNDATIONS OF THE TWO BELIEF-SYSTEMS

The creation-vs-evolution conflict is just one part of a larger battle. We need to see the whole picture in order to

Supernatural Origin

There is an all-powerful God, who can intervene in this world.

The Bible is the true word of God.

The universe, our world, and all its inhabitants were created by God.

The complexities we see in everything around us are strong evidences of God's creative power, and testify to the truth of the Biblical account.

Divine creation includes:
- Sudden origin of earth, stars, complex animals, and people.
- Physical laws of nature, also moral laws, were started just after creation, so that everything keeps on right.

Humans were created on Day 6.

God is still capable of intervening in His own creation. He often answers prayers, etc., and sometimes has done mighty miracles.

The creative period only took 6 days.

Age of universe	< 15,000 years
Age of earth	< 15,000 years
Age of humankind	< 15,000 years

The Great Flood of Noah covered the entire earth. Most of the sedimentary strata, with their fossils, were caused by this flood. A remnant of each kind of animal life was saved in Noah's ark.

We were created in the image of God, and have an everlasting life, either in heaven or hell, both of which are real places.

God loves us, and sent His Son, Jesus, to pay the penalty for our sins. The Bible tells us to believe and accept Jesus as Saviour.

Materialistic Origin

If there is a God, He doesn't interfere in the affairs of this world.

The Bible is mythology and folklore.

All that we see, including humans, developed in a purely materialistic way.

There cannot be any design in nature. That would require a designer (an intelligent supernatural power) — a violation of the starting premise.

Material origin includes:
Cosmological evolution (big bang, etc.)
Planetary and terrestrial evolution (the sun and solar system developed slowly from cosmic gas and dust).

Biological evolution (including chemical origin of life), then molecules-to-man. Humans evolved from ape-like ancestors.
Social evolution (situational ethics, no absolute morality).

This development took a long time.
Age of universe	~15,000,000,000 years
Age of earth	~4,500,000,000 years
Age of humankind	~3,000,000 years

"Uniformitarianism" can explain all the surface features of the earth. There was never a worldwide catastrophe that destroyed almost all of the earth's surface, or killed almost all of its life.

Our bodies are simply blobs of chemicals, and when we die that's the end of it. There is no eternal soul and so afterlife.

The idea of a God becoming man, coming back to life, and going back to heaven, is nonsense.

properly evaluate the smaller portions. To be logically consistent, a person should choose one of the two sets of beliefs outlined in the two columns on the two previous pages, then follow on to the one below that. Each point of belief is a logical consequence of those listed above it, although, of course, most of us are not completely logical in our emotional thoughts; many people believe some points in each column.

Many people, theistic evolutionists, agnostic typologists, and others, try to pick bits and pieces from both sides, attempting to compromise secular science with the biblical account, but these two are like oil and water — they don't mix well. This writer followed that path for years, with considerable frustration.

STRUCTURE OF THIS BOOK

Even though, as we showed at first, the basis for believing either in creation or evolution is primarily one of religion rather than of science, most people don't recognize this because secular educators have done a good job of spreading their propaganda of "science has proved that the world and its inhabitants gradually came into being by an evolutionary process."

This is demonstrated by the 1992 "Science Framework for California Public Schools," which uses the two words "evolution" and "science" as synonymous, and says that evolution is a fact. We'll show later that their definitions have the effect of ruling out the existence of the God of the Bible, and that they don't base their use of the term "scientific facts" on real physical evidence so much as on the beliefs of the majority of scientists.

In order to show the gross error of this teaching and its perverse effect on the mind of students, most of the discussions in this book concern scientific evidences, their foundations and consequences. The remainder of this book is organized into five broad categories:

1. First, I'd like to give you some of my own background as a way of explaining my search for life's origin.

2. In chapter 2 we'll try to define a number of terms that are commonly used, in discussing theories of origins. These have been used quite loosely at times, causing a number of misunderstandings.

3. Chapter three discusses several scientific evidences that favor the idea of creation.

4. Chapter four simply explains what most creationists believe about the great flood of Noah. Much of this is based on the Bible rather than on scientific evidence.

5. In Chapter five we'll show a number of technical arguments against some of the widely believed, but poorly based, so-called evidences of evolution.

6. Chapter six contains a number of religious arguments intended for those who try to "straddle the fence" with some sort of theistic evolution compromise.

A list of some books that I've found helpful is given at the end. Each has my own brief evaluation.

The reader will notice that this book contains both scientific and religious arguments. That's reasonable, because both of these are directly applicable. However, in saying that, we're opening the possibility that critics may repeat that tired old cliché "see, that proves that creationism is just religious." But I've separated the two kinds of arguments so that reasonable persons can see that this cliché is nonsense.

DOES THIS BOOK ACTUALLY PROVE ANYTHING?

The reader should realize that none of these arguments about evidences are intended to either prove or disprove either creation or evolution. This would be impossible, since "the beginning" is beyond our reach. The only way to have good knowledge about such ancient events is to read historical accounts written by those who were there at the time.

However, it is my intention to show that the widely

taught notion of the absolute truth of evolution is a gross exaggeration. The facts show that a belief in creation is certainly a reasonable alternative, if not more realistic. I believe this to be true either from a scientific or religious point of view.

DEFINING SOME TERMS

Before we get into specific evidences, we need to be on common ground about the meaning of several words. Sometimes people from both camps toss words around carelessly, create wrong impressions, and cause misunderstandings. Even though these are oversimplified here, they're close enough, and are easy to read.

MICRO-EVOLUTION, which is also called SPECIA-TION, is a known fact of nature. Two examples are often given: 1) the varieties of flowers or domestic animals that breeders can achieve, and 2) the finches on the Galapagos Islands, which led Charles Darwin to write *The Origin of Species*. An original few finches apparently became isolated there, and the next many generations diversified, so that now there are a number of species differing in size, bill shape, and color. But these are all still finches, and the breeder's new rose is still a rose; there are fixed limits to any such process.

MACRO-EVOLUTION is the theory that all of the varieties of creatures that we observe today developed by a gradual set of changes, over tremendously long times, from common ancestors. Usually this includes the concept of life itself having developed from lifeless chemicals. (Darwin didn't suggest this in his writing; that came much later.) Micro-evolution is often mistakenly used as evidence for macro-evolution. But those are two vastly different things; there's no evidence that large changes (above the "family" level) could ever occur.

The term "macro-evolution" is often simplified to just "evolution." Despite statements to the contrary, there's not the slightest physical evidence for this, and much evidence against it. Creationist Louis Pasteur, in the late 1800s, showed that life can't arise from non-life. But he was opposed by the evolutionists of his day.

The science of classifying creatures into descriptive groups is called TAXONOMY. Its hierarchy includes kingdom, phylum, class, order, family, genus, and species.

There are about 30 PHYLA in the animal kingdom. Most of these are made up of the tiny marine creatures that most people never heard of. Three phyla that are familiar are mollusca (snails, clams, etc.), arthropoda (spiders, lobsters, insects, etc.), and chordata (one of whose SUB-PHYLA, vertebrata, contains all fish, birds, reptiles, and mammals). Several of the phyla contain two or more sub-phyla.

Each phylum or sub-phylum is divided into several CLASSES. For example, the sub-phylum vertebrata contains eight classes, including amphibia, reptilia, aves (birds), mammalia, and four classes of fishes.

Usually each class contains several ORDERS. For example, some well-known orders within class mammalia include rodentia (mice, squirrels, etc.), carnivora (flesh-eating mammals — dogs, bears, etc.), and primata (ape-like creatures including humans).

Often an order will consist of several FAMILIES, a family will typically include several GENERA (its singular is GENUS), and each genus will often have several SPECIES. Not all categories of creatures are sub-divided with this much precision.

As an example of a complete scientific classification, a particular creature that I've seen eat goldfish from our backyard fishpond might be categorized as follows:

> kingdom — animal
> phylum — chordata
> sub-phylum — vertebrata
> class — aves (birds)
> order — ciconiiformes (heron, stork, ibis)

family — ardeidae (herons)
genus — butorides
species — striatus

This is too long a list for common use, so its scientific name will usually be shortened to butorides striatus (or b. striatus), whose common name is "green-backed heron."

The evolution idea, to replace the concept of a Creator God by a materialistic view, can be traced back to at least 500 B.C., but scientific attempts to explain how that might have happened didn't come until about 1700. Lamarck and Erasmus Darwin were two early theorists.

LAMARCKISM tried to show a mechanism of how evolution might have occurred. It said that acquired characteristics, such as that of the long neck of a giraffe, caused by stretching to reach higher branches for food, might be passed on to the next generations. This idea was disproven when the facts of genetics, and how they affected heredity, became known.

The term DARWINISM (that's often called Darwinian evolution) is often misused. Darwin proposed two different concepts in his famous first book. His Special Theory proposed what amounts to micro-evolution, as described above. It's based on three ideas — that natural variations occur normally in individuals, that these variations can be inherited, and that environmental factors give survival advantages to those who possess certain of these variations. That last part is often called NATURAL SELECTION. There is some truth in natural selection; this is a strong factor in helping creatures to adapt to their surroundings, and was put into operation at the time of creation.

Herbert Spencer, not Darwin, coined the phrase "survival of the fittest," but this has been criticized as circular reasoning or a tautology (because "Which are the fittest?" — "Those that survive.")

Darwin also proposed his General Theory as an extension of his Special Theory. This is very similar to macro-evolution, and essentially says that all forms of life developed in this way. This theory became known as Darwinism. Because this would require a vast number of intermediate forms, and these are completely absent from the fossil record, most scientists agree that this idea couldn't be exactly correct. The phrase "Darwinism is dead" was coined at the Conference on Macro-evolution, Field Museum, Chicago, in November of 1980. Darwinism has been replaced by NEO-DARWINISM, which gives mutations the role previously held by natural variations.

Neo-Darwinism, sometimes called Modern Synthesis, is the recent attempt to make macro-evolution more credible. It became popular during the 1940s. It involves three main points: 1) chemical evolution from non-life to life, 2) a common ancestry (phylogenetic relationship) for all creatures, and 3) random mutations acted upon by natural selection. But, again, there's very little in the way of real proof in its favor, and quite a bit against it.

By 1960 many scientists realized the problems that Neo-Darwinism faced. In 1966 a world conference titled "Mathematical Challenges to the Neo-Darwinian Interpretation of Evolution" was held at the Wistar Institute Symposium in Philadelphia. In his opening remarks, chairman Sir Peter Medawar, said:

> The immediate cause of this conference is a pretty widespread sense of dissatisfaction about what has come to be thought as the accepted evolutionary theory in the English-speaking world, the so-called Neo-Darwinian theory.

Their worries centered around the extremely high probability that mutations would cause damage, not improvement, in future generations. This problem has not gone away.

The THEORY OF PUNCTUATED EQUILIBRIUM

was proposed in the late 1970s by S.J. Gould and N. Eldredge as an attempt to offer an explanation for the absence of transitional fossils. It says, in effect, that small groups somehow became isolated, and went quickly through some sort of Neo-Darwinian evolution to develop into new kinds of creatures; this was then followed by a long period of stasis, or lack of change. They don't offer much proof for this, except they say that short periods of change would leave few transitional fossils.

TYPOLOGY is the belief held by most of the 19th-century founders of biology — Cuvier, Agassiz, Owen, Linnaeus, Lyell (at first), and others. This holds that there are types or classes of organisms, each having a number of variations, but each separated from other classes by fixed boundaries. One of the best modern explanations for typology is *Evolution: A Theory in Crisis*, by Michael Denton. This is an excellent reference book for anyone who's interested in learning more about the so-called "facts" of evolution.[4] Denton is a molecular biologist, a religious agnostic, and a typologist.

Typology looks at the realities of the modern world but omits "the beginning," or how that world came to be. To this writer, it is the best materialistic view of biological reality. If I were not a creationist, I would probably be a typologist, just because of all the physical evidences.

There are two flavors of CREATIONISM. These both believe that organisms are divided into typological classes, with no evolutionary development between, but they go a step further and say that there was a beginning, and a supernatural Creator who started it all. Biblical creationists use the Bible as their proof, and say that "In the beginning, God created the heavens and the earth." Most scientific creationists believe that also, but use arguments based on physical evidences. The flood during Noah's day holds an important place in creationists' explanation of geology. (This writer considers himself to be both a biblical and a scientific creationist.)

Neither of these creationist versions qualifies as a proper scientific theory, because neither can be experimentally verified or disproved. But, then, neither can evolution be experimentally confirmed or denied. All three are belief systems, based on foundational assumptions that can't be proven.

Another word that needs some sort of definition is UNIFORMITARIANISM. This was first proposed by James Hutton in the late 1700s and was amplified by Charles Lyell in his 1830 book *Principles of Geology*. It says that our present world was shaped by the same "Laws of Nature" that we see today, and that this took an extremely long time. The key phrase is "the present is the key to the past."

This has become a widely believed idea that excludes all supernatural intervention, whether creation or modification. It has led to the common belief that any suggestion of a divine creation or the biblical great flood of Noah is automatically "outside the realm of science," and therefore can't even be considered. This dual idea of uniformitarianism and an extremely long age of the earth are vital foundationstones for belief in evolutionism.

Closely linked to the concept of uniformitarianism is the arrangement of the earth's strata into a "paper series," separated according to the kinds of fossils each stratum contains. This sequence is called the GEOLOGIC COLUMN, and divides earth history into eras, periods, and epochs (see the chart on the next page).

The eras are named according to the assumed age of the life forms found therein — Paleozoic means "ancient life," Mesozoic means "middle life," and Cenozoic means "recent life." We can see that the assumption of evolution is implicit within these definitions. The various eras, periods, and epochs are supposed to represent the history of the entire world, but in only a few spots in the world do these all appear; whereas many spots have out-of-sequence strata.

MAIN DIVISION AND EVENTS OF GEOLOGICAL TIME			
ERAS	PERIODS	CHARACTERISTIC LIFE	ESTIMATED YEARS AGO
CENOZOIC	Quaternary: Recent Epoch Pleistocene Epoch	Rise of modern plants and animals, and man.	25,000 975,000
CENOZOIC	Tertiary: Pliocene Epoch Miocene " Oligocene " Eocene " Paleocene "	Rise of mammals and development of highest plants.	12,000,000 25,000,000 35,000,000 60,000,000 70,000,000
MESOZOIC	Cretaceous	Modernized angiosperms and insects abundant. Foraminifers profuse. Extinction of dinosaurs, flying reptiles, and ammonites.	70,000,000 to 200,000,000
MESOZOIC	Jurassic	First (reptilian) birds. First of highest forms of insects. First (primitive) angiosperms.	70,000,000 to 200,000,000
MESOZOIC	Triassic	Earliest dinosaurs, flying reptiles, marine reptiles, and primitive mammals. Cycads and conifers common. Modern corals common. Earliest ammonites.	70,000,000 to 200,000,000
PALEOZOIC	Permian	Rise of primitive reptiles. Earliest cycads and conifers. Extinction of trilobites. First modern corals.	200,000,000 to 500,000,000
PALEOZOIC	Pennsylvanian	Earliest known insects. Spore plants abundant.	200,000,000 to 500,000,000
PALEOZOIC	Mississippian	Rise of amphibians. Culmination of crinoids.	200,000,000 to 500,000,000
PALEOZOIC	Devonian	First known seed plants. Great variety of boneless fishes. First evidence of amphibians.	200,000,000 to 500,000,000
PALEOZOIC	Silurian	Earliest known land animals. Primitive land plants. Rise of fishes. Brachiopods, trilobites, and corals abundant.	200,000,000 to 500,000,000
PALEOZOIC	Ordovician	Earliest known vertebrates. Graptolites, corals, brachiopods, cephalopods, and trilobites abundant. Oldest primitive land plants.	200,000,000 to 500,000,000
PALEOZOIC	Cambrian	All subkingdoms of invertebrate animals represented. Brachiopods and trilobites common.	200,000,000 to 500,000,000
PROTEROZOIC	Keweenawan Huronian	Primitive water-dwelling plants and animals.	500,000,000 to 1,000,000,000
ARCHEOZOIC	Timiskaming Keewatin	Oldest known life (mostly indirect evidence).	1,000,000,000 to 1,800,000,000

The Geologic Column

When a geologist or paleontologist wants to identify a particular stratum, he doesn't usually check for rock type or chemical composition (granite, limestone, etc.); instead he looks for INDEX FOSSILS. These are remains of creatures which are thought to have lived during certain eras and then to have become extinct. Most index fossils are invertebrates such as various species of trilobites and mollusks.

Obviously, this method of using index fossils for dating applies only to sedimentary rocks (those laid down as grains of sediment deposited by wind or water action, then later lithified — solidified into hard, solid rock). Igneous rocks (those that have cooled from melted magma) couldn't contain fossils.

CATASTROPHISM is the concept that many of the evidences we see in the earth today were not caused by slow actions of ordinary forces, but by sudden and violent events. Creationists coined this word, thinking of such things as the great flood of Noah; that was probably the event that accounts for the majority of fossils and sediments in the crust of the earth. Some other typologists such as Cuvier believed that several catastrophes have occurred.

But the word has now been picked up by all scientists, and includes such catastrophes as volcanoes, earthquakes, and other "normal" violent events. Of course, catastrophists agree that almost always the "laws of nature" act in a uniform and reliable way — otherwise, science would be meaningless. But people who believe in a personal God who can actually do something also realize that, on occasion, He can intervene into His creation.

THE CHANGING MEANING OF SCIENCE ITSELF

We need to discuss something that's often misunderstood by most people but is so important that it deserves a section of its own here. The word "SCIENCE" itself has changed its practical meaning in the past century or so, because of the shifting philosophy of the majority of scientists in regard to the question of origins.

Webster defines science as "systemetized knowledge derived from observation, study, and experimentation carried on in order to determine the nature or principles of what is being studied." This definition hasn't changed much down through the years, but the body of data and theories constantly changes, and often the laws themselves are rewritten.

The classical concept of the "scientific method" involved forming a theory to explain a physical situation of interest, then performing experiments to verify or disprove that theory. But "the beginning" is beyond experimental reach, and any divine intervention (not experimentally repeatable) would violate the theory of uniformitarianism.

So "science" has taken the position of excluding any intervention by God by definition (even at the risk of abandoning the truth), and instead, trying to explain everything in nature in a completely materialistic manner. The so-called "law" of uniformitarianism has become foundational; it can never be questioned. Philosophical conformity within that constraint has replaced experimental validity. No longer is the basic question of materialistic or supernatural origin being seriously discussed, because "that's beyond the reach of science." They simply say that a materialistic origin is a "fact." (But it's really only an assumption.)

This new concept that redefines "science" as excluding an activist God and all of His absolutes is demonstrated by this quotation from the textbook *Physical Science*:

> A theory that is not fruitful is a "bad" theory because it does not lead to further knowledge. For example, *the theory that the earth was specially created as is, is a "bad" theory,* not because it is not true, but because it does not lead one towards a better understanding of nature. Such a theory is barren, for it gives a final explanation to all things, that they are as they are because they were created

that way. *A believer in such a theory has no incentive to investigate nature except to describe it*, for he already has all of the answers as to why things are as they are.

"Difficult for the layman to understand is that *the scientists' criterion for a 'good' theory does not depend upon whether it is true or not. He measures it only by its consequences: "... consequences in terms of other ideas and other experiments. Thus conceived*, **science is not a quest for certainty**; it is rather a quest which is successful only to the degree that it is continuous.[5] (Emphasis added)

That author demonstrates a woeful lack of knowledge when he says that believers in creation have no incentive to investigate nature. Most of the "founding fathers" of modern science were sincere Bible-believers. A few are listed here:

Leonardo Da Vinci, (1452-1519)
Samuel F.B. Morse (1791-1872)
Johann Kepler (1571-1630)
Matthew Maury (1806-1873)
Francis Bacon (1561-1626)
James Joule (1818-1889)
Blaise Pascal (1623-1662)
Louis Agassiz (1807-1873)
Robert Boyle (1627-1691)
Gregory Mendel (1822-1884)
Nicolaus Steno (1631-1686)
Louis Pasteur (1822-1895)
Sir Isaac Newton (1642-1727)
John Ambrose Fleming (1849-1945)
Carolus Linnaeus (1707-1778)
Joseph Clerk Maxwell (1831-1879)
William Herschel (1738-1822)
George Washington Carver (1864-1943)

Charles Babbage (1792-1871)
Michael Faraday (1791-1867)
Georges Cuvier (1769-1832)
Wernher von Braun (1912-1977)
William Thompson, Lord Kelvin (1824-1907)

Many of these men wrote books of their faith in God and the Bible, in addition to their scientific works. Sir Isaac Newton wrote more volumes on theology than on science, including one defending the Ussher Chronology for the age of the earth. He wrote, "I find more sure marks of authenticity in the Bible than in any profane history whatsoever." Johann Kepler (who discovered the laws of planetary motions) said that in his astronomical research he was just "thinking God's thoughts after Him." Matthew Maury (called the "father of oceanography") read Psalm 8:8, ". . . whatsoever passeth through the paths of the seas." From that, he began to search for paths in the seas, and became the discoverer of vast regular worldwide ocean currents. Blaise Pascal gave us a significant quotation — the "Wager of Pascal," as follows:

> How can anyone lose who chooses to become a Christian? If, when he dies, there turns out to be no God and his faith was in vain, he has lost nothing — in fact, he has been happier in life than his non-believing friends. If, however, there is a God and a heaven and hell, then he has gained heaven and his skeptical friends will have lost everything in hell!

Of course, the majority of scientists today go about their normal work investigating the facts of the present-day laws of nature without getting involved in speculations about origins. Most are highly motivated, and many maintain trust in God. But not many give glory to God in their technical writings. If they did, their articles probably wouldn't be published. The publicity goes to those who secularize in new ways, often with an imaginative new theory involving origins. And evolutionist journals won't publish articles that promote God's creation, in the same way that creationist journals don't touch the ones that push evolutionary concepts. Both sides discriminate, naturally.

Astronomer Robert Jastrow began his book by saying:

> When an astronomer writes about God, his colleagues assume he is either over the hill or going bonkers.

He closes with quotations from several well-known scientists who express discomfort with the big bang theory simply because its discontinuity implies some sort of "First Cause" (a fancy name for God). Then he wrote:

> There is a strange ring of feeling and emotion in these reactions. They come from the heart, whereas you would expect the judgments to come from the brain. Why?
>
> I think part of the answer is that scientists cannot bear the thought of a natural phenomenon which cannot be explained, even with unlimited time and money. There is a kind of religion in science; it is the religion of a person who believes there is order and harmony in the Universe, and every event can be explained in a rational way as the product of some previous event; every effect must have its cause; there is no First Cause. . . . This religious faith of the scientist is violated by the discovery that the world had a beginning under conditions in which the known laws of physics are not valid, and as a product of forces or circumstances we cannot discover. When that happens, the scientist has lost control.

He then discusses how science has pushed back the limits of knowledge so as to learn much of how nature has operated, but the closer it nears "the beginning," the more impenetrable the barrier becomes. Then he continues:

> At this moment it seems as though science will never be able to raise the curtain on the mystery of creation. For the scientist who has lived by his faith in the power of reason, the story ends like a bad dream. He has scaled the mountains of ignorance; he is about to conquer the highest peak; as he pulls himself over the final rock, he is greeted by a band of theologians who have been sitting there for centuries.[6]

In the past several decades, public belief in creationism has expanded tremendously. Many scientists consider this a threat and, in late 1981, began a counter-attack at meetings of the National Academy of Sciences and the National Association of Biology Teachers. "Committees of Correspondence" were established in every state, together with an umbrella organization called the "National Center for Science Education." Their efforts were involved in assisting a number of scientific, educational, and liberal religious organizations to issue resolutions that endorsed evolution and strongly criticized "scientific creationism." They also published a booklet, "Voices For Evolution."

Several individuals and several groups of scientists have written books lambasting creationism, often using extremely vitriolic language.

These efforts were supposedly for the purpose of keeping creationism out of public school science classes, but their propaganda campaign had the practical effect of making "science" and "evolution" synonymous in the public mind. This automatically attributed belief in God's creation to mythology. By proclaiming that evolutionism is scientifically true, then belief in creation must be false.

This fundamental change in the practical meaning of the word "science" has encouraged many evolutionary enthusiasts to proclaim that evolution is a fact, and that creationism is a non- scientific religious belief. Some have even made the statement that "creation-science is an oxymoron" (that is, two opposing ideas linked together). Unfortunately, if one adheres to this restriction in their new definition of "science," then both "creation science" and "scientific truth" have become oxymoronic by definition.

This writer agrees that religious dogmas of creationism involving the Bible or describing the Creator have no place in public school science classes. By the same token, neither does the dogmatic teaching of purely naturalistic evolution as the only possible explanation for our existence belong in these classes. If the negative evidences against evolution are prohibited, then students are being unfairly indoctrinated into an atheistic mindset; this is, in effect, a state-mandated "establishment of religion," (which is supposed to be prohibited by the First Amendment of the U.S. Constitution).

A great many people, including most "main-line" theologians, try to get along with both sides by some sort of merger such as "theistic evolution," "progressive creation," or the "gap theory." For many people, this compromise is satisfactory and even desirable. But hard-line believers on both sides of the fence have trouble with these sorts of compromise ideas. For them, "the beginning" must have been either by the action of an omnipotent Creator or an uncompromising materialistic naturalism.

Phillip Johnson shows that compromise is opposed by evolutionists just as much as it is by fundamentalist Bible-believers:

> Theistic or "guided" evolution has to be excluded as a possibility because Darwinists identify science with a philosophical doctrine known as naturalism. NATURALISM assumes the entire realm of nature to be a closed system of material causes and effects, which cannot be influenced by anything from "outside." Natural-

ism does not explicitly deny the mere existence of God, but it does deny that a supernatural being could in any way influence natural events, such as evolution, or communicate with natural creatures like ourselves. Scientific naturalism makes the same point by starting with the assumption that science, which studies only the natural, is our only reliable path to knowledge. A God who can never do anything that makes a difference, and of whom we can have no reliable knowledge, is of no importance to us.

Naturalism is not something about which Darwinists can afford to be tentative, because their science is based upon it. As we have seen, the positive evidence that Darwinian evolution either can produce or has produced important biological innovations is nonexistent. Darwinists know that the mutation-selection mechanism can produce wings, eyes, and brains not because the mechanism can be observed to do anything of the kind, but because their guiding philosophy assures them that no other power is available to do the job. The absence from the cosmos of any Creator is therefore the essential starting point for Darwinism. . . .

Naturalists will usually concede that any theory can be improved, and that our understanding of naturalistic evolution may one day be much greater than it is now. To question whether naturalistic evolution itself is "true," on the other hand, is to talk nonsense. Naturalistic evolution is the only conceivable explanation for life, and so the fact that life exists proves it to be true.[7]

SCIENCE, TECHNOLOGY, AND EVOLUTION

Most people are rightly impressed by the marvelous scientific accomplishments of today. These have become so common that we accept them without a second thought. Such things as solid-state electronic devices, satellite navigational aids, medical miracles, space probes that send high-resolution photos of the rings of Saturn, nuclear weapons and other mass destroyers — these have become simply a fact of life. These technological wonders have convinced many people that scientists surely must have super knowledge, and therefore they couldn't be wrong about such things as evolution or the long age of the universe. But these people are confusing two different subjects; all of the wonders above come from technology, not from the sort of science that pretends to understand ancient history just from the facts of today.

Most people don't realize that most scientists can go about their normal work without ever utilizing the doctrines of evolution. That theory, and also the age of the universe, doesn't have anything to do with the design of a new computer, a nuclear weapon, or a space vehicle. Even though geologists are often the most insistent about ancient ages, they can perform seismology and other ground analysis studies dependent only on what they measure at the present time and place. They may believe in evolution, but they don't depend on it in their normal work, except when they engage in "historical science" type of work. This is true for almost all other fields of scientific discipline. The thoughtful person should not allow his admiration for technology to blind him to the weakness of historical science.

A RELIGIOUS REACTION

Firm believers in anything, whether it be naturalism or Christianity, tend to be unforgiving toward those of the opposite view. Many biblical believers just aren't concerned with details of scientific procedure or belief, but simply point to biblical verses such as the ones below, which say that the "natural" human mind isn't capable of understanding godly things unless it is enlightened by the guidance of the Holy Spirit: The Bible tells us:

> The fear of the Lord is the beginning of wisdom (Prov. 9:10).

> For the preaching of the cross is to them that perish foolishness; but unto us which are saved it is the power of God (1 Cor. 1:18).

> For the foolishness of God is wiser than men; and the weakness of God is stronger than men (1 Cor. 1:25).

To the devout Christian, this belief overwhelms secular logic, but for many who have a more inquiring mind and/or a scientific background, it's not a very satisfactory solution to the creation/evolution controversy. That's part of the reason this book has been written — to show some of the reasons and details of both sides.

Of course, it's obvious that this writer makes no claim to impartiality. I am a Christian, retired after spending a lifetime working as an engineer in scientific fields. I spent the first 20 years of my working career as a believer in evolution, then slowly learned the technical problems of that belief. It took years of studying the issues on both sides before I finally became fully convinced of the superiority of the creationist position.

Endnotes

[1] Douglas Futuyma, *Science on Trial: The Case for Evolution* (New York, NY: Pantheon Books, 1983), p. 12-13.

[2] Phillip E. Johnson, *Darwin on Trial* (Washington DC: Regnery Gateway, 1991), p. 113.

[3] Johnson, *Darwin on Trial*, p. 131.

[4] Michael Denton, *Evolution: A Theory in Crisis* (Bethesda, MD: Adler & Adler, 1986), p. 93-118).

[5] Verne H. Booth, *Physical Science* (New York, NY: Macmillan Publishing Co., 1962), p. 147-148.

[6] Robert Jastrow, *God and the Astronomers* (Reader's Library, Inc., 1978), p. 11, 113-116.

[7] Phillip Johnson, *Darwin on Trial*, p. 114,-115, 121.

Notes

Notes

Chapter 3

ARGUMENTS FAVORING CREATION

CHAPTER INTRODUCTION

A critic once told me that I lacked focus; he said that I used too many random facts, and didn't have an overall coherent "theory of creation." By that I think he meant that I should have some hypothetical framework of just how the creation occurred. Of course he had in mind the sorts of stories that evolutionists use to describe their preferred ideas.

Anti-creationist Philip Kitcher describes such stories as follows:

> The heart of Darwinian evolutionary theory is a family of problem-solving strategies related by their common employment of a particular style of historical narrative. A Darwinian history is a piece of reasoning. . . . Suppose we want to know why a contemporary species manifests a particular trait. We can answer that question by supplying a

Darwinian history that describes the emergence
of that trait.[1]

In other words, if evolutionists want to describe something that happened in the hypothetical evolutionary development of some modern creature, they simply make up a
story — a "piece of reasoning" they call a "historical
narrative." This story becomes a "Darwinian history," and
is incorporated, along with other such stories, into the big
framework that becomes the "theory of evolution." Most of
these stories have very little actual physical evidence that
might serve as proof; the only requirement is that such a
story seems to be reasonable. But it's really only imaginative!

In 1967, a worldwide conference was held at
Philadelphia's Wistar Institute. The subject was problems
with evolution theory. Dr. M. P. Schützenberger was obviously thinking of the above "Darwinian histories," when he
said:

> For any specific question you can provide
> me with a specific answer, but I would claim that
> in most of the circumstances there was no general
> principle on which you could decide in advance
> which type of specific explanation you would use
> for it. I think this is exactly what it means to be a
> non-falsifiable theory.[2]

It's just this sort of "might-have-been" story, mas-
querading as a scientific theory, that creationists want to
avoid. The vast majority of creationists believe the Bible's
account of creation to be true, although they won't agree on
the details. But almost all will be careful to separate belief
that God did it from proof as to how He did it. For example,
chapter four of this book discusses the Great Flood of Noah.
It begins with the statement, "This chapter is not intended
as even a partial proof for creation, but rather as a simple
explanation of some of the beliefs that most creationists

hold concerning the flood."

For this reason, creationists generally don't even try to offer any sort of "grand unifying theory" to explain how the creation occurred. We don't put out fascinating stories such as the popular magazines like *Scientific American* offers. This chapter deals with solid evidences that seem to support sudden creation. Chapter five deals with solid evidences that seem to conflict with evolution theory.

THE FOSSIL RECORD

Creationism predicts that since all kinds of life were created in much the present form, we may find fossil evidence of some extinctions, but there were never any "half-this-half-that" transitional creatures. The fossil record should show this, and indeed it does.

In fact, no verifiable transitional fossils have ever been found above the "family" level, although there is good evidence that some new species have appeared. Speciation is discussed in a later section in this chapter. It is a known fact of science, widely used by breeders and horticulturalists on many types of plants and animals.

A later section in chapter five discusses archaeopteryx, claimed by evolutionists to be a transition between class reptilia and class aves. It's said that this is the best example of a transitional fossil known to science. But there is much evidence that this is a completely false claim — it's not transitional at all.

Almost all fossils can be identified and classified in the same way as those creatures living today. Most knowledge-able evolutionists now admit that this disproves the original Darwinism — evolution by natural selection working on normal hereditary variations, thus producing all of the wide varieties of life we see today, and that these are descendants from one, or a very few, original forms.

The problem of gaps in the fossil record was recognized by Charles Darwin himself; he wrote:

But, as by this theory innumerable transitional forms must have existed, why do we not find them imbedded in countless numbers in the crust of the earth?[3]

Darwin then explained that he thought these gaps existed because of the "imperfection of the geologic record," (not enough fossils had been collected). Early Darwinians expected that these gaps would be filled as the exploration for fossils continued. But the majority of paleontologists now agree that this expectation has not been fulfilled.

David M. Raup is dean of the Field Museum of Natural History in Chicago; this museum has one of the largest collections of fossils in the world. Thus, its dean should be eminently qualified to summarize the situation regarding gaps in the fossil record. He said:

Well, we are now about 120 years after Darwin, and the knowledge of the fossil record has been greatly expanded. We now have a quarter of a million fossil species, but the situation hasn't changed much. The record of evolution is still surprisingly jerky, and ironically, we have fewer examples of evolutionary transition than we had in Darwin's time. By this I mean that some of the classic cases of Darwinian change in the fossil record, such as the evolution of the horse in North America, have had to be discarded or modified as a result of more detailed information — what appeared to be a nice simple progression when irrelatively few data were available now appears to be much less gradualistic. So Darwin's problem has not been alleviated in the last 120 years and we still have a record which does show change, but one that can hardly be looked upon as the most reasonable consequence of natural selection.[4]

Stephen J. Gould is one of today's most outspoken advocates of evolution, yet he admits, "All paleontologists know that the fossil record contains precious little in the way of intermediate forms; transitions between major groups are characteristically abrupt."[5]

Because of this lack of evidence that evolution has occurred, Drs. Stephen J. Gould and Niles Eldredge proposed the Theory of Punctuated Equilibrium. This suggests that small segments of populations became isolated and experienced mutational changes that quickly led to formation of new species. Upon their reintroduction into the general population there was a long period of stasis (no change). It's said that since the new types developed quickly in a small group, it's not likely that any transitional fossils would now be found. Yet this theory makes no attempt to explain how such evolutionary development may have occurred. It seems that a simpler way of explaining the absence of transitional fossils is simply to believe in the Theory of Direct Creation.

But if the fossil record doesn't show those "innumerable transitional forms" that Darwin expected, why do so many of today's textbooks seem to say that the fossils show evidence of evolution? Is there actual falsification of facts? Well, not exactly misrepresentation — wishful thinking might be a better term. David Raup of Chicago's Field Museum is one of the world's most respected paleontologists, and a believer in evolution. Yet he wrote the following in a letter to *Science* magazine:

> A large number of well-trained scientists outside of evolutionary biology and paleontology have unfortunately gotten the idea that the fossil record is far more Darwinian than it is. This probably comes from the oversimplification inevitable in secondary sources: low-level textbooks, semi-popular articles, and so on. Also, there is probably some wishful thinking involved.

In the years after Darwin, his advocates hoped to find predictable progressions. In general, these have not been found — yet the optimism has died hard, and some pure fantasy has crept into textbooks.[6]

Another paleontologist who recognizes this problem with the inaccuracy used by textbooks in discussing fossils is Niles Eldredge of the American Museum of Natural History in New York. In speaking of the famous "horse series" of fossils, he said, ". . . horse evolution. . . . That has been presented as the literal truth in textbook after textbook. Now I think that that is lamentable." This full quotation, with its documentation reference data, is given in the section entitled "Horse Series Fossils" in chapter five of this book.

DINOSAUR FOSSILS

Of all the fossils discovered through the ages, none have stirred the public imagination as much as have these giant dragons. And almost every museum exhibit on dinosaurs uses them to proclaim their fable of "millions of years ago." Yet dinosaur fossils actually speak more clearly of creation than of evolution. Mace Baker wrote:

> The record of the dragons, contrary to the theory of evolution, does not demonstrate the gradual emergence of one kind into another. . . . The geological record — the contents and nature of the sedimentary strata — does not obviously support any notion of millions of years, nor any distinct time parameters monopolized by mammals, reptiles, or humans.[7]

The fossils of dinosaurs are all classified within class reptilia, and are either in order saurischia (lizard-hipped) or order ornithischia (bird-hipped). They're further divided into several dozen families, and a few hundred species.

Saurischias ranged in size from some of the small

chicken-sized coelurosaurs to the large vicious-looking tyrannosaurs and the huge "gentle-giant" sauropods. Ornithischias were mostly large, and included the hadrosaurs (duckbills or spoonbills), many of which had strange bony crests on their heads, as well as the ceratops (horned dinosaurs), ankylosaurs (armored dragons), stegasaurs (having plates along their backs), and others.

The interesting thing about this assortment of strange creatures is that they all fall into distinct groups — never any that were "half and half." Evolutionists assert that certain types lived early in the Triassic period, then died out and were replaced by other types, on and on for some 150,000,000 years to the end of the Cretaceous period, when suddenly all dinosaurs became extinct.

If this were true, surely there would be some evidence of this; but there is absolutely none. Every one of the crested hadrosaurs has a full-size crest; never is there a trace of one that's just forming. In the ceratops sub-order, there are several different kinds of neck frills and differing numbers of horns, but no sign of one type developing into another. All appeared to be fully formed. This all points to a Creator, not to random evolution.

Evolutionists speak of certain varieties living in certain periods, and others living in other periods. This sounds meaningful, until we remember that their method of dating strata is to see what sorts of index fossils are found in each one. These are arranged according to the assumed stage of evolution. This is circular reasoning at its worst. The director of the Field Museum vastly understated the case when he wrote:

> The charge that the construction of the geologic scale involves circularity has a certain amount of validity.[8]

Others have attempted many times to explain this problem in the logic of dating, with little success. Mostly it's ignored, as if it might go away after enough repetition. For example, one writer said:

> The intelligent layman has long suspected circular reasoning in the use of rocks to date fossils and fossils to date rocks. The geologist has never bothered to think of a good reply, feeling that explanations are not worth the trouble as long as the work brings results. This is supposed to be hard-headed pragmatism. . . . The rocks do date the fossils, but the fossils date the rocks more accurately. Stratigraphy cannot avoid this kind of reasoning, if it insists on using only temporal concepts, because circularity is inherent in the derivation of time scales.[9]

There's much speculation today about what caused the "sudden" extinction of dinosaurs. Scientists can't agree. Many speak of an asteroid striking the earth, causing world-wide atmospheric problems, however others disagree and point to the many creatures that did not become extinct at that time. There are two points we should realize: first, the suddenness of their demise is due to circular reasoning (see above), and second, most of the dinosaur fossils are found in huge "dinosaur graveyard" regions all over the world. These give strong evidence of having been buried in some huge watery catastrophe, such as a Great Flood. The post-flood environment was probably so different from what those on the ark had been suited for that extinction became inevitable.

MOLECULAR BIOLOGY

In recent years, molecular biology has enabled the study of the chemistry inside the DNA molecule. This, too, shows many distinct groups that do not show any signs of gradual development or transition. Dr. Michael Denton, who is not a creationist, but is a religious agnostic, wrote a book that's devastating to evolution theory.

Denton first describes how the ideas of evolution developed and are supposed to work, and gives many detailed descriptions of different facets of these ideas, showing the difficulties of matching evolutionary theory with fact. He discusses the gaps between the various phyla, and shows that there's not just "a missing link," but hundreds of gaps that can never be filled. These parts of Denton's book are written in a way that can be read and easily understood by almost anyone. They make very fascinating reading.

Then he moves into a more technical subject which some would find to be difficult reading. He describes the new techniques of examining the amino acid sequences within various proteins of different kinds of creatures. This method actually quantifies those differences into numerical values, thus giving a scientific measure of the degree of difference. Again, he describes the distinct gaps that occur, and discusses how this is strong evidence against any sort of evolution:

> The prospect of finding sequences in nature by this technique was, therefore, of great potential interest. Where the fossils had failed and morphological considerations were at best only ambiguous, perhaps this new field of comparative biochemistry might at last provide objective evidence of sequence and of the connecting links which had been so long sought by evolutionary biologists.

> However, as more protein sequences began to accumulate during the 1960s, it became increasingly apparent that the molecules were not going to provide any evidence of sequential arrangements in nature, but were rather going to reaffirm the traditional view that the system of nature conforms fundamentally to a highly ordered hierarchic scheme from which all direct evidence

for evolution is emphatically absent. Moreover, the divisions turned out to be more mathematically perfect than even most die-hard typologists would have predicted.[10]

Denton is an agnostic, an Australian medical doctor and molecular biologist. He is not a creationist, but calls himself a typologist.

The book *Of Pandas and People* was written as a supplemental biology textbook. It discusses six areas: Chemical Origin of Living Cells, Genetics and Evolution, Origin of Species, Fossils, Homology, and Molecular Biology. In each, the evidence for evolutionary descent is compared with the evidence for intelligent design. Religious arguments are not used. The closing paragraph of the book says:

> Any view or theory of origins must be held in spite of unsolved problems; proponents of both views acknowledge this. Such uncertainties are part of the healthy dynamic that drives science. However, without exaggeration, there is impressive and consistent evidence, from each area we have studied, for the view that living things are the product of intelligent design.[11]

SPECIATION IS NOT EVOLUTION

As was discussed in chapter one, speciation (or micro-evolution) is a well-known fact. It is utilized by plant and animal breeders to develop new and "better" varieties of animals and plants. But that's not macro-evolution — the gradual development of completely new creatures. And there are definite limits as to how far this process can be taken:

> All competent biologists acknowledge the limited nature of the variation breeders can produce, although they do not like to discuss it much when grinding the evolutionary ax.[12]

Speciation also happens in nature, anytime that populations encounter new environmental conditions. For example, even though it can't be proven, "Darwin's finches" were probably proliferations of a few storm-driven birds that once landed on the isolated Galapagos Islands.

In some cases, two or more species have merged into one. National Geographic's *Field Guide to the Birds of North America,* on page 426, says that the Northern Oriole was formerly two different species — Baltimore Oriole in the east, and Bullock's Oriole in the west.

But it's very important to notice that all of the new finches remained finches, and the two old species of orioles are still orioles. Only minor changes in color, song, or bill shape took place. These are examples of modification to adapt to environment, and the potential for such change was present in the genetic code of the original finches. These principles are discussed in more detail in the section entitled "How Did the Human Races Develop?" in chapter four.

COMPLEX ORGANS

Suppose you're hiking in the wilderness, miles from civilization, and find a gold wristwatch lying near the trail. As you pick it up, do you exclaim, "Look what nature accidentally formed," or do you say, "Oh look, someone lost his watch?" Of course we'd all choose the latter. In 1802 William Paley, a theologian with an interest in science, wrote a book called *Natural Theology.*[13]

The main theme centered on the analogy that a fine watch must have been carefully made by an intelligent watchmaker. In like manner, he said that the intricacies of nature proved there must be a highly intelligent Creator God.

Paley's book was widely acclaimed for many years. Then, as materialism took over scientific philosophy, Paley became the focal point for scorn. Scientists scoffed, and expounded the glory of evolution as the driving force that made the universe, our earth, and all forms of life itself. But now the tables are turning back. Many scientists are realizing that evolution cannot account for many of the intricacies of life. Complex organs such as the eye and the brain are hardest to explain.

For example, Sir Fred Hoyle and Dr. Chandra Wickramasinghe don't believe in God and are not creationists (they think life was imported from outer space), but they wrote:

> The speculations of *The Origin of Species* turned out to be wrong, as we have seen in this chapter. It is ironic that the scientific facts throw Darwin out, but leave William Paley, a figure of fun to the scientific world for more than a century, still in the tournament with a chance of being the ultimate winner.[14]

Many others have recognized the problems in believing that complex organs could be the product of accidental mutations. But, being driven by faith in naturalism, they're forced to say, "Well, it must have happened somehow."

Charles Darwin, for example, acknowledged this problem in his original book when he wrote:

> To suppose that the eye with all its inimitable contrivances for adjusting the focus to different distances, for admitting different amounts of light, and for the correction of spherical and chromatic aberration, could have been formed by natural selection, seems, I freely confess, absurd in the highest degree.[15]

Yet he went on and tried to show that it must have happened. But he didn't give any sort of explanation as to how it might have happened, only that in the vast passage of time the accumulation of gradual changes accomplished what was like a miracle.

But the problem has gotten worse. By now, thousands of fossils of trilobites have been found and widely studied. These extinct marine arthropods had eyes that seem to have been even more complex than our own. And they are considered to be among the very earliest forms of life, having no obvious predecessors. There were so many trilobites that they are referred to as members of the "Cambrian explosion" of early life.

The complexity of the human eye is quite small when compared to that of the brain. Not only does it control the eye and a vast array of other bodily organs and the body itself, it is a storehouse of information that most of us barely utilize. Michael Denton discussed this in considerable detail:

> The human brain consists of about ten thousand million nerve cells. Each nerve cell puts out somewhere in the region of between ten thousand and one hundred thousand connecting fibres by which it makes contact with other nerve cells in the brain. Altogether the total number of connections in the human brain approaches 10^{15} or a thousand million million . . . a much greater number of specific connections than in the entire communications network on Earth.[16]

It seems absolutely foolish for someone to imagine that such complexity could have developed, by chance, without a Designer who had vastly more intelligence. In order for a watch to exist, there must have been a watchmaker.

THE LAWS OF THERMODYNAMICS

These are considered to be the most important laws of science. They are usually expressed in somewhat the following form:

> 1. Matter and energy cannot be created nor destroyed — only changed from one form to another.

2. Any such change causes an increase of entropy, that is, a decrease in complexity.

These two fundamental laws are defined only for closed systems, but no one has ever been able to imagine any other system for which these laws are not true over a long time span, unless there is outside intelligent energy input. Raw energy input (sunlight, etc.) is not enough.

Creationists have used this as one of their most telling arguments; evolutionists usually respond by saying the earth is an open system, and an increase of entropy here is compensated for by a decrease somewhere else. But there is no known place in the universe that shows such a related decrease.

We've seen stars explode and die (supernovae), but we've never seen a new star born. Astronomers see many dust clouds in space, and say that this material is in the early stages of being the birth of a new star. But this is only a speculative theory. No one has ever seen it happen. They say that would take too long.

NOTE: Notice that the first evidences cited here (the fossil record and molecular biology) show that apparently macro-evolution has never occurred. The laws of thermodynamics give a theoretical reason why macro-evolution could never occur.

PLANETARY MAGNETIC FIELDS

The only workable theory ever proposed that explained in detail the source and behavior of earth's magnetic dipole was by creationist Sir Horace Lamb in 1887. This postulated that, in the beginning, an electric current had started flowing in the molten core, and has been exponentially decaying ever since.

Since Gauss's first measurement of earth's magnetism in 1835, repeated tests have shown a steady decay (about 6 percent since then). The data from these measurements follow the same curve that's obtained by plugging the known physical constants of the earth's core into Lamb's equations. A backward extrapolation of these equations shows that 10,000 years ago, the earth would have been much too hot to support any kind of life. This is one of the many limits showing the earth could not be much more than about 10,000 years old.

Cosmic evolutionists rely on the flimsy "dynamo theory" to explain a planet's magnetic field, since it's the only way to escape the short-age prediction of the more reasonable creationist explanation.

The dynamo theory says that a rotating planet with an electrically conductive core will generate a magnetic field. But this theory has never been demonstrated, and can't even be precisely formulated.

Using the dynamo theory, most astronomers had said that Uranus's magnetic field would be very weak. But two years before Voyager II arrived at Uranus, the Creation Research Society published physicist R. Humphrey's prediction that Uranus had a strong magnetic field. When Voyager II arrived, it confirmed the creationist's prediction, and the January 1986 newspapers were filled with the surprise of astronomers.

AGE OF THE MOON

One thing that astronomers agree on is that the moon's origin is still a mystery. Various evidences don't fit together properly for them. We know that a certain amount of "space dust" (micrometeorites, etc.) is continuously falling on the earth and the moon. On earth, rain allows this to mix with normal dirt. But the moon has no rain. Before the first moon landing, there was a strong worry about the thick layer of dust that should be there if it had been falling for billions of years.

Isaac Asimov wrote of this dust problem, and described what he thought might happen:

> I get a picture, therefore, of the first space-

ship, picking out a nice level place for landing purposes coming in slowly downward tail-first and sinking majestically out of sight.[17]

The moon lander was designed with very broad pads, so it wouldn't sink in the dust. Creationists predicted that dust would be less than a few inches thick, since it had only been falling for a few thousand years, and they were proven to be right. The evolutionists have revised their theories to try to explain this, but the question is still a hot issue.

It's well-known that the interaction between the moon and the earth's tidal bulge is causing the moon to gradually recede from the earth. If it had been doing this for long, it must have started too close to the earth for a stable orbit. Here's one evidence for a youthful moon (thousands, not billions, of years old).[18]

Also, the sides of the moon's craters are very steep near the edges. And, as Morton and others pointed out, if they were much older than a few tens of thousands of years, the fairly loose rock would "creep," making them more level.[19]

PLEOCHROIC HALOS

Dr. Robert Gentry, at Oak Ridge National Laboratory, studied the halos (spherical discolorations) made by radiation damage caused by the decay of alpha-emitting isotopes that are embedded in the micas in granite. Their diameters show what isotope had decayed. He found many halos from polonium (a "daughter-product" of uranium and thorium), but in a number of cases there was no trace that any uranium or thorium had ever been present. The polonium must have been there when the rock first hardened.[20]

But rock must be solid for a halo to form, and polonium has a very short half-life, so the rock couldn't have hardened slowly, like the evolutionist model of a gradually cooling earth or magma demands, else the polonium would have decayed away before it had a chance to make a halo. It must have actually been primordial polonium — it had to have been placed there in the beginning! Thus the earth must have been formed as a solid in a very short time, no more than a few minutes. This writer finds pleochroic halos to be one of the most solid evidences for God's miraculous creation.

ATMOSPHERIC HELIUM

An alpha particle consists of two protons and two neutrons, tightly bound together. This is just like the nucleus of a Helium-4 (^{4}He) atom. Thus, every alpha particle emitted by an atom such as radium, thorium, or uranium actually becomes a helium atom. When a ^{238}U atom ends up as ^{206}Pb (one of the most common heavy-metal dating reactions) it emits eight alpha particles (that become eight ^{4}He atoms) in the process. These 4He atoms diffuse out of the earth's crust at the rate of about 2×10^6 atoms/cm^2-sec, and end up in the earth's atmosphere.

Another helium isotope is ^{3}He, which arrives in our atmosphere via the solar wind at the rate of about 10 ^{3}He atoms/cm^2-sec; a minor source of ^{3}He is from the decay of tritium.

Helium accumulates in the atmosphere, and its concentration can be measured. There's now about 3.71×10^{15} grams there. But, if this had been happening for billions of years, there should be a lot more. Those scientists who believe in an ancient earth are very puzzled.

Professor of Metallurgy Dr. Melvin Cook in 1966 calculated that the helium content of our atmosphere shows the maximum age of the earth to be between 10,000 and 100,000 years.[21]

There have been a number of studies since then, trying to explain that question: "Where did all that helium go?" But, as J.W. Chamberlain said in his book *Theory of Planetary Atmospheres*, [the helium escape problem] ". . . will not go away and it is unsolved."

ICR's Dr. Larry Vardiman discusses the factors involved in atmospheric accumulation and escape of helium and other gases. He gives a number of references to these studies. But he says that the maximum age of the atmosphere is still far too young — 1.8 million years from ^{4}He studies, and 370 thousand years from ^{3}He studies. He makes an alternative suggestion that is quite significant:

> An obvious alternative to the evolutionary model, but one which runs counter to the basic assumption of the evolutionary / uniformitarian model, is that the earth's atmosphere is relatively young (less than 10,000 years). The helium we observe in the atmosphere is primordial with possible minor increases due to short-term decay of radioactive uranium and thorium in the earth's crust and some unknown consequences of the collapse of a vapor canopy during the flood.[22]

CARBON-14 DATING

The earth is constantly bombarded by high-energy cosmic radiation from deep space. As cosmic rays enter the atmosphere they collide with gas molecules, knocking off neutrons. Many of these neutrons interact with Nitrogen-14, producing Carbon-14 and a free proton.

$$^{14}N_7 + {}^1n_0 ==> {}^{14}C_6 + {}^1p_1$$

Prior to the advent of atomic bombs, this was the sole source of all the C^{14} on Earth.

Oxidation (combination with oxygen) takes place fairly quickly, producing carbon dioxide ($C_{14}O_2$), and this diffuses and mixes with the normal carbon dioxide ($C_{12}O_2$) that is a vital part of the earth's atmosphere. Animals take in CO_2 by respiration; plants take it in through photosynthesis, and thus the carbon becomes part of the food chain, and part of all organisms.

In this way, all living organisms contain carbon, and most of this comes from the CO_2 in the atmosphere. Most of it is the normal C_{12}, which is a stable isotope. However, a small fraction is ^{14}C, a radioactive isotope that emits a beta particle (nuclear electron) with a half-life of 5,730 years.

$$^{14}C_6 ==> \; ^{14}N_7 + \; ^{0}e_{-1}$$

As long as the plant or animal is alive, its bodily carbon has the same $^{14}C/^{12}C$ ratio as does the atmosphere around it. However when it dies it no longer takes in a fresh supply and, after a long time, much of its internal ^{14}C is depleted through radioactive decay. If we know the initial $^{14}C/^{12}C$ fraction of an ancient sample, and measure the current fraction, we can calculate how long it has been since that sample was part of a living organism. This is the principle of Carbon-14 dating.

Willard F. Libby invented this system, and wrote the definitive book on the subject. He discussed the important factors, especially SPR and SDR. He showed that the Specific Production Rate (SPR) of C_{14} is 18.8 atoms per gram of total carbon per minute. But he showed the Specific Decay Rate (SDR) to be only 16.1 ± 0.5 disintegrations per gram per minute. These two numbers should be the same, if the atmosphere is in equilibrium. The difference shows that buildup in the biosphere hasn't had time to catch up with production in the stratosphere. This troubled Libby, since he believed the world was many millions of years old, and C_{14} half-life is 5,568 years (this has since been revised to 5,730 years). He wrote:

> If one were to imagine that the cosmic radiation had been turned off until a short while ago, the enormous amount of radiocarbon necessary to the equilibrium state would not have been manufactured and the specific radioactivity (SDR) of living matter would be much less than the rate of production (SPR) calculated from the neutron intensity.[23]

Of course, most creationists believe that this manufacture has only been going on for several thousand years, and that Libby was unknowingly agreeing with the Bible's account of a recent creation. But he chose to ignore this discrepancy and attribute it to experimental error. He recalculated his original numbers and settled on an SDR of 15.3 dis/gm-min, and said that it must have remained at that value for at least 20 or 30 thousand years.

But several other scientists have rechecked this work, and all have verified the non-equilibrium. Their SPR numbers have ranged up to 27 atoms/gm-min. They've all shown that the SDR is near 15 dis/gm-min in most living things, all over the world. This seems to be a strong indication that the age of the atmosphere should really be measured in thousands, not millions, of years.

Professor Robert L. Whitelaw (Virginia Polytechnic Institute), who teaches Mechanical and Nuclear Engineering, realized that by using these SDR and SPR numbers, and accepting their difference as real, he could calculate the actual time at which this system must have started. He used the values obtained for SDR and SPR by several other scientists also, and calculated the starting point as being between 7,000 and 16,000 years ago. Also, by using these actual SDR and SPR numbers, he found correction factors for any published radiocarbon ages. These are shown on the chart below.[24]

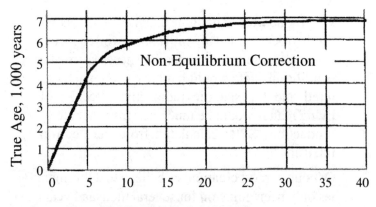

All samples that have been dated by the ^{14}C method are published in the *Radiocarbon Journal*. Whitelaw selected those samples published from 1950 through 1979 that fell into five categories: 1) land animals, including humans, from the Americas; 2) the same except from Europe, Asia and Africa; 3) trees; 4) marine fossils found in ocean areas; and 5) marine fossils found on continental areas. For each, he applied the described correction.

He then grouped this collection of revised ages into 500-year age groups and plotted five histograms, showing the number of objects that died in each 500-year period. These graphs are shown on the following page. They all show one surprising effect — there was an unusually high number of deaths between 5,000 and 5,500 years ago, followed by a much lower number of deaths during the next 500 years. This seems to show strong evidence that some worldwide catastrophe took place at that time and killed a large fraction of the earth's land and sea creatures, as well as most of the trees. And that is just when the Bible says the Great Flood of Noah occurred. Doesn't this seem to be a scientific verification of Scripture?

Other evidences coming from this large set of radiocarbon dates are:

1. Even before correction for non-equilibrium, almost all ages connected with human artifacts are no more than about 12,000 years.

2. These seem to be mostly from the Middle East and the Mediterranean basin.

3. Almost all sea-creatures whose dated remains were found on continental areas had died just over 5,000 years ago.

4. There were many samples of coal and oil that gave ages less than 50,000 years, even though most scientists believe these were formed very much longer ago than that. The ^{14}C dating method is not considered usable for objects thought to be

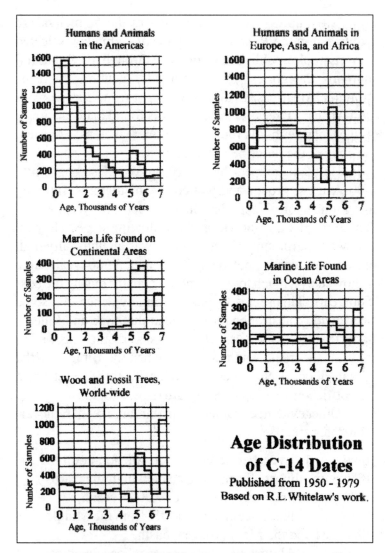

more than about 50,000 years old, since almost all of the ^{14}C would have decayed during that time (its half-life is 5,730 years).

A number of other creationist scientists have written about the creationist aspects of ^{14}C dating; most agree on the importance of the non-equilibrium problem, but not all agree with Whitelaw's method of correction. Whitelaw's summary is a good starting point for those who wish to learn more about creationist views on this dating method.[25]

Before the mid-1980s, dating utilized sensitive radio-activity detectors and counters; this required that a sample must have 10 to 20 grams of carbon. Many valuable artifacts were ruled off-limits because too much material would be destroyed by the measurements. Now, with particle accelerator mass spectrometers, only a small fraction of a gram of carbon is needed. This greatly improves the statistical accuracy of the isotope measurement, but does nothing to address the all-important non-equilibrium question: "How much ^{14}C did the sample contain when it was alive?"

POPULATION GROWTH

We can use population growth figures to get an interesting insight into the question, "How long have people been on this earth?" First, we should list some of the known historical numbers of how many people have lived here.

United States Population Growth			World Population Growth		
Year	Pop. x10^6	Rate %/yr	Year	Pop. x10^6	Rate %/yr
1800	5.31		1 A.D.	300	
		3.0			.032
1850	23.2		1650	510	
		2.41			.41
1900	76.2		1700	625	
		1.93			.26
1910	92.2		1750	710	
		1.40			.50
1920	106.		1800	910	
		1.52			.43
1930	123.		1850	1130	
		0.71			.70
1940	132.		1900	1600	
		1.36			.90
1950	151.		1950	2510	
		1.71			1.62
1960	179.		1972	3575	
		1.26			2.55
1970	203.		1982	4600	
		1.09			1.68
1980	226.		1987	5000	
				(estimated)	

Population figures taken from 1987 World Almanac.

Except for the one involving the world population in A.D. 1, which is just a conjecture, growth rates range from 0.26 to 3.0 percent per year.

The Bible describes one growing population. Let's see if it's numerically reasonable. When Jacob's family moved to Egypt, it had 70 members; when the Israelites left Egypt 430 years later, in about 1446 B.C., they had grown to between one and two million people, which greatly worried the Egyptians. If we calculate that growth rate, we find it to be between 2.25 percent and 2.41 percent per year, which is within the range of the modern figures quoted above, and therefore is completely reasonable.

The Bible also describes Noah's family as consisting of eight people who survived the Great Flood (which many believe to have been in about 2350 B.C.). These were the only people left to repopulate the earth. Some 4,340 years later, we now have a world population of some five billion people. This is a growth rate of about 0.47 percent per year, about the same as is known to have been true a few hundred years ago.

On the other hand, if we consider any sort of evolutionary growth over a period of a few million years, we arrive at ridiculously low growth rates. For example, if an original pair of "pre-humans" started a million years ago, and increased to five billion humans today, the rate of that growth would have been only an average of 0.00217 percent per year.

At that rate, the time required for the group to double its size would be 32,000 years. At such low growth rates, these "people" would quickly have become extinct, considering that a lifespan was probably less than a hundred years, at most. In the early millennia, an accidental death of a single adult of child-bearing age would have been devastating.

We can see that population considerations seem to make the evolutionist position to be almost impossible for a reasonable person to consider, whereas the growth rates according to the creationist time scale are well within the limits of actual numbers that we see today.

For those who are mathematically inclined, population growth rates can be calculated by one of the following equations:

Population Growth Equations

Equation	Where
$P_N / P_0 = (1 + R)^N$	P_0 = orig. population,
$N = \dfrac{\log (P_N / P_0)}{\log (1 + R)}$	P_N = final population,
	R = growth rate / year,
$R = (P_N/P_0)^{1/N} - 1$	N = number of years.

BUTTERFLY METAMORPHOSIS

Duane Gish of the Institute for Creation Research often debates evolutionist scientists. These clashes are usually held on university campuses, before audiences of a thousand or so. One of his always-successful ploys is to pose this challenge: "If evolution is true, how do you account for the metamorphosis of a butterfly? What could be its ancestor? How could it have evolved by small steps?" He's never gotten an answer, because this seems such an obvious case for the intelligent design of a unique kind of creature.

Poirier and Cumming wrote a beautiful article recently describing the life cycle of the monarch butterfly.[26]

This amazing insect begins life as an egg, laid on the underside of a milkweed plant. After a few days, the tiny larva emerges and lives for three weeks on the leaf, growing to some 2,700 times its original weight. It's become a 2" long caterpillar, with yellow, white and black stripes. It then spins a pad, attaches itself to the leaf and hangs motionless, head down, for about a half day.

Suddenly it jerks convulsively, sheds its outer skin, head, and 16 legs, and is quickly transformed into a jade-green pupa, or chrysalis, with gold spots. While in this state, all of its interior parts dissolve into an amorphous green liquid, except for its tiny red pulsating heart. In 8-14 days its outer shell opens and the newly formed butterfly unfolds. It's ready to fly within a couple of hours. It now has six legs, four beautiful orange wings with black borders, a 4" wing-span, and compound eyes that have 6,000 lenses.

Monarchs are the only insects known to migrate over distances as far as 3,000 miles, from spots all over the U.S. and Canada. Most of them winter in the Neovolcanic Mountains of Mexico, hibernate for four months in freezing temperatures, and then return to their origin.

How can evolutionism explain the God-given instinct that guides them unerringly to the same wintering ground their parents used, even though they've never been near it before? What "accidental force" could bring them back to the same region they came from? And how could blind chance account for the remarkable multiple transitions from egg to caterpillar larva, the dissolving and re-forming into the pupal chrysalis, and finally their emergence into the beautiful monarch butterfly? No reasonable materialistic explanation has ever been proposed; only the mind of an infinitely intelligent Creator could account for this.

OUT-OF-SEQUENCE STRATA IN GRAND CANYON

The Grand Canyon shows more strata than any other spot in the world. Yet there are hundreds of millions of years missing from these strata, compared to the evolutionist's standard "geologic column" (see page 66); also at least two different so-called ages alternate and repeat. Here is good evidence against the accuracy of that "column" as a measure of age.

As one descends the Grand Canyon, the top-most rocks are very old, according to the geologic column classification. The entire Cenozoic and Mesozoic eras are missing; these supposedly occupied the last 225 million years. It's said that these missing times saw the rise and fall of dinosaurs, then the development of huge mammals, and finally of all the creatures we see around us today. But it's all gone now.

The topmost rock layer is the 300-foot thick white Kaibab limestone, which contains marine fossils said to be of Permian age (280 to 225 million years old). This was evidently deposited under water. Below that is the red clay and shale of the Toroweap formation. Much of its visible part is a talus slope. This is also considered Permian.

Next is the beautiful cream-colored Coconino sandstone, which forms a 300-foot ribbon around almost the entire Grand Canyon. It is cross-bedded and, according to evolutionary geologists, is said to have been deposited during a time when strong winds blew sand first one way and then the other. Many animal tracks are preserved in this stone — from quadrupeds that had broad clawed feet but no dragging tail. Geologists say these probably came from some sort of amphibian. But how could amphibians have flourished in a dry, sandy, windswept climate?

The reddish Hermit shale is next, forming a talus slope that rests on the 850-foot thick Supai formation. This is composed of alternating layers of shale and sandstone, stained red by iron oxide, and containing land-type fossils, also said to be of Permian age. This vast Supai extends for hundreds of miles over most of Arizona and much of New Mexico. The explanation most often heard for the Supai is that this came from a river delta, but there are many reasons to doubt this — no trace of a large river has been found.

The conventional evolutionist explanation for both the Coconino and the Supai would seem to contradict the creationist belief that most of the above-bedrock formations of the Grand Canyon were produced by the Great Flood of Noah. However, modern research has changed this picture. See the section entitled "How Was The Grand Canyon Formed?" in chapter four. This also discusses research about the Coconino quadruped trackways, showing that these must have been made by newt-like animals walking uphill in flowing water (trying to escape the flood water?).

If the strata followed the sequence predicted by the geologic column, the next lower layers should be Pennsylvanian. But this entire 45-million year period is missing. The Supai lies conformably on the 500-foot thick Redwall limestone, whose natural light gray color is stained by water that has percolated through the red Supai. This Redwall formation has an abundance of marine fossils, said to show early Mississippian age (345-325 million years old).

There is good evidence showing that these limestone formations were deposited very quickly, during the Great Flood of Noah. See the section entitled "Where Did The World's Limestones Come From?" in chapter four.

The geologic column would predict that below Mississippian should be Devonian, then Silurian, and then Ordovician — representing over 150 million years of time. But these are all completely missing, over all of Arizona, except for a few small lenses of Devonian material, apparently deposited in holes (like Karst topography) in the Cambrian Muav below.

As we descend below the Redwall limestone, we find, crossing what seems to be a completely conformable boundary, the Muav limestone, which has many trilobites and other Cambrian fossils. But that missing 150 million years is a problem. L.F. Noble expressed this puzzle as follows:

> No representatives of the Ordovician, Silurian, or Devonian were discriminated in the area studied, the Muav limestone being succeeded without apparent stratigraphic break by the Redwall limestone.[27]

One of the biggest stratigraphic problems in the entire canyon is found near the bottom on the northern side. Here there are several alternating layers of Cambrian Muav interspersed between layers of Mississippian Redwall. This interbedding of two periods widely separated in supposed age cannot be explained by the uniformitarian geologist; it's like evolution went back and forth. Yet they lie conformably.

The early Cambrian Tapeats sandstone lies below the Muav, and rests on the red Precambrian Hakatai shale. Below that are the foundation rocks — Bass limestone, Vishnu and Brahma schists — all considered early Precambrian, Proterozoic or Archean. These are highly metamorphosed (changed by extreme heat and pressure), twisted, uplifted, and showing signs of violent stresses, probably caused by several opposing fault movements.

SOFT SEDIMENT DEFORMATION

ICR's Dr. John Morris describes "soft sediment deformation," showing it as an evidence for a young earth.[28]

As we've seen, the Tapeats sandstone is at the bottom of the Grand Canyon, and is supposedly some 550 million years old. It is overlain by several other formations, the topmost of which is the Kaibab limestone, said to be a little over 200 million years old. These layers of rock were all uplifted some 70 million years ago, according to the standard geologic column dating. This uplift formed the Kaibab Plateau.

But over to the side of the plateau, the strata all bend sharply down, becoming almost vertical in places. In one area the Tapeats changes from horizontal to nearly vertical in only about 100 feet. Yet this rock, which today is very brittle and hard, shows no signs of rupture — no cracks from all that bending. This makes it hard to imagine that the bending occurred after the rock had hardened, but yet according to the standard geological dating system it had to be some 480 million years old.

Creationists, on the other hand, believe that this entire

system of sedimentary rock was laid down under water during the time of the Great Flood. The Tapeats, at the bottom, was one of the first deposits. Then, as the floodwaters surged first one way and then another, one formation after another was formed, ending with the Kaibab. During the recovery phase, while new ocean basins and continental regions were developing, uplift occurred as the earth adjusted to the weight of the shifting water. Since the deposits were still fairly soft, they could bend without cracking.

This uplifting trapped a huge body of water in an area covering what now comprises several adjoining states to the north and east of Grand Canyon. It wasn't long before a small stream opened in the plateau, and that large lake began to drain. The huge Grand Canyon system was quickly eroded as this vast amount of water surged through. In this way, the canyon was eroded in a short time, possibly only a few days.

We've recently seen an example of this sort of canyon production. In 1980 the Mount St. Helens volcano in southwestern Washington blew up with a violent explosion. The Toutle River was filled with a vast amount of pyroclastic ash mud that began to form rock; Spirit Lake was dammed, and its water level rose over 400 feet. After a couple of years, a heavy rain made the dam overflow, cutting a small channel, and Spirit Lake began to quickly dump its excess water. Within a couple of days, a canyon was formed that now looks very much like the Grand Canyon of Arizona, except it's about 1/40 as large. But the Toutle Canyon happened as a result of only one relatively small volcano. Think how much more vast was the Great Flood of Noah, which covered the entire earth. That could have easily carved the entire Grand Canyon of Arizona.

PALYNOLOGY

The study of palynology (fossil spores and pollens) has also produced strong evidence against the uniformitarian concept (and thus is evidence favoring creation). Evolution theory teaches that complicated plants like conifers didn't evolve until the early Mesozoic era. Yet many samples of gymnosperm (seed-bearing) pollen from pine, spruce, hemlock, and fir have been found in strata all the way from the Precambrian Hakatai shale near the bottom, to the Permian Hermit and Supai shales, and even in some shaley layers within the Mississippian redstone.

Clifford Burdick's early work in the area of fossil pollens was rejected by the University of Arizona only because it violated the uniformitarian concept. But a second team got similar results. Later, a field trip by Loma Linda University scientists again confirmed Burdick's work. His book, *Canyon of Canyons*, first published by the Bible-Science Association in 1974, shows a number of photographs of fossil pollens, as well as many views of the canyon.

This controversial conclusion, showing that apparently these "complex" trees were created very early in earth's history, seems to be correct, even though most scientists reject it because of prejudice. It would seem that a better explanation for the deposition of these rock layers might involve the Great Flood of Noah.

This tremendous amount of surging water would have contained much calcium (from the feldspars in basaltic magma that came up from the "breaking open of the fountains of the deep"). There would also have been a lot of dissolved carbon dioxide (steam and CO_2 are the main constituents of volcanic gases). These combine in water to form limestone ($CaCO_3$). In this way the massive quantities of limestone were probably laid down during the first months of that flood. Different kinds of fossils do not represent widely differing ages, but simply depend on the ecological regions from which the waters came, as they surged back and forth.

ANOMALOUS ARTIFACTS
(modern objects in ancient strata)

There have been many findings of sandal prints in pre-Cambrian rock, man-made objects smoothly embedded in coal beds, etc. These show that either man has been around a lot longer than most people think, or that the system of dating strata is badly in error, or both. Petrified trees have been found, standing vertically through several so-called different-aged strata.[29]

In 1972 Dr. Don Elston was a member of a U.S.G.S. team that explored the Sierra Ancha mountains of central Arizona. They discovered a mass of crab-like arthropod fossils in rock that had been age-dated at 1.2-billion years. But arthropods are not supposed to have evolved until the Cambrian period, thought to have begun 570 million years ago.

Caves where Cro-Magnon people lived in Rhodesia contain paintings of animals that look like dinosaurs, showing that man and dinosaurs must have lived during the same time. Similar carvings exist on the walls of the Hava Supai branch of the Grand Canyon, in Mexico, and elsewhere. William Meister found fossilized trilobites embedded in what seemed to be a sandal print, in Middle Cambrian rock of the Wheeler Formation in Antelope Springs, Utah.[30]

PALUXY RIVERBED

For many decades the Cretaceous limestone of the Paluxy riverbed in Texas has produced curious tracks. Many books and articles have described dinosaur tracks and human footprints, side by side in the same strata. See, for example, *Tracking Those Incredible Dinosaurs . . . and the People Who Knew Them* by John Morris, CLP Publishers, 1980.

These were first found in 1908, when floodwaters eroded the clay that covered the limestone below. During the 1930s, a number of local people cut out blocks of stone containing footprints, and sold them to tourists. Many trails were found, showing alternating left and right prints, and apparently having all the earmarks of genuine tracks. But a few people became skilled at carving fake tracks, and selling them.

In 1938, Roland T. Bird, a paleontologist at the American Museum of Natural History in New York, went to Glen Rose and investigated. He documented many of the exposed trails, identified several as having been made by sauropods (possibly an apatosaurus), excavated one entire trail, and placed it on display at his museum. Other tracks have been displayed at the University of Texas at Austin.

The same limestone also contains tracks that appear to be human. Some show traces of sandals, others retain toemarks. But few scientists have been willing to call them "human," because, as Roland Bird said, if he were to acknowledge the presence of man tracks in Cretaceous strata, all the textbooks would have to be rewritten. Yet there's been no other identification.

In June of 1987, Dr. Carl Baugh and others found a tooth, embedded in marl (clay and gravel mix) between two limestone layers on the bank of the Paluxy River, each of which contained dinosaur tracks. Several dentists independently examined the tooth and identified it as an apparent human deciduous maxillary right central incisor — a child's tooth. Tests were made by professional anatomists, and initial results of the morphology pronounced it human-like. But more careful analysis of the microstructure of the tooth enamel found a fish-like micro-rod structure. It's now classified as being of "unknown origin." Meanwhile, more tracks of both dinosaur and human-like origin have been found. Excavation is continuing, in the hopes of finding more definite proof.

Why do creationists hope to find proof that dinosaurs and humans lived during the same time? Is it really that important? Yes, it is one of the major points of difference between the two viewpoints. Biblical creationists believe that God created birds, fish, whales, and other sea life on the fifth day of Creation Week, and land animals including humans the very next day. This clearly says that all forms of animal and plant life must have co-existed.

Evolutionists, on the other hand, rely on the concept that life developed gradually, beginning with simple one-celled organisms. They say that many millions of years elapsed before reptiles (including dinosaurs) appeared, and more millions before ape-like creatures "evolved." They say that humans only appeared between one and three million years ago.

Controversy has dogged these tracks, with evolutionists trying to discredit them and creationists trying to emphasize their validity. In the mid-1980s this became more intense when several of the human-like tracks began to show a discoloration that was shaped like three-toed dinosaur tracks surrounding the human-like portions. This only showed up after several years of sun, water, and weather. Those opposed to the idea that humans and dinosaurs could coexist made accusations of fraud or poor science. The widely circulated film "Footprints in Stone" was withdrawn in 1986 by Films for Christ, who issued a statement that these were certainly genuine tracks, not carvings, and seemed to show human-like traits. But, in view of uncertainties, they should not be used as "proof" of co-existence.

In 1986 the Bible-Science Association established a Task Force, headed by Robert Helfinstine, to investigate the tracks, discolorations, and other artifacts. Their report covered many aspects of investigations.[31]

About the same time that they began their investigation, two more teeth were found, not far from where the first one had been. The Task Force made a number of conclusions:

1. The footprints, both dinosaur and human-like, were definitely tracks of animals, not erosion-marks or other

natural phenomena. Many of them were in distinct trails, with alternating right-left characteristics. In many cases, toemarks were clearly visible. When tracks were removed and cross-sections were cut, microscopic examination showed stress lines below them, in a pattern that made it clear the limey mud had been stepped on, compressed by the weight of the animal, and spread out, forming an upraised edge.

2. There were a number of cases where a human-like print had been formed inside a dinosaur print. Tests by barefoot people running in wet mud were performed, and it seemed clear that stepping inside a previously laid larger track made it easier to run. The general character of such experimental tracks matched those found in the stone. The smaller human-like tracks were not always centered within the dinosaur track, and some even overlapped an edge, as if someone had been in a hurry. They weren't able to clearly explain the discolorations, but apparently some sort of filling had taken place between the time of the original dinosaur track and the human-like track, and this fill didn't show until weathering had occurred.

3. Many scientists didn't believe it possible that these could actually be human tracks, because of the relative ages in which these species are thought to have lived. However, no one has been able to suggest what kind of animal other than humans might have made them. Any mammal that co-existed with dinosaurs would violate uniformitarian's dating rules, just as much as would humans.

4. All three of the teeth have been identified by dentists, pathologists, and paleontologists as having a very strong appearance of being genuine human teeth. But Scanning Electron Microscope analysis of the enamel showed a micro-pattern more nearly fish-like. Some suggested it may have come from a Pycnodont or a Sargodon, but all have agreed that these fish families have teeth shaped radically differently from the three Glen Rose teeth. For example,

these teeth have roots, but pycnodont teeth are rootless and are mounted on pedicles (small posts). A radio-immuno-assay test was conducted on genetic material in the root structure of one of the teeth, and this material showed similarity to mammals but not to fish. At present, the conclusion is that these must be of unknown origin, since no teeth are known that have detailed human-like morphology, mammal-like genetic material, and fish-like enamel micro-structure. Maybe they can think of a way to explain how surrounding minerals or a genetic peculiarity of a sub-race of humans might explain the unusual tooth enamel.

5. What appears to be a fossilized human finger was found in the same marl layer as the teeth, between two limestone layers that are both considered Cretaceous. This has all the shape details of a finger, including a fingernail. X-ray analysis was inconclusive, because the material was too dense. But when the finger was sawed in two, the cross-section showed the bone, marrow, and skin structure. It was shown to 16 medical doctors, and all agreed that it had all the characteristics of a normal human finger. Complete fossil-ization of flesh is unusual, but paleontologists have found well-preserved fossilized worms in this same general re-gion. The only way fossilization could have occurred would be by quick total immersion in the limey mud, so as to prevent decay.

6. In 1936 a hammer was found some miles away, embedded in a Cretaceous concretionary sandstone, dated (by orthodox methods) to be 135 million years old. Prelimi-nary tests showed the appearance of good technology, but lack of funds limit further testing.

7. In 1987, while digging for dinosaur and human tracks, two long coalified roots were found, and positively identified as from a Lepidodendron, a fern-tree type of plant which grew to heights of 60 to 100 feet. It is listed as of Permian age, and had never before been found in Cretaceous material. What's even more unusual is that it was polystrate,

that is, one end was embedded in the lower limestone layer, most of it (9 feet, 8 inches) was in the marl layer above (where the teeth were found), and part of it grew through the upper limestone layer. This clearly demonstrates that all three of these layers were deposited quickly, not spread through millions of years. Lepidodendrons were considered to have grown some 150 million years earlier than any Cretaceous formations. Thus, although this has little to do with the co-existence of humans and dinosaurs, there is a clear sign of strong disagreement with conventional "geologic column" dating, and a solid evidence for deposition during a tremendous flood.

MOUNT ST. HELENS

On the morning of May 18, 1980, in southwest Washington, the Mount St. Helens volcano exploded in the most spectacular display ever fully recorded by scientists. The total energy release was estimated to be equivalent to one Hiroshima-sized atom bomb every second, for nine hours — a total of some 400,000,000 tons of TNT. It leveled 150 square miles of forest, and dumped 1/8 cubic mile of rock into nearby Spirit Lake, causing a tidal wave 860 feet high. The level of the lake ended up 200 feet higher than before, held by a newly created rock/earth dam. Elevation of the mountaintop dropped from its original 9,500 to about 9,150 feet. This catastrophe has proved to be a gold mine of evidences showing the likelihood of the flood of Noah. Geologists, amazed by studies in the next dozen years, saw evidences of rapid production of effects previously thought to have taken many thousands of years to accumulate.

Geologist Dr. Steve Austin, of the Institute for Creation Research, is featured in a video that describes how these evidences fall into four main divisions. These are described below.[32]

Stratigraphic Layering — The majority of evolutionists believe that the layers, or strata, in the earth's crust took millions of years to deposit; they actually use these strata to date various fossils. But Mount St. Helens proved otherwise. A new cliff was formed, showing 30 feet of clear bedded layering. Geologists expected that one event of this kind would make just one thick layer, but this cliff looked just like many others that are estimated to be millions of years old. Geologist Steve Austin said, "If you had told me several years ago that this could have happened this quickly, I would never have believed it."

Quick Deposit of Petrified Forests — About a million logs ended up floating on Spirit Lake, in a huge logjam. Divers later found that many logs were floating vertically, with their root-end down. These were at varying depths, and some were already buried in the deep mud at the bottom. Silt was constantly being added to the bottom, burying logs at varying depths.

So what does this prove? Consider the famous Yellowstone petrified forest, which scientists believe was formed by many successive forests, each of which was killed by some catastrophe, then petrified, and centuries later was replaced by another forest. They base this claim on the different heights at which petrified trees were found. They say that this entire area took many tens of thousands of years to form, and it's one of the "showcase examples" proving the long age of the earth.

But think what Spirit Lake will probably look like at some point in the future, a few dozen years after it has drained and the land has dried out. We already know that logs can petrify quickly, under the right conditions of being deeply buried in wet soil — conditions very much like these logs are in today. Here we'll someday be able to see a petrified forest, with logs standing vertically, roots down, in varying depths of soil — just like those in Yellowstone. If we didn't know better, it would certainly look like it took many thousands of years, but this one has only taken about a dozen years so far.

Quick Formation of Coal — Most scientists say that coal has formed from forests growing in peat bogs, over millions of years. But examination of the texture of actual peat bogs shows many roots intertwining through the mass; yet actual coal beds don't show roots — they often have flecks of bark. Several recent studies have concluded that the vast coal deposits of the eastern U.S. probably formed from large masses of water-deposited vegetation. Now the logs on Spirit Lake are actually demonstrating how this might have occurred.

Wave action on this logjam is chafing the logs against each other, rubbing bits of bark off. Much of this bark has settled to the bottom of the lake, and has already formed a bog several feet thick. The bottom parts have been compressed, and already show a texture very much like coal. A few more years under pressure will probably see real coal forming in the lower parts. Here is a much more likely story of how our massive coal beds were really formed. And it's only taken a few years to do it.

Erosion of Massive Canyon — Most of the older stories of how the Grand Canyon of Arizona was formed involve slow erosion by the Colorado River meandering through the bottom. But for years hydrologists have said it really couldn't have happened that way — no normal river would have produced such a wide canyon. And meandering rivers don't carve deep canyons; they're more like the lower Mississippi, moving slowly through a flat flood plain. Now Mount St. Helens has produced a better explanation.

One effect of the explosion of Mount St. Helens was a huge mudflow that overflowed Spirit Lake and dammed up the Toutle River. This partially lithified dam breached about two years later, and a torrent of water gushed out, almost draining the lake, eroding away the dam, carving a canyon almost 200 feet wide, and leaving just a small stream flowing down its middle.

Mount St. Helens gives us a small-scale demonstration

showing that the Grand Canyon of Arizona could have been produced by a dammed-up lake breaching its dam not long after the Great Flood, and dumping its stored water. A contour map of the western United States shows that if such a dam once existed near the northern part of the present Grand Canyon, it could back up a lake that covered several states. And there are extensive evidences of shorelines of several huge ancient lakes in this very region.

The dam may well have been formed by the Kaibab Uplift that held back a portion of the floodwaters for a few tens of years during the last parts of the flood's drying. Here is strong backing for the concept that the Grand Canyon could have been formed in only days, not millions of years.

CHAPTER SUMMARY

This chapter has discussed a number of physical evidences tending to show that the best explanation of this world and its contents is sudden creation by a supernatural power — the one we call God. But we haven't said much about the personality or purpose of this power.

Chapter five takes up the discussion from the other side of the picture. Many of its topics are rebuttals of arguments often used by evolutionists in trying to bolster their belief. There we'll try to show the flaws in their approach; some are from errors in logic and some are leftover evidences once thought to be true but which now have been disproven. Some are even hoaxes. These two chapters are complementary, each leading to the same result, but from the opposite direction. One deals with positive evidences; the other deals with negative.

The true answer to the question "How did we get here?" has got to be a variant of one or the other of these two answers — there's really no other choice. Any evidence showing evolution to be false is evidence favoring creation. That's why we have two chapters, dealing with both sides of the issue.

Endnotes

[1]Philip Kitcher, *Abusing Science — The Case Against Creationism*, (Cambridge, MA: The MIT Press, 1982), p. 50.

[2]M.P. Schützenberger, *Mathematical Challenges to the Neo-Darwinian Interpretation of Evolution* (Philadelphia, PA: Wistar Institute Press, 1967), p. 70.

[3]Charles Darwin, *The Origin of Species*, 6th edition (New York, NY: Macmillan, 1927), p. 163.

[4]David M. Raup, "Conflicts Between Darwin and Paleontology," Field Museum of Natural History Bulletin, January 1979, p. 25

[5]Stephen J. Gould, "The Return of Hopeful Monsters," *Natural History*, Vol. 86, June 1977, p. 22-30.

[6]*Science*, Vol. 213, p. 289.

[7]Mace Baker, *Dinosaurs* (Redding, CA: New Century Books, 1991), p. 10.

[8]David M. Raup, "Geology and Creationism," Field Museum of Natural History Bulletin, Vol. 54, March 1983, p. 21.

[9]J.E. O'Rourke, "Pragmatism Versus Materialism in Stratigraphy," *American Journal of Science,* Vol. 276, January 1976, p. 47 & 53.

[10]Michael Denton, *Evolution: A Theory in Crisis* (Bethesda, MD: Adler & Adler, 1985), p. 277-278.

[11]Percival Davis, Dean H. Kenyon, and Charles B. Thaxton, *Of Pandas and People: The Central Question of Biological Origins* (Richardson, TX: Foundation for Thought and Ethics, 1989), p. 150.

[12]William Fix, *The Bone Peddlers: Selling Evolution* (New York, NY: Macmillan Publishing Co., 1984), p. 184-185.

[13]William Paley, *Natural Theology* (England: 1802; reprint edition Houston: St. Thomas Press, 1972).

[14]Hoyle and Wickramasinghe, *Evolution From Space: A Theory of Cosmic Creationism* (New York, NY: Simon and Schuster, 1981), p. 96-97.

[15]Charles Darwin, *The Origin of Species*, Everyman Library No. 811 (New York, NY: E.P. Dutton & Sons, 1956; reprint edition, Sussex, England: J.M Dent and Sons, Ltd., 1967), p. 175.

[16]Denton, *Evolution: A Theory in Crisis*, p. 330-331.

[17]Isaac Asimov, "14 Million Tons of Dust Per Year," *Science Digest*, January 1959, p. 36.

[18]See W.H. Munk and G.J.F. MacDonald, *The Rotation of the Earth* (England: Cambridge University Press, 1975), p. 198; also C.F. Yoder, et al, "Tidal Dissipation in the Earth and Moon from Lunar Ranging," Conference on the Origin of the Moon, (Houston, TX:

Lunar and Planetary Institute, 1984), p. 31.

[19]*Creation Research Society Quarterly*, Vol. 28, p. 105-108),

[20]Robert V. Gentry, *Creation's Tiny Mystery* (Knoxville, TN: Earth Science Associates, 1986).

[21]Melvin A. Cook, Prehistory and Earth Models (London, Max Parrish and Co. Ltd., 1966), p. 340.

[22]Larry Vardiman, "Up, Up, and Away! The Helium Escape Problem," Institute for Creation Research *Impact*, May 1985, p. iv.

[23]W.F. Libby, *Radiocarbon Dating*, (Chicago, IL: University of Chicago Press, 1952, 1955), p. 7.

[24]Robert L. Whitelaw, "Time, life, and history in the light of 15,000 radiocarbon dates," *Creation Research Society Quarterly*, Vol. 7, 1970, p. 56-71, 83.

[25]G.E. Aardsma, "Radiocarbon, Dendrochronology, and the Date of the Flood," Proceedings Second International Conference on Creationism, (Pittsburgh, PA, 1990), p. 1-10.

[26]Jules Poirier and Kenneth B. Cumming, Design Features of the Monarch Butterfly Life Cycle, *I.C.R. Acts & Facts Impact*, #237, March 1993.

[27]U.S.G.S. Bulletin #549.

[28]John D. Morris, "Is There Geological Evidence For The Young Earth?" Institute for Creation Research *Acts and Facts*, November 1991, p. d.

[29]F.M. Broadhurst, "Some Aspects of the Paleoecology of Non-Marine Faunas and Rates of Sedimentation in the Lancashire Coal Measures," *American Journal of Science*, Vol. 262 (Summer 1964), p. 865.

[30]William Meister, *Creation Research Society Quarterly*, 1968, p. 97-102.

[31]*Texas Tracks and Artifacts*, by Robert F. Helfinstine (1136 5th Ave. S., Anoka, MN 55303) and Jerry D. Roth (9860 256th Ave., Zimmerman, MN 55398), 1994.

[32]Steve Austin, Mount Saint Helens video (Green Forest, AR: Master Books).

Notes

Notes

THE GREAT FLOOD OF NOAH

This chapter is not intended as even a partial proof for creation, but rather as a simple explanation of some of the beliefs that most creationists hold concerning the flood. Much of this information is also shown in a beautiful video, *The World That Perished.*[1]

This chapter is organized into a question-and-answer format because that's how most people react when we say that the flood really happened as the Bible says.

FIRST, WHY IS IT IMPORTANT TO BELIEVE THAT NOAH'S FLOOD WAS REAL?

For some readers, the importance lies in the concept of believing that the Bible is true and is God's written record of world history, as it claims to be. This is discussed further in chapter six.

Many other readers may not care about the Bible's truth. For that group, the flood's importance lies in the fact that this great catastrophe is the best way of explaining the appearance of the world around us. No other explanation can adequately account for the fossil distribution and massive sedimentation that exists. Many of the earth's features, such as the Grand Canyon, dinosaur graveyards, and so-called out-of-sequence strata are impossible to adequately explain in any way other than by recognizing a massive worldwide flood.

DO CREATIONISTS AGREE ON THE FLOOD MECHANISM?

Genesis 7 and 8 describe a bare outline of what happened. Some of the basic facts include:

Noah spent a hundred years building the ark, following God's detailed plan,

The "fountains of the great deep" were broken up,

It rained for 40 days and nights,

There were eight people in the ark — Noah, his wife, his three sons, and their wives,

God caused pairs of all air-breathing animals to come to the ark,

The water covered the entire earth, and all its mountains,

All air-breathing creatures drowned except for those that were in the ark,

They were all in the ark for about a year,

Then the ark came to rest on "the mountains of Ararat," and they disembarked.

Other than those bare facts, there is not complete agreement on the physical and geologic details; a number of hypotheses have been proposed. These include an asteroid crashing into the earth, high-pressure water just below the crust creating pressure due to steam heating, the weight of ice-caps in polar regions, and a number of others. Some of these ideas are mentioned in the following pages.

At least one group of scientists is trying to collect and evaluate all flood theories, and methodically arrive at the "best" ones. But the truth can never be proven (until we learn it in heaven) because, as we've said before, "the beginning is beyond the reach of science." The effects of the flood were so devastating that we can't know for sure what the earth was like before it occurred.

WAS THE FLOOD ACTUALLY WORLDWIDE?

The Bible is very specific in many spots, for example:

> And the waters prevailed exceedingly upon the earth; and all the high hills, that were under the whole heaven, were covered.... And all flesh died that moved upon the earth.... All in whose nostrils was the breath of life, of all that was in the dry land, died (Gen. 7:19-22).

A good indication that it was not just some local flood is the fact that even today the crust of the entire earth shows the drastic effects of the flood. Sedimentation is not restricted to just a small area; there are thousands of feet of fossil-filled strata in all parts of the world. Slow accumulation of dead creatures does not result in fossils — that takes a catastrophe. A worldwide flood provides the best explanation for what we see around us.

Also, the folklore of several dozen races, from all over the world, contain stories of a Great Flood that destroyed everyone except one family that escaped in some sort of large boat. Most of them say that animals were also on the boat. These legends are from Polynesia, China, North and South America, Greece, Babylonia, and many small tribes the world over. Most people would not give much credence to individual tales of this sort, but the fact that there are so many legends, with basic similarities, from many widespread areas, says there must have actually been some such event.

WHERE DID ALL THAT WATER COME FROM?

Most creationists believe that at least part of the water came from a dense water vapor canopy surrounding the earth, as is implied in Genesis 1:7:

> And God made the firmament, and divided
> the waters which were under the firmament from
> the waters which were above the firmament: and
> it was so.

This water vapor canopy would have the beneficial effect of making an even, tropical climate everywhere, and would shield out the harmful cosmic radiations that we now receive. When God triggered the flood most of this moisture was depleted.

But the bulk of the floodwater almost certainly didn't come from the vapor canopy. Calculations show that if a quantity of water larger than that required to precipitate just a couple of inches of rainfall over the earth is in a vapor form, the earth's surface temperature would be too hot for habitation. One recent paper that carefully examines some of the technical details of water vapor canopies is "Radiative Equilibrium in an Atmosphere With Large Water Vapor Concentrations" by David E. Rush and Larry Vardiman.[2] A number of other references are also given therein.

This is due to the "greenhouse effect." Water vapor is an extremely efficient radiation absorber.

Where, then, did the tremendous volume of water for the flood come from, if not from a mass of vapor in the sky? Genesis 7:11,12 says:

> In the six hundredth year of Noah's life, in
> the second month, the seventeenth day of the
> month, the same day were all the fountains of the
> great deep broken up, and the windows of heaven
> were opened. And the rain was upon the earth
> forty days and forty nights.

Many people have wondered what "the fountains of the great deep" meant. But, in the late 1950s, the mid-Atlantic ridge was discovered, and a huge gash was found that almost circled the earth. It runs from near the North Pole, down through the Atlantic, passes south of Africa through the Indian Ocean, continues between Australia and Antarctica and north through the Pacific, ending in the Gulf of California off western Mexico. When this broke, massive volcanism must have erupted, pouring lava, steam, and sediment into the stratosphere. This probably furnished most of the floodwater.

This tremendous explosion, cracking open the entire crust of the earth for thousands of miles, must have released energy that we can't imagine today. Our largest volcanoes are tiny in comparison to that one. Of course, it would have thrown volcanic debris high into the air, triggering a downpour that depleted the water vapor canopy. But there must have also been huge amounts of water released from underground reservoirs — enough to account for most of the floodwaters.

We see vestiges of that underground water today, in every volcanic event. Measurements made during Hawaii's

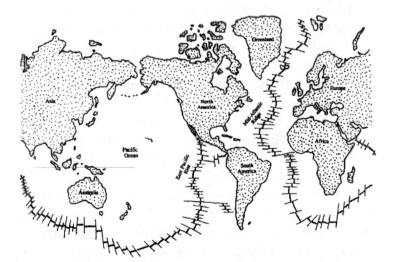

The Mid-Oceanic Rift
(Divergent Plate Boundaries)

1983 Kilauea eruption show that about 5 percent of the mass ejected was in the form of gases, and most of this was water steam. Gases consisted of about 70 percent water, 15 percent CO_2, 5 percent nitrogen, 5 percent sulphur, and some chlorine, argon, and hydrogen. There was very little helium, and that's interesting, since helium is produced by radioactive decay of uranium and thorium and, if the earth is actually billions of years old, we might expect much more helium than was seen.

Dr. Walter Brown has written a rather complete description of how this explosion of the "fountains of the deep" might have been the physical means of bringing on the Great Flood. He suggests there was actually a shell of water 5/8 mile thick several miles below the surface of the earth. This would have been very hot, and under extreme pressure. Brown suggests that when this pressure exceeded the tensile strength of the crust above, it burst, triggering the flood and all of its aftereffects. This book also contains many descriptions of evidences that favor the creation concept and that tend to disprove any sort of long, evolutionary development of the earth and its inhabitants.[3]

All signs today look like this must have been a cataclysmic event. When the internal pressure exceeded the tensile strength of the crustal material, it burst violently upward. The ocean bottom still bulges upward for several hundred miles on both sides. Big cracks extend outward all along its entire length, as if when the rift burst and the sides rose, the crust was stretched and split. Today's sea-floor map shows that magma has pushed the sides apart somewhat unequally from one split to the next.

Most geologists consider that magma coming up from this rift today is causing slow sea floor spreading, pushing the continents apart. To compensate for movements at these divergent boundaries, other regions are slipping together and some plates are sliding back under others, in a subduction process. They consider that, over a period of several hundred million years, these tectonic movements have occurred at about the same rate we presently measure.

But rates of sea floor spreading in the past cannot be proven today. All of the attempts at estimating past rates and ages involve circular reasoning, based on the uniformitarian concept. Many creationists consider that much of this tectonic activity happened quickly, at the time of the flood. After the flood subsided these movements continued, but have been slowing ever since. Today's movement is so slight (in the order of an inch each year) that it takes sensitive satellite measurements to detect it.

COULD THE ARK HAVE HELD ALL THOSE ANIMALS?

Yes, the dimensions are given in Genesis 6:15; it was about 450 feet long — the biggest ship ever built until the late 19th century. It had a floor space of over 100,000 square feet, and a volume over 1-1/2 million cubic feet — equivalent to over 500 standard railroad stock cars.

Ernst Mayr has estimated there are slightly more than a million species of animals. But most of these can live in water, so Noah didn't have to carry them; he took only air-breathing animals. Whitcomb and Morris show that when the coelenterates, fishes, sponges, tunicates, mollusks, and protozoans are eliminated, as well as many of the amphibians, aquatic mammals, reptiles, worms, and arthropods, there would be plenty of room.[4]

Most of the insects, spiders, worms, etc. are tiny.

A reasonable estimate of about 50,000 sheep-size animals would be more than enough, and would fit in about 40 percent of the ark's volume. The rest would contain plenty of room for food and for Noah's living space.

WERE THERE DINOSAURS ON THE ARK?

Yes, all of the animals, including dinosaurs, were created during creation week. When the flood came, God directed pairs of all air-breathing animals to the ark. The larger varieties may not have been fully mature, but infants. Probably many animals were in a state of hibernation on board, reducing their food needs and space requirements.

WERE ALL THE MOUNTAINS REALLY COVERED?

Yes, that's what the Bible says. However they were probably not nearly as high as they are today. Part of the drying process must have involved uplifts of land and depressions of ocean bottoms. There's evidence of violent collisions between continental masses. These could build mountains. Many are also volcanic. Mount Ararat, where the ark landed, is a 17,000 foot volcano; some of its rock shows that pillow lava hardened under water.

I think Psalm 104:5-9 (RSV) refers to the drying of the flood when it says:

> Thou didst set the earth on its foundations, so that it should never be shaken. Thou didst cover it with the deep as with a garment; the waters stood above the mountains. At thy rebuke they fled; at the sound of thy thunder they took to flight. The mountains rose, the valleys sank down to the place which thou didst appoint for them. Thou didst set a bound which they should not pass, so that they might not again cover the earth.

WHERE DID ALL THAT WATER GO?"

This is related to the previous question. Creationists and evolutionists agree that the earth has changed shape since its origin — the big difference between their views regards the speed with which that change took place.

Genesis 1:9-10 refers to the initial separation of the dry land and the seas; it sounds like there was only one land mass. Geologists also speak of the early earth having just one continent that divided into pieces that then moved by tectonic activity into the present configuration. That movement is still going on.

From either the short-age or long-age view, such movements must have caused collisions that crumpled the land masses and caused mountains to develop. The shifting continents rest upon the relatively rigid plates, and float on the magma below. All this activity resulted in changing water levels, uplifts, and shifting ocean bottom. As mountains formed, continental edges shrank, and ocean areas increased. The waters flowed back and forth as the land reshaped itself, like a mass of "silly putty" that's left in the sun. It finally settled into its present shape.

HAS THERE BEEN TIME FOR POPULATION GROWTH?

Most creationists believe that the Great Flood happened between about 3300 and 2300 B.C., less than six thousand years ago. Does this leave enough time for civilization to grow to the present stage of development?

The simple answer is "Yes, an average population growth rate of less than 1/2 percent per year would allow this." That's less than we see around us today.

For a more detailed analysis of population growth rates see the "Population Growth" section in chapter three. This section also shows calculations for the Israelite's population growth while they were in Egyptian exile. That, too, is reasonable.

HOW DID ALL THE HUMAN RACES DEVELOP?

In order to answer that, we must first find what constitutes a race, and then see a little about how genetics operates. Speaking at the A.A.A.S. conference on "Science and the Concept of Race," Ernst Mayr said:

> But if we look at some recent textbooks on physical anthropology, we find that in one textbook they recognize five human races, in the next textbook they recognize sixty-five human races. Races there are; how to delimit them, how to draw

the line between them is not only difficult, it is impossible.[5]

Speaking at the same conference, Bentley Glass said:

> Races are subdivisions of a species. There is no real distinction between races, in the anthropological or zoological sense, and subspecies. Races (or subspecies) are always separated from each other in space or time. In other words, contemporaneous races or subspecies always are separated from each other geographically.[6]

If a few individuals from some much larger group are isolated, the variety within the small group's gene-pool is reduced. Some genes that are subordinate in most members of the original large group will be completely missing in the smaller group. Therefore, later generations from the small group, if left in isolation, will never develop some of the diversity of the original large group. Glass called this the "Founder's Effect," and explained:

> Small populations therefore come to differ radically in their gene frequencies from the populations of their origin. . . . Whenever a new colony is established by a very few individuals, it cannot be fully and proportionately representative of the gene pool from which it is drawn.[7]

Noah and his family almost certainly had medium brown skin, and had a full complement of genes that included all that today's peoples have. But his descendants became isolated groups as they spread over the world. Each isolated group must have had fewer of certain recessive genes than some of the other groups; in time these became completely absent, so all members of that group would share an appearance different from other groups. In other words, they would become a different race.

This effect became especially enhanced after the dispersion following the Tower of Babel. At that time, God caused a confusion of languages and deliberate moves to far-off places for each small group. This isolation would quickly cause proliferation of races.

We could formulate two general rules for formation or dissolution of races, as follows:

1. If a small portion of an initially broad population is isolated for many generations, then a "race" is produced. Members of this race share common characteristics that are different from those of descendants of some different isolated group.

2. Conversely, if two "races" that had previously been isolated for many generations are brought together and then intermarry, later members of this newly merged broader society lose the sharp differences of the original races, and get characteristics that cover a wider range of shared average appearances.

These principles are proven daily by the work of plant or animal breeders. We know, for example, that each puppy in a litter born to a pair of pure-bred Irish Setters will look like an Irish Setter, but if the male happened to be a Beagle and the female an Irish Setter, the puppies will be mixed — they won't look alike, but will be some intermediate between the two breeds (or races). Professional breeders are careful to never allow interbreeding, because that could damage the purity of future generations.

This principle can be extended to the descendants of God's original creation. The Bible does not refer to "species" of animals, but rather to "kinds." A "kind" probably should correspond to either a genus or a family, in modern taxonomic terminology.

For example, there was probably a single pair of "dog kinds," from which all of the subspecies (or breeds) of domesticated dogs, most of the wolves, some foxes, and other species developed. This helps to explain how Noah's ark could have held the ancestors of all of the land animals that have lived since then; at the time of the flood there may not have been as many kinds or species as there are now.

We've had many species become extinct since the flood, but we've also had many new species develop. Speciation is a well-recognized action and is not an evidence for evolution (see the discussion in chapter two). Many of the now-extinct species had probably developed since the flood, and later became victims of the changes in their environment. The extinction of the dinosaurs was almost certainly caused by changes in environment.

While we're on the subject of racial characteristics, let's respond to occasional speculations about what Jesus looked like. This one is easy. Jesus was a "sabra" Jew (or native Israeli), whose ancestry is documented in the Bible all the way back to Adam and Eve. Even though He had no physical descendants, there are a great many people today who have a similar genetic background. So we can know that He almost certainly had a medium-olive complexion, dark curly hair, and a robust physique (He was a carpenter and an outdoorsman who walked almost everywhere He went). In accordance with custom, He probably had a dark beard, neatly trimmed. Of course, most people have a mental image of "their Jesus," and that's okay. The important thing to us is what He said and did, not what He looked like.

WHAT ABOUT THE ICE AGE?

This is a question that scientists have asked many times. They've studied present glaciers and evidences of past ice movements to try to learn what caused it all. But their success is quite limited. The geology textbook *Essentials of Geology* says:

> A great deal is known about glaciers and glaciation. . . . However, scientists have not yet developed a completely satisfactory explanation

for the causes of ice ages. . . . [Several theories are then described.] In conclusion, it should be emphasized at this point that the ideas just discussed do not represent the only possible explanations for glacial ages. Although interesting and attractive, these proposals are certainly not without critics nor are they the only hypotheses currently under study. Other factors may, and in fact probably do, enter the picture.[8]

Geologists have applied the theory of uniformitarianism to explain how the Ice Age might have come about. But all agree that large-scale glaciation cannot occur with today's weather patterns, so in this case the present is certainly not the key to the past, and thus the cause of the Ice Age is beyond the realm of science. Thus, we must look to history for the answer. And the biblical description of the Genesis flood is the best starting point.

First, what sort of climate is required to produce an ice age? Most people think that a long period of cold weather is the first step. But that's not really true. Two necessary factors are 1) very large amounts of winter snow, and 2) very cool summers, so that the snow won't melt off. This combination will ensure the formation of glacial ice sheets.

Large amounts of snow are not caused by very cold winters, as can be shown by looking at a number of areas today. Instead, a large reserve of water vapor near moderately cold air is known to cause heavy snowfall. This could even imply winters that are warmer than we have in many northern climes today.

Let's consider what the earth's oceans were probably like in those days. Before the flood, the vapor canopy around the earth caused a greenhouse effect that warmed everything, including the oceans. Then, the trigger for the flood was the "breaking up of the fountains of the deep." This subterranean water must have been hot, and mixed with steam, warming the ocean even more. Thus, we can be fairly sure that the post-flood oceans were relatively warm for some time — perhaps several hundred years. This would have stimulated evaporation and furnished plenty of water vapor for huge snowfalls. Oceanographers have confirmed, by oxygen-isotope ratios and other methods, that the early oceans were warmer than those of today.

Now, let's consider that the continental temperatures were probably colder than they are today. Marvin Lubenow, in his excellent book about early hominid fossils, describes how the ice age climate must have caused the unusual bone structure of Neanderthal man.[9] He gives five reasons why air temperatures were probably quite cool during the early post-flood centuries:

1. Depletion of the vapor canopy during those 40 days and nights of rain removed the insulating blanket of warm, moist air that had existed prior to the flood.

2. Volcanism is mentioned in Genesis 7:11; this probably continued for many years due to the shifting and settling of the earth's surface. It's also possible that tectonic movements occurred during this post-flood period; heavy volcanism and mountain-building would certainly have taken place then. This would have filled the air with volcanic ash, reflecting the sun's rays back into space.

For example, in 1815 the volcanic eruption of Mount Tambora (Indonesia) blanketed the entire earth with volcanic debris, darkening the sky and causing noticeable cooling — some have called 1816 "the year without a summer."

3. Since the flood stripped the earth of most of its vegetation, the bare ground would have reflected much of the sun's radiation.

4. Evaporation from warmer oceans would have produced heavy cloud cover, and this would also have reflected the sun's rays.

5. As glaciation progressed, much of the earth became covered with highly reflective ice; this would also cause cooling due to loss of absorbed solar radiation.

Lubenow goes on to show that this same atmosphere, with its volcanic debris and excessive cloud-cover, would filter out most of the ultraviolet radiation from the sun. Since this is the component that interacts in the human skin to produce vitamin D, it's likely that people living in those times would experience a vitamin D deficiency, and therefore would suffer from rickets, a bone-deforming condition caused by lack of vitamin D.

Pathologist Rudolf Virchow examined the original Neanderthal fossil in 1872. His careful analysis showed that that person had suffered from rickets as a child and arthritis as an adult, but was otherwise a normal human. But his diagnosis was ignored because those bones fit the preconceived hope of evolutionists for an intermediate between apes and humans. However, several more modern studies, including one by Francis Ivanhoe in the August 1970 issue of *Nature*, confirmed Virchow's diagnosis. This is now generally accepted to be correct. Thus, we see that the unusual features of the Neanderthal and Homo erectus fossils were most likely caused by the severe climate of the Ice Age; this, in turn, was the aftermath of Noah's Great Flood.

Probably the most thorough creationist study of the Ice Age was by Michael Oard, of the National Weather Service.[10]

I.C.R.'s Dr. Larry Vardiman has also published monographs on studies of ancient ice and its dating. Oard estimated that it took about 500 years for the maximum glacial coverage to occur, and that most of it was gone in some 200 years.

HOW MANY ICE AGES?

Michael Oard discusses the ice age(s) in his book and also in an *Acts and Facts* article.[11]

Early scientists believed in only one ice age, but study of glacial gravel terraces in the Alps led most to say there must have been four. Later, fluctuations in oxygen isotope ratios in deep-sea cores led to a belief in many ice ages, possibly up to 30 during the late Cenozoic.

But earth scientists have learned a lot since the early days; the Alps terraces are now viewed as possibly "a result of repeated tectonic uplift cycles — not widespread climatic changes per se."

And today's oxygen isotope measurements are interpreted according to uniformitarian ideas; the influence of surging floodwaters during any possible worldwide flood is completely ignored. Such a flood would undoubtedly cause many layers of crossbedded sedimentation, which would be interpreted today (by most uniformitarianists) as sequential deposits over long periods of time. Thus, it's likely that the timing of these measurements doesn't mean much.

Oard describes the stringent requirements for an ice age, and that scientists still can't explain how one could even occur; to explain many would be almost impossible. He says that the main characteristics of glacial till can be best explained by recognizing a dynamic ice age having fluctuations and surges. This would have the leading edge of glaciers advancing and retreating, leaving stacked till sheets. Oard closes by saying, "In summary, the mystery of the Ice Age can be best explained by one catastrophic ice age as a consequence of the Genesis flood."

WHAT MADE PETRIFIED WOOD?

We've all been fascinated by samples of this "stone that looks like wood," or "wood that feels like stone" (both descriptions are true). Their origin is still not known in complete detail. It's clear that these began life as trees, and that, in some way, organic molecules in the wood were replaced by minerals. Wood is not the only substance that can petrify; most ancient bones have been mineralized in a somewhat similar manner. These aren't called "petrified," but the process is similar.

Sometimes evolutionists have cited petrified wood as another example of "millions of years ago," but this isn't correct. Let's look at the probable mechanism of how these "stone logs" came to be, and see how they can show the likelihood of a huge flood, such as the Great Flood of Noah. Either of two minerals are usually involved — silica (SiO_2) and/or calcium carbonate ($CaCO_3$), both of which are common constituents of rocks. There are often trace amounts of other substances which give color. Some think that a molecule-by-molecule replacement occurs, but it's more likely in most cases that a mineral solution in water saturates the wood and then is deposited on the cell walls, from the saturated solution.

Emmett Williams has described in some detail the beliefs of various scientists about petrification.[12]

He gives an extensive list of references, and quotes from several of them. He shows that water is the single most-needed factor for petrification to occur, together with a source of minerals. A log would decay away if it was simply buried.

Williams cites the reference work by Leo and Barghoorn to show water's role:

> The role of water in petrifaction is of paramount importance. Water is a necessary agent for ash alteration and mineral diagenesis. Saturation of the sediment serves to exclude oxygen, thereby inhibiting deterioration of tissue structure, through the maintenance of reducing conditions. Waterlogging dispels entrapped air, and maintains the wood in a swollen and plastic state, thereby maintaining maximum permeability.[13]

Lab tests have shown that petrification can occur in a short time. Emmett Williams cites an Australian report in which the authors were asked how long it takes to make petrified wood.[14]

They replied, "We suspect tens, perhaps hundreds, rather than thousands, of years in view of the reported finding of a nail embedded in a specimen of petrified wood."

The professor in a geology class I took made a remark that is more true than I had once thought. He said, "Every field of science has its buzzwords, but geology seems to have more than its fair share." Two examples of such words are "autochthonous" and "allochthonous." Therein lies a controversy. Did petrified wood grow in the region where it was found, or was it carried there by some mechanism such as floodwater? Experts have found examples of each case.

An autochthonous origin (petrification in growth location) is the usual explanation given for the famous Yellowstone petrified forest. Rangers describe 27 layers of logs, many of them in vertical position, and say that this must represent 27 sequential forests, that would have taken at least 30,000 years to form. This presentation is said to have been responsible for many people's belief that the world must be very old.

But this explanation ignores all the non-vertical logs with missing roots. Most of the logs are found lying horizontally. W.J. Fritz suggested these trees had an allochthonous origin (that is, they grew elsewhere and were transported to their petrification site). He wrote:

> Besides vertical stumps . . . logs that are parallel and diagonal to the bedding also occur in abundance . . . In all sections, with the exception of several small intervals in the Specimen Ridge section, fossilized horizontal logs are most abundant and make up 60 percent to 100 percent of the total.[15]

He went on to describe how volcanic ash flows that were saturated with water probably moved down the Lamar River valley, uprooting trees, carrying them along, and finally depositing them in what is now the Yellowstone

Park: ". . . uprooted trees growing in high-elevations, cool-temperate habitats. . . . During transport, roots and branches were broken off."

In other writings he compared this to the 1980 Mount St. Helens eruption (see the discussion in chapter three of this book). This description of volcanic eruptions, heavy ash flows, and tremendous water movement is exactly what one would expect from the Great Flood of Noah. The biblical account is quite consistent with present evidence. On the other hand, it doesn't seem reasonable that 27 forests were consecutively grown, covered with water and minerals for hundreds of years, petrified, and finally exposed to air again, ready for the next forest to make its appearance and go through the same cycle. Petrified forests confirm the Bible story.

WHERE DID THE WORLD'S LIMESTONE COME FROM?

About 10 percent of all the world's sedimentary rock is limestone, which is mostly calcite ($CaCO_3$), the mineral that makes Portland cement. The source of limestone is debatable; it can be produced by slow accumulation of tiny marine organisms whose shells are rich in calcite, but it can also be made inorganically. Lutgens and Tarbuck express this common view:

> Limestones having a biochemical origin are
> by far the most common. As much as 90 percent
> of the world's limestone may have originated as
> accumulations of biochemical sediment.[16]

Here is one of the reasons that most geologists say the earth is very ancient, since there are thick limestone deposits all over the world, and biochemical sediment accumulates very slowly — some estimate about one foot per thousand years.

The belief that most limestone has a biological origin

is partly based on the lack of any other credible explanation. Most geologists base their thinking on the processes they can see around them today, rather than accepting the possibility of the Genesis flood. But there are evidences that cast doubt on this biological source of most of the world's limestones.

Many modern shallow oceans produce "lime muds" on their bottoms, from the slow decay of the shells of tiny marine organisms such as foraminifera. These muds have typical grain sizes of some 20 microns in diameter. They are mostly aragonite with up to 10 percent calcite.

In a recent *Impact* article, ICR's head geologist Dr. Steven Austin shows that many massive limestones, such as the 500-foot thick Redwall limestone formation of the Grand Canyon, differ considerably from these modern lime muds.[17]

This limestone has a much smaller typical grain size — about 4 microns. And it's almost all calcite, with a little dolomite mixed in. It contains sand-size and larger shell fragments. There are also quartz sand particles scattered evenly throughout, which imply moving water; sand is not distributed in placid water.

The Redwall has no evidence of coral reefs, made up of organisms that slowly cemented themselves together. These are often found in stone that was deposited in calm shallow seas. But, north of Grand Canyon in the same Redwall formation, there are many Nautiloid fossils — straight slender shells up to two feet long; these have a dominant orientation, as if they were buried quickly in rapidly flowing water. There are also many disks from crinoid stems, and some fossils of crinoid heads. These indicate rapid burial, not slow sedimentation.

These are evidences against the very slow deposition of this massive limestone formation. They're also evidences against the idea that this continent was once covered by a shallow placid ocean. But how would creationists explain this limestone? What's the source of the chemicals required for direct inorganic deposit of massive limestones?

Dr. Walter Brown gives one very plausible explanation. He points out that the gases emitted by modern volcanoes are about 70 percent water steam and 15-20 percent carbon dioxide (CO_2). Also one of the principle minerals in a basaltic lava is plagioclase feldspar, which comes as a mixture of two varieties — anorthite, which contains calcium ($CaAl_2Si_2O_8$), and albite, which contains sodium ($NaAlSi_3O_8$). If anorthite has an opportunity, there's a strong likelihood that its calcium will be exchanged for sodium, thus releasing a lot of free calcium.[18]

Genesis 7:11 tells us that, as the Great Flood began, "the fountains of the great deep were broken up." This must have involved massive volcanic activity in the oceans — possibly even the direct rupture of the mid-Atlantic rift and other divergent zones. Much water, steam, and CO_2 came up, as well as large amounts of basaltic lava, including its feldspar. Ocean water has a lot of salt ($NaCl$) in it, ready to react with the anorthite feldspar and release free calcium.

Now, calcium reacts easily in water to form calcium hydroxide ($Ca(OH)_2$):

$$Ca + 2\ H_2O \longrightarrow Ca(OH)_2 + H_2$$

and this in turn reacts with carbon dioxide to form calcite ($CaCO_3$):

$$Ca(OH)_2 + CO_2 \longrightarrow CaCO_3 + H_2O$$

Calcite is the mineral that's found as the main ingredient of limestone, so here's a probable source for at least some of the limestone formations produced during the Great Flood.

Incidentally, notice that a large amount of hydrogen is released in the calcium + water reaction. This would quickly combine with the oxygen of the atmosphere to form water. Thus a considerable amount of oxygen must have been lost from the atmosphere at this time. This means that the pre-flood atmosphere must have had more oxygen than we have now. This is in sharp contrast to the "ancient reducing atmosphere" assumed by evolutionists (for which there's no evidence anyway). And an atmosphere with more oxygen would be more healthful, helping to account for the giant size of many ancient fossils, and for the long life spans mentioned in Genesis 5.

A flood massive enough to cover the world's mountains would be big and violent beyond imagination, and would certainly involve huge amounts of volcanism, lava, steam, and calcite production, shown in the above paragraphs. This would happen almost instantaneously as lava met ocean water. It's a good explanation for formations such as the Redwall and Kaibab limestones of the Grand Canyon region.

Why isn't this kind of explanation accepted by most geologists? Because it is based on the biblical account of the Great Flood, and that flood was a singular event, not seen in recent history. Such a flood would be a violation of the principle of uniformitarianism, dear to most geologists' hearts. For that reason, it's not usually accepted as a viable explanation. But there's no reason why it can't be really a true account, and there are many evidences to show that it did actually happen. As in other cases, evidences are often interpreted so as to agree with one's preconceived philosophical beliefs.

HOW WAS THE GRAND CANYON FORMED?

This is a big question, and we only have space for a small answer, which will be somewhat speculative. However, quite a few scientists are working on this project, and several evidences have been found that upset the current uniformitarian assumptions that have been "standard answers" for a long time. A few of these will be mentioned later.

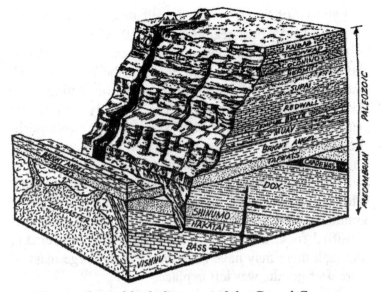

*This geologic block diagram of the Grand Canyon
shows the relationship of the sedimentary strata
above to the Great Unconformity and the granite
and schist basement rocks below.*

The geologic diagrams and much of this discussion is based on a beautiful book by Dr. Steven Austin, *Grand Canyon: Monument to Catastrophe.*[19]

Austin is the head geologist of the Institute for Creation Research. We will divide the answer into two parts: 1) how did the rocks get there in the first place? and, 2) how was the canyon carved?

First, let's consider how the rocks comprising the canyon walls were formed. There are two separate regions, with a sharp distinction between them. Look at the geologic block diagram above. Notice that all the lower strata slant, showing uplift, and have then been eroded smooth and level at their top. These strata are probably of pre-flood origin, possibly formed during the separation of land and water on Day 3 of the creation. They are called the "Unkar Group," and consist of limestone, shale, siltstone, and sandstone. These are said to be Precambrian, since they have no fossils.

Further east, not shown in this block, are rocks called the "Chuar Group." There are signs that these were formed under water, and some say that this part of the continent was covered by an ocean at that time. This probably occupied the period from the end of Creation Week until the beginning of the Great Flood. These rocks, too, don't have any fossils, and are considered to be Precambrian.

Why are all these strata slanting? At some point in time, after the sedimentary strata were deposited, a mass of granitic magma pushed upward, and lifted large regions of stratified rock. No signs of a volcanic eruption remain, although there may have been one. But the large mass of Zoroaster granite was left in place.

Since this was molten hot at the time of the intrusion, it caused metamorphism in the surrounding rocks, leaving the Vishnu schist and Trinity gneiss (pronounced "nice"). Metamorphic rocks are caused by the effects of great heat and pressure which modify the structure of existing, usually sedimentary, rock. They are hard and have lost the identifying grains of their original type.

Above this collection of granite, metamorphic rock, and slanting strata is the extremely flat "Great Unconformity," that separates two obviously very different regions. This level probably marks the onset of the Great Flood of Noah. It is the result of tremendous erosion that scoured the existing earth surface. This unconformity extends for thousands of miles, throughout most of the North American continent. There must have been violent tectonic activity, breaking loose large parts of the earth's crust.

At the same time, there must have been a tremendous amount of water to scour all the clastic debris away and leave the surface almost as flat as a tabletop. Even though it covers many thousands of square miles, the variation in local flatness is only a few hundred feet. It would take a

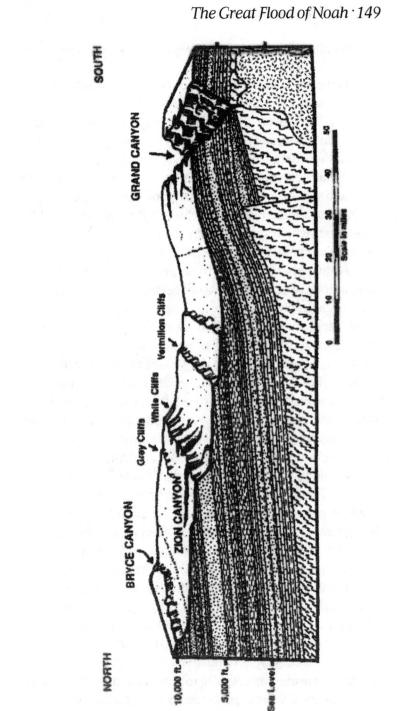

catastrophe of the magnitude of the start of the flood to account for this.

Now let's change scale and look at a cross-section of strata from mid-Utah to mid-Arizona.[20]

The sketch on the preceding page is taken along a north-south line, and is exaggerated in the vertical direction, so as to show detail. Notice that layer upon layer of sedimentary strata occur, and that all are very widespread, extending for hundreds of miles. These were probably all deposited during the Great Flood, at least up through the Kaibab limestone, which forms the level ground at the top of the Grand Canyon.

Notice also that all of these strata are parallel, but all have a slope of several thousand feet in a few hundred miles. The southern portions were all lifted, and then much of the upper strata has been eroded away, leaving several long spectacular cliff formations. Notice, too, how extremely broad all of these strata are. They cover vast areas; whatever caused all of this sedimentation must have been huge.

Some readers will be surprised that we say all this large volume of sedimentary rock was deposited during just one year. This contradicts the materialist's uniformitarian ideas. But there's evidence to back up this contention.

Geology texts usually say that most limestone was deposited slowly, typically one foot per thousand years, from shells of small marine organisms. "Lime muds" are accumulating slowly today in a number of warm-water locations.

But Steve Austin discusses the arguments used by proponents of an ancient earth and by recent-creationists.

He shows that lime muds that accumulate slowly are mostly composed of aragonite (calcium carbonate with 20-micron grain size), whereas most of the world's limestones are made of calcite (calcium carbonate with 4-micron grain size). He describes a number of technical journals that discuss the problems in trying to reconcile these conflicting data. Apparently the experts are not as agreed on the origin of limestone as are the elementary textbooks.

Austin also describes the 1966 discovery of a bed of fossil nautiloids, extinct mollusks that had long straight cigar-shaped shells up to two feet long and a few inches in diameter. These were conformably buried in fine-grained limestone in a side canyon of the Colorado River. One interesting thing is that the shells in this group of fossils were aligned in a north-westerly direction, an indication that they were buried in lime-rich water that was flowing with a strong current. This is a strong argument against the usual interpretation of slow deposition in a placid sea over a period of millions of years.

Another strong argument used by those opposed to the concept of the Great Flood concerns the sandstones of the canyon. They say these formed slowly, but they can't agree on how they were formed. Dr. Austin tells of how some have suggested a river delta origin for the Supai group[21] which has thick layers of sandstone interbedded with shale and limestone. These beds have many fossils of both marine and terrestrial types. But deltas have a wedge shape, and that's totally absent here. Also, there are no traces of channels which might represent a riverbed. Finally, the very large lateral extent of these deposits makes a delta origin almost out of the question.

The Coconino sandstone formation offers different problems. This prominent cream-colored ribbon is the most visible part of much of Grand Canyon, encircling almost the entire canyon. It's composed of quartz sand, and ranges from 300 to 1000 feet thick. It's usually considered to have resulted from wind-blown sand dunes during a long period of dry desert conditions. It's strongly cross-bedded, showing that the wind (or water?) moved in currents, first one direction and then another. Obviously such a dry desert couldn't have occurred during the Great Flood. But Austin describes problems with that interpretation, and tells of modern laboratory research that almost disproves it.

One major question concerns the huge volume of sand, and where it came from. The Coconino extends eastward, covering most of New Mexico (where it's called the Glorietta formation) and parts of Texas, Colorado, Oklahoma, and Kansas. It's estimated to contain 10,000 cubic miles of sand. And yet there is no obvious source of this sand, although there are strong evidences that it came from the north and west.

Sand can't precipitate from water; it must be eroded from a bedrock such as granite, or from some other sandstone. But almost all of the vast beds of Grand Canyon sandstones (except for the Tapeats) rest directly on limestone, which contains no sand. It must have come from an unknown source, a very long distance away. But it's hard to imagine that wind could transport sand that far.

The Coconino contains many crossbeds, inclined layers in alternate directions. These have traditionally been interpreted as evidence that they developed from sand dunes in a dry windy desert. But Austin describes several reports in geology and petrology books and journals. These researchers have studied bedding angles, grain size distribution, and performed laboratory experiments with large flumes, where sand was driven by both air and water of various depths and velocities. They've concluded that it's more likely the Coconino was deposited under water, and that some of it must have had high velocities.

A third set of studies provides strong evidence of underwater deposition. The Coconino has many animal tracks, often in trails or trackways. These appear to have been made by some sort of amphibian or reptile. Many tracks show distinct claw-marks. Dr. Leonard Brand and others at Loma Linda University performed an extensive set of experiments involving tracks made by several kinds of salamanders and newts under controlled laboratory conditions.[22]

These were done in both wet and dry sand of various

slopes, under several depths and flow velocities. They also video-taped the creatures as they contended with the currents. Their conclusion showed clearly that the Coconino trackways must have been made by newt-like animals walking under water while being pushed by a strong current.

These laboratory experiments all seem to offer conclusive proof that the Coconino sandstones were not from desert dunes but were deposited under deep water, in flood-like motions.

We've dwelt on this question of "how were the rocks laid down?" in some detail, because it effectively disposes of the necessity of "millions of years," that has saturated the minds of so many people. We all learned this in school and nature magazines. TV and other media have bombarded us with the idea that our earth is ancient. Most people accept that as a fact. And yet, it probably isn't a true picture. It's only the secular concept of uniformitarianism that requires so many eons of time, and there are many evidences that this doctrine isn't true! God's word tells us that "In the beginning, God created the heavens and the earth." It goes on to state clearly that this only took six days, and that it was only several thousand years ago. We've let secular forces blind us to the truth of reality. But now that creationist scientists have begun to uncover the actual evidences we're beginning to see what really happened. It's a young earth, after all.

Now let's think about the second phase of the question. How was the Grand Canyon carved out? Early explorers considered this a badlands region — a worthless barrier to travel, 277 miles long, 4 to 18 miles wide, and over a mile deep — a sudden hideous slash in the middle of a land that was mostly almost flat. The only way to get from one side to the other would be to fly like a bird.

Ever since this gigantic chasm was first discovered, the standard elementary textbook explanation for its formation has been that the mighty Colorado River slowly carved the canyon during a period of many millions of years. This is called the "Antecedent River theory." But geologists today realize that this could not be the right answer. Rivers don't work that way, and there's no trace of the sediment that would have been deposited.

When a symposium of geologists officially rejected that theory in 1964, another idea became somewhat popular. It was called the "Precocious Gully theory." This said that originally the Colorado River flowed southward toward the east end of the present canyon, but then followed the course of the present Little Colorado River southeasterly. Then somehow a small channel called the Hualapai drainage began flowing westward near the present Grand Canyon, and somehow broke through and "captured" the Colorado River. That larger volume of water completed the carving of the canyon. But this theory has more problems than the first one did. It hasn't had much success in gaining converts.

The best explanation seems to be contained in an ancient legend of the Havasupai Indians, who still live in villages near the bottom of the canyon. They say that this canyon formed after the world was covered by a Great Flood. This is one of hundreds of flood legends among ancient peoples all over the world. These events have recently been studied in more careful detail.

Look at the regional map on the following page. The Kaibab Upwarp is a long region of anticline, centered near the eastern end of the Grand Canyon, and forming a long north-south arch. It must have been caused by a large mass of magma that pushed up by tectonic activity, probably near the end of the flood. This Kaibab Upwarp was almost certainly an important contributory cause of the catastrophic formation of the Grand Canyon. It formed a huge dam that later ruptured and spilled its stored water, eroding several hundred cubic miles of newly-formed rock.

Near the end of the flood, the entire earth was covered with water, and the runoff and drying up began. Waters surged back and forth, as strong winds blew and the earth's surface shifted beneath the weight of moving water and sediment. Gradually the waters collected into regions resembling today's oceans, and the land began to dry off. As it dried, it cooled. This begins the period of the Ice Age, described in a previous section in this chapter. In many of the northern areas, the snowpack built up until it formed massive glaciers that probably lasted for several hundred years. Much of the melt-off collected in large lakes.

Austin's book shows that if a line is traced along the 5,700-foot contour line on a map of the western U.S., and if the region within that line were to fill with water, a 30,000-square-mile lake would cover a large portion of the Colorado plateau.[23]

This would contain more than 3,000 cubic miles of water. The only gap in that present contour line is at the Grand Canyon.

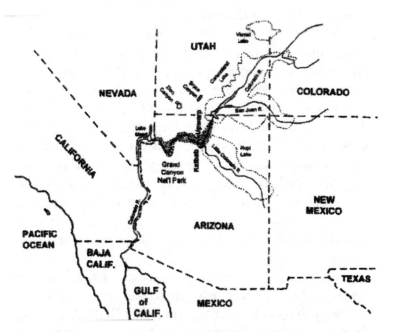

Three lakes that could have held the water that eroded the Grand Canyon after the flood of Noah.

Stated in a different way, if the Kaibab Upwarp didn't have the Grand Canyon slashing through it, it would form the westward bank of this 30,000-square-mile lake. It would form a dam.

The map on the preceding page has dotted lines that define three proposed lakes within that area — Hopi, Canyonland, and Vernal. These probably did exist in prehistoric times, although they haven't been clearly documented. But in the Hopi Lake region there is good evidence of Pliocene-epoch lakebed. Fossils of fresh-water fish, amphibians, and beavers have been found in several spots. The shorelines have eroded away. The other two lake beds have not been found, but many of the surface features appear to have been shorelines that were subject to rapid erosion. These appear to be "relict features" (things that were formed in earlier times but still survive today in a new environment). There has not been sufficient erosion since they were shaped to smooth out their sharp edges.

There are two ways that a dam can fail — overtopping (when the water level is high enough to spill over) and piping (where a porous spot begins leaking through). In either case, once water begins flowing, rapid erosion quickly forms a catastrophic failure. Tremendous volumes of water dump quickly. If Hopi Lake broke through the Kaibab Upwarp, the resulting volume flow could easily carve the initial channel that marks Grand Canyon. The resulting shift in isostatic balance could then rupture the area that is now Marble Canyon, adding the massive waters of Canyonland Lake to that flow, and complete the carving of Grand Canyon. This entire process might have taken a few weeks.

Geologists have only learned within the last half-century of the extreme erosive power that high-volume flow of water can exert. For example, in 1923 J.H. Bretz proposed that Grand Coulee, Washington, had been carved out by the failure of an Ice Age dam in the Idaho panhandle. He said this would allow a prehistoric Missoula Lake in western Montana to dump, thus carving the 50-mile-long Grand Coulee and the Washington scablands. It took 40 years for his theory to be accepted because of uniformitarian objections, but now it is the accepted explanation.

Other examples of massive excavations being caused by catastrophic flows of suddenly-released water include the failure of the Glen Canyon Dam spillway tunnel in 1983, the 1976 failure of the Teton Dam in Idaho, the 1982 breaching of a Toutle River mud dam that had been formed by Mount St. Helens' volcanic eruption two years earlier. Even the 1993 Mississippi River flood, which was considered relatively placid, ruptured two dams in Kansas and one in Iowa. In each case, canyons were excavated deep into limestone bedrock.[24]

When large volumes of high-velocity water flows occur, such as from the rupture of a dam, erosion processes are not simply from frictional wearing away of a rock surface. Processes such as cavitation literally explode a rock surface into powder, and hydraulic plucking and vortex kolks blast large boulder-size pieces out of solid bedrock. Sapping can quickly carve rounded short side canyons alongside a major flow channel. The Grand Canyon has many of these, with no evidence that a stream ever flowed through them. The Goosenecks of the San Juan River, near the east end of the Grand Canyon, are extreme deeply incised meanders of what is now a small river, yet they have vertical walls several hundred feet high. Large flume experiments have shown that this could only have made by large volumes of high-velocity water in a one-time event.

These processes have only been understood within the last few decades, and are just beginning to be applied as evidence that corroborates the rapid carving of Arizona's Grand Canyon. This all goes together to form powerful evidence of the worldwide Great Flood of Noah, as described in the Bible.

SOME HARDER QUESTIONS

This chapter has discussed questions about the Great Flood of Noah — a singular event in world history, and thus one to which the scientific method doesn't apply because it can't be repeated and tested. We've given answers in the way that a believer in biblical creation might explain them. Some of these answers are speculative, but they're compatible with all the physical evidences available, however, many non-believers choose to find other explanations, even if some don't fit the evidences as well.

Since we've been dealing with some hard questions, let's look at some others that most creationists won't even try to answer with any sort of positive explanations. Nonbelievers often use these questions to scoff at the idea of creationist belief. But, just for fun, let's see how a creationist might respond. Of course, I should say here that not all would agree; many other responses are possible.

QUESTION: If the sun wasn't created until the fourth day, what was the source of the light that defined "day" and "night" during the first three days? How can a biblical believer say that these were 24-hour days?

We've got to admit that this is a question that can't be answered in detail. My favorite analogy is a comparison with the prophetic description of heaven at the end of the age, contained in the last chapters of the Bible. We can read in Revelation 21:23-22:5:

> And the [heavenly] city had no need of the sun, neither of the moon, to shine in it; for the glory of God did lighten it . . . And the gates of it shall not be shut at all by day: for there shall be no night there. . . . and they need no candle, neither light of the sun; for the Lord God giveth them light.

I can't explain that one either, but it seems that God himself will be the source of the light in Heaven. Jesus said in several spots, "I am the light of the world." We usually think of this as a figurative statement, but it could have a broader meaning.

Some people have tried to rationalize this problem by saying that God first filled space with "raw energy," and that this took the form of electromagnetic radiation, which is a kind of light. I can't argue with this.

The part of the question that involves 24 hours is a little easier; all it takes is to accept that there was some source of some kind of light (or energy), and that the earth was rotating. Since the definition of an hour is 1/24 of the rotational period of the earth, we don't even have to know the speed of rotation to say that a "day" was 24 hours long. It was simply one day/night period.

Does the fact that I can't always give detailed answers, known to be correct, to all these questions mean that my belief in creation is poorly founded? No, not at all. After all, there are questions about the big-bang theory that even its most ardent believers can't answer, and usually won't even try. These include:

QUESTION: (for evolutionists) What was the source of all the mass of the universe before the big bang occurred? How did it get crammed into a space the size of a pinpoint just before the big bang?

Some cosmologists have suggested an oscillating universe, that is, first there was a big bang, followed by an expansion that's still going on, but in a few billion years that expansion will slow and stop, and contraction will begin. After billions of years of such contraction, all the mass of the universe will arrive back at one point, compressed by gravitational attraction, and a "big crunch" will occur, something like an enormous black hole. At some later time there'll be another big bang, and this sequence might go on almost forever. Many scientists disagree.

People with this belief often neglect the Second Law of Thermodynamics, which says that disorder will always increase. The cycle would then come to a slow stop. But even if we allow this explanation to stand, it still can't explain the original source of all the mass; all it does is postpone the question back further in time.

My conclusion is that questions that are apparently unanswerable don't really invalidate either of the two basic belief systems. They don't furnish any sort of proof that the foundational assumptions are necessarily wrong; they just indicate our lack of total knowledge.

All scientists will agree that science doesn't have all the answers; science is just a systematic search for more knowledge. The big difference between creationist scientists and evolutionist scientists is the foundation on which their belief systems rely.

One is based on a belief that there is a Creator God who can and did intervene in the affairs of this world, temporarily interrupting the principle of uniformitarianism; the other depends on faith in a materialistic explanation that has no "First Cause." Once one of these foundations is chosen, commitment to the rest of the belief system will follow automatically.

Endnotes

[1] *The World That Perished*, Films For Christ Association, 2628 West Birchwood Circle, Mesa, AZ 85202.

[2] David E. Rush and Larry Vardiman, "Radiative Equilibrium in an Atmosphere With Large Water Vapor Concentrations," *Creation Research Society Quarterly*, Vol. 29, No. 3, December 1992, p. 140-145.

[3] Walter T. Brown Jr., *In The Beginning* (Phoenix, AZ: Center For Scientific Creation, 1989), p. 59-83.

[4] John Whitcomb and Henry Morris, *The Genesis Flood* (Grand Rapids, MI: Baker Book House, 1970), p. 65-70.

[5] Ernst Mayr, *Science and the Concept of Race, American Association for the Advancement of Science* (New York, NY: Columbia University Press, 1968), p. 16.

[6] Bentley Glass, *Science and the Concept of Race*, p. 88.

[7]Ibid., p. 91.

[8]F.K. Lutgens and E.J. Tarbuck, *Essentials of Geology* (Columbus, OH: Charles E. Merrill Publ. Co., 1982), p. 161, 163.

[9]Marvin L. Lubenow, *Bones of Contention: A Creationist Assessment of the Human Fossils* (Grand Rapids, MI: Baker Book House, 1992), p. 146-156.

[10]Michael J. Oard, *An Ice Age Caused by the Genesis Flood,* (San Diego, CA: Institute for Creation Research, 1990).

[11]Michael J. Oard, "The Ice Age and the Genesis Flood," Institute for Creation Research *Acts and Facts,* June 1987.

[12]Emmett L. Williams, "Fossil Wood From Big Bend National Park, Brewster County, Texas: Part II — Mechanism of Silicification of Wood and Other Pertinent Factors," *Creation Research Society Quarterly*, Vol.30, No.2, September 1993, p. 106-111.

[13]R.F. Leo and E.S. Barghoorn, "Silicification of Wood," Botanical Museum Leaflets, Harvard University 25(1):1-47, p. 27.

[14]G. Scurfield, C.A. Anderson, and E.R. Segnit, "Silica in Woody Stems," *Australian Journal of Botany*, 22:211-229, 1974, p. 396.

[15]W.J. Fritz, "Reinterpretation of the Depositional Environment of the Yellowstone 'Fossil Forest,' " *Geology* 8:309-313, 1980, p. 312.

[16]F.K. Lutgens and E.J. Tarbuck, *Essentials of Geology* (Columbus, OH: Charles E. Merrill Publishing Co., 1986), p. 83.

[17]Steven A. Austin, "Were Grand Canyon Limestones Deposited by Calm and Placid Seas?" Institute for Creation Research *Impact*, December 1990.

[18]Walter T. Brown, Jr., *In The Beginning* (Phoenix, AZ: Center for Scientific Creation, 1989), p. 79-80.

[19]Steven A. Austin, *Grand Canyon: Monument to Catastrophe* (Santee, CA, Institute for Creation Research, 1994).

[20]Austin, *Grand Canyon*, p. 12.

[21]Austin, *Grand Canyon*, p. 29-36.

[22]L.R. Brand and T. Tang, "Fossil Vertebrate Footprints in the Coconino Sandstone (Permian) of Northern Arizona: Evidence for Underwater Origin," in *Geology* 19(1991): 1201-1204. Cited in Austin, *Grand Canyon*, p. 31-32.

[23]Austin, *Grand Canyon*, p. 92-107.

[24]G.W. Wolfrom, "The 1993 Midwest Floods and Rapid Canyon Formation," *Creation Research Society Quarterly,* Vol.31, No.2, September 1994, p. 109-116.

Notes

Notes

Notes

Chapter 5

ARGUMENTS AGAINST MACRO-EVOLUTION

CHAPTER INTRODUCTION

This chapter will discuss some of the oft-quoted "evidences" that purport to show that macro-evolution has occurred. We'll try to tell how these so-called evidences are inadequate. A number of quotations from eminent scientists are given to document our explanations.

A REMINDER: Almost everyone agrees that micro-evolution, or speciation, is a real process that allows breeders to produce new varieties, and that it occasionally occurs in nature. But the idea of macro-evolution — that an accumulation of such small changes has led to all of the kinds of animals and plants in the world today — is erroneous. That's what this chapter is all about.

Creationists have often been criticized for trying, helter-skelter, to tear down bits and pieces of evolutionary ideas. Some critics, who don't understand the real foundations of the conflict, have tried to say that there shouldn't be a problem; that creation is just religious, while evolution is a fact or scientific theory.

But it's a little like a football team; if it's to be effective, it must have at least two lines of offense and a good defense. It's not very effective for creationists, with limited access to the public, to make some good points while evolutionists, with almost complete control of the public schools, TV, and other media, continue to make their claims. They teach our children the fanciful tales about how evolution occurred, but don't allow rebuttal of their claims. These stories actually don't have factual evidence to back them up. We need to get that story out.

Creation and evolution are two mutually exclusive, diametrically opposing concepts. If one is true, the other must be false. If one is to be demonstrated, the other must be destroyed. That's why creationists base their most telling arguments on the weaknesses of evolution.

The famous British evolutionist Sir Arthur Keith wrote:

> Meantime, let me say that the conclusion I have come to is this: the law of Christ is incompatible with the law of evolution — as far as the law of evolution has worked hitherto. Nay, the two laws are at war with each other; the law of Christ can never prevail until the law of evolution is destroyed.[1]

ANCIENT FOSSILS

This is the most common "evidence" shown in the public media. Evolutionists have made it seem that fossils from extinct creatures prove evolution. That is obviously incorrect. Many species have become extinct, but in order to show evolution there must be transitional fossils that show increasing complexity. Most paleontologists now agree that none have been found above the "family" level, and most will admit that this disproves the old Darwinism, and possibly Neo-Darwinism as well. Let's look at a few well-known fossils.

A. Neanderthal Man — is now considered a genuine human race, many of whom had rickets from poor nutrition.

B. Cro-Magnon Man — was definitely a genuine human, artistic and religious.

C. Piltdown Man — has been proven to be a deliberate hoax.

D. Java Man — has been proven to be a deliberate hoax.

E. Nebraska Man — was just a hoax of over-optimism; a single tooth from an extinct pig was proclaimed to be the remains of an early human.

F. Peking Man — probably was a hoax. (The fossils were lost during World War II, so it's still a debatable subject.)

G. Zinjanthropus — studies show this was just a primitive ape, not ancestral to humans.

H. "Lucy" — was probably just a primitive arboreal ape — no relation to humans.

I. Australopithicines — modern multi-variate computer analysis shows these were primitive apes that are now extinct.

J. Archaeopteryx — some evidence shows signs of a hoax, but it was probably a primitive bird. This is discussed more fully in a later section in this chapter.

K. Coelacanth — formerly this 6-foot-long fish was used as an early Cretaceous "Index Fossil," extinct for 80 million years, but living specimens have now been found near Madagascar. It was said to be ancestral to the amphibians, but is really a true fish. (*See Creation Research Society Quarterly*, December 1992, page 160.)

L. Horse Series — this collection of unrelated fossils was assembled to look like a series. Dr. Niles Eldredge, curator of vertebrate paleontology at the American Museum of Natural History where this was displayed, said it is "lamentable" that this is still shown in textbooks by people "who know of its speculative nature."[2]

Some may object to the several uses of the word "hoax" above, but creationists are not the only ones to make this accusation. Dr. W.R. Thompson, F.R.S., was an entomologist, a believer in evolution, and director of the Commonwealth Institute of Biological Control, Ottawa. He was chosen to write the Introduction to the "Everyman's Library No. 811" version of Darwin's *The Origin of Species*. He wrote:

> The success of Darwinism was accompanied by a decline in scientific integrity. This is already evident in the reckless statements of Haeckel and in the shifting, devious, and histrionic argumentation of T.H. Huxley. A striking example, which has only recently come to light, is the alteration of the Piltdown skull so that it could be used as evidence for the descent of man from the apes; but even before this a similar instance of tinkering with evidence was finally revealed by the discoverer of pithecanthropus, who admitted, many years after his sensational report, that he had found in the same deposits bones that are definitely human. Though these facts are now well-known, a work published in 1943 still accepts the diagnosis of pithecanthropus given by Dubois.[3]

THE PILTDOWN FRAUD

When this writer was in high school and college during the late 1930s and early 1940s, the Piltdown skull mentioned above was called the "missing link." It was described as an ultimate proof that humans had descended from an ape-like ancestor. We were taught that bones and teeth found in a quarry in Piltdown, England, clearly showed both ape and human characteristics. Later, during the 1950s, word leaked out in technical journals that these bones had been faked. However, the public wasn't informed in big headlines — this was too much of an embarrassment to the scientific establishment. Much later the real story finally came out.[4]

Prof. Brian Gardiner of Kings College, London, published an article in a May 1996, issue of *Nature*, the respected British science journal. He named the perpetrator as Martin A.C. Hinton, a curator at London's Natural History Museum.

The saga of Piltdown Man, or Eoanthropus (dawn man), began when Charles Dawson, a lawyer and amateur geologist, gave some bones to Arthur Smith Woodward, head of the geology department of the British Museum. He led Woodward to the spot where he had found them. Woodward found more fossils there, and reconstructed them into a partial skull that had the brain capacity of a modern human, but the jaw and teeth of an ape. He announced his discovery to the Geological Society in London in 1912, and it was subsequently published in textbooks the world over.

Much later, in 1952, chemical analysis by Kenneth Oakley of the British Museum showed that all the teeth and bone fragments were modern, and had been stained with iron and manganese to look old, while the teeth had been filed to alter their shape. It was clearly a deliberate fake. The skull was from a modern human, while the jaw had come from an orangutan.

There has been much speculation as to who was responsible for this hoax. Dawson's name figured prominently, but he probably didn't have the skills to do this. Hinton, Woodward, Pierre Teilhard de Chardin, and several other prominent scientists have been named by some, but nothing was proved until the *Nature* article appeared. Now it seems the full story is available. A trunk was found in the 1970s, stored in a loft at the British Museum. It contained many bones, teeth, and fossils. It had belonged to Martin A.C. Hinton during the time he had worked at the Museum.

Some years later, Prof. Gardiner obtained it, studied it, and uncovered the full hoax story.

Hinton apparently had been angry at his boss, Arthur Smith Woodward, because of a pay dispute. He took revenge in an attempt to embarrass Woodward in the eyes of the scientific world. Some time previously Hinton had stained some bones for Dawson, so he knew the techniques. As curator in the geology department, he knew enough about fossils to know what would be considered fascinating to Woodward and the scientific world. And he knew the geology of the Piltdown area. He prepared the bones to look like fossils, and planted them in the quarry, then led Dawson to them. The stage was set.

But Hinton was known to be a practical joker, and also as a scavanger who never threw anything away. When the contents of his trunk were examined, years later, it was filled with old bones, including four tubes of human teeth that had been stained. Analysis showed that these stains were the same as those on the Piltdown hoax. The verdict was in. All of the original actors in this drama are now dead, but the damage will be long remembered.

NEANDERTHAL MAN

The story of the "Neanderthal ape-man" shows how a preconceived idea can distort actual evidence. The first of these fossils was found in 1857 in a limestone cliff in the Neander valley near Dusseldorf. It looked human, but had massive brow-ridges, something like those of an ape.

In 1872 pathologist Rudolf Virchow examined the bones and said they were from a middle-aged human who had rickets and arthritis. Then other fossils were found, all having those same brow-ridges. In 1908 Professor Marcellin Boule of Paris' l'Institut de Palaeontologie Humaine, a strong Darwinist, published a "reconstruction" of the La Chapelle-aux-Saints Neanderthal fossil. Boule ignored the larger-than-modern skull volume, a factor that should have suggested

Neanderthal was highly intelligent. His reconstruction was pictured as being naked, hairy, and living in a cave.

Of course, fossils can't show such things as color, clothing, or hair. But this caught the public imagination — Virchow's diagnosis was forgotten, and soon museums all had exhibits based on Boule's "ape-man" image. For several decades Chicago's Field Museum display was the best-known, and public imagination was "fired up" by the idea that ancient ape-men had been found.

But finally, in 1957, anatomists Straus and Cave made a detailed study of Neanderthal fossils. Their careful analysis showed that the toes were not prehensile, the pelvic structure was not at all ape-like, and the bones all showed strong evidence of severe arthritis. In 1970 medical specialist Ivanhoe showed that a widespread vitamin-D deficiency would have caused all of the bone peculiarities. It's thought that they must have lived at a time when there was insufficient sunlight, and now it's believed they lived during the Ice Age.

The Field Museum put in a newer exhibit that shows Neanderthals that look fully human (if they had been placed in a modern setting they would appear like anyone else on a city street). But the Museum has also kept its old cave-man exhibit. More details on Neanderthal fossils are given in Ian Taylor's *In The Minds of Men: Darwin and the New World Order.*[5]

Chapter 4 of this book has a section about "What Caused the Ice Age?" This includes a fair discussion of how the heavily overcast sky must have caused widespread rickets, the probable cause of the bone deformations that led to the belief that Neanderthals were some sort of link between apes and humans.

Marvin Lubenow's book, *Bones of Contention,* is devoted to a discussion of all of the so-called "early hominid fossils." This has probably the most complete listing of all 4,000 fossil individuals found to date. He gives the age, as agreed on by paleontologists, the places where these were found, and how they were all classified. For the more important fossil sets, he describes some of the controversies that surround each. Everyone who's interested in the idea of human evolution should read this book.[6]

An appendix goes into much detail about the dating of KNM-ER-1470, an important and very modern-looking skull that was originally dated at 2.9 million years old. For about ten years scientists debated various aspects of how to reconcile the several methods of "absolute" radioactive dating methods for this skull that seemed to conflict with each other and with evolution theory. There was even debate over whether this individual should be referred to as Homo erectus, H. habilis, or H. sapiens; finally H. habilis won out. However, there are some who argue that this entire taxon is faulty.

Dr. Lubenow explained some of the problems faced by taxonomists and paleontologists, while dealing with KNM-ER-1470. He wrote:

> The very modern morphology and the very old date (2.9 m.y.a.) of skull 1470 presented an intolerable situation for human evolution. The ten-year controversy concerning the date of this fossil was finally "settled" in 1981, when the accepted date became 1.9 m.y.a. The account of this controversy, showing that the dating methods are not independent of evolution or independent of each other, is found in the appendix of this book. That case study of the dating of the KBS Tuff and of skull 1470 offers clear evidence that when the chips are down, factual evidence is prostituted to evolutionary theory.[7]

MASS EXTINCTIONS

To the evolutionist, one of the great mysteries about the fossil record is the sudden appearance and disappearance of many kinds of creatures. Darwinian theory would predict a gradual increase in the complexity of different kinds. It also suggests that as one "new and advanced" creature became dominant (due to its better adaptation through natural selection) other less-well- adapted kinds would be displaced and become extinct. This should be gradual.

But paleontologists know that the fossil record shows no trace of this. Several large-scale "mass extinctions" account for the demise of the majority of creatures that are no longer with us. Human encroachment accounts for most of the others.

Short-age creationists such as myself say that most of the so-called mass extinctions took place during or shortly after the Great Flood of Noah. That these appear to the evolutionist to be several groupings of creatures that actually were all made extinct at the same time is the result of the extreme circularity in their reasoning process. Their dating of a rock strata is determined by the index fossils contained in that strata.

For example, no matter at what depth a rock is buried, if it contains the fossil of a certain species of fish it is automatically said to be of Devonian age. A different geographical region might have been inhabited by reptiles instead of fish. In this case, certain reptilian fossils would cause those strata to be labeled Cretaceous. Yet they might have lived at the same time as the "Devonian" fishes.

The groupings of taxa that became extinct are better explained by the bio-geographical distribution of their natural habitat, rather than the age during which they lived. We must remember that strata of different "ages" are not consistently found vertically stacked, one above the other. When they are, and are in the wrong order, they're always considered anomalies, and often blamed on overthrusts. But most of these "overthrusts" show no trace of thrusting.

However, the worst problem about the ancient fossils is not how or when they became extinct; it's how they came into being in the first place.

DESCENDANTS WITHOUT ANCESTORS?

The theory of evolution says that the earliest forms of life were simple one-celled organisms that evolved from raw chemicals in the early oceans. These led to simple creatures like algae and bacteria, which left fossils in rocks said to be a couple of billion years old. The next step, according to evolutionists, was the development of the various invertebrates, such as sponges, worms, and the marine creatures that have shells. One or more of these invertebrate phyla then supposedly evolved into fish, which are thought to be the earliest forms of vertebrate life. If this long development is true, then millions of fossils should show it.

But the Cambrian period of geologic time was marked by the sudden appearance of many different forms of life. The Cambrian is believed to have started some 570 million years ago and to have lasted for about 70 million years. During this relatively narrow window of time, creatures belonging to almost every phyla suddenly appeared, at about the same point in geologic time. There's no sign of gradual development — they were just suddenly there, with no trace of ancestors.

Science writer Richard Dawkins, who is a virulent anti-creationist, wrote, "It is as though they were just planted there, without any evolutionary history."[8]

Invertebrate paleontologist Niles Eldredge, of the American Museum of Natural history, put it this way:

> This rather protracted "event" shows up graphically in the rock record; all over the world, at roughly the same time, thick sequences of rocks, barren of any easily detected fossils, are overlain by sediments containing a gorgeous array of shelly invertebrates; trilobites (extinct relatives of crabs and insects), brachiopods, mollusks. All of the typical forms of hard-shelled

animals we see in the modern oceans appeared, albeit in primitive, prototypical form, in the seas of six hundred million years ago. . . .

Indeed, the sudden appearance of a varied, well-preserved array of fossils . . . does pose a fascinating intellectual challenge.[9]

Rocks considered older than Cambrian do have signs of life, but these were all algae and bacteria — "prokaryotes" (or single-cell types having no nucleus or organelles). No one has proposed any reasonable explanation of how these simple forms could have gradually evolved into "eukaryotes" (those having a nucleus and complex structure; usually multi-cell creatures). Most of these even had shells.

This sudden appearance of almost every phyla and invertebrate class except insects is known as the "CAMBRIAN EXPLOSION." It's a mystery that no evolutionist has explained; how could more than 5,000 species, including sponges, corals, jellyfish, worms, mollusks, trilobites, and crustaceans have come into existence without any kind of development?

Trilobites are the most widely known index fossils of the Cambrian period. These have all been long extinct, but they were not simple primitive types of life. They were marine arthropods, exo-skeletal, with head, thorax and abdomen. They breathed through gills, and their bodies were segmented. There were many shapes of trilobites — some up to 45 centimeters long. Their eyes were highly complex multi-lens types; trilobite eyes alone are enough to play havoc with evolution theory.

The Cambrian Explosion is the name given to the sudden appearance of many classes of highly complex invertebrates, supposedly descended from algae and bacteria, but with absolutely no trace of intermediates. Another sudden appearance, just as mysterious and impossible to explain, is the origin of fishes.

Fish are considered to be the earliest vertebrates (that

sub-phylum also includes amphibians, reptiles, birds, and mammals) and, if evolution is true, must have evolved from one or more of the invertebrate phyla just discussed. But again, there are absolutely no intermediate forms found in the rocks; it's like fish were just suddenly there, having no ancestors.

In his 1966 presidential address to the Linnaean Society, ichthyologist (fish expert) Errol White said:

> But whatever idea authorities may have on the subject, the lungfishes, like every other major group of fishes I know, have their origins firmly based in nothing.[10]

Dr. Duane Gish is the best-known creationist spokesman and debater, and thus is the one who receives the most criticism. In his book *Creation Scientists Answer Their Critics* he gives detailed responses to many of the charges brought against him, and in so doing becomes an excellent source of information that documents creationist claims. On the subject of gaps in the fossil record, especially this huge absence of ancestors to the vertebrates, he wrote:

> I thoroughly searched a number of the most prominent anti-creationist books and could find no mention whatsoever concerning the origin of fishes. This was true of the earlier book edited by Godfrey, her later book, the book edited by Zetterberg, the book by Kitcher, and the book edited by D.B. Wilson. Futuyma and Eldredge each briefly mention fishes, but neither mentions a single word about the huge gap between fishes and invertebrates nor attempts to give any explanation whatsoever as to why each major group of fishes appears fully formed at the start. These anti-creationists have enshrouded this profound discontinuity in the history of life in an enormous fog of silence. They not only make no attempt to

offer "Just-so" stories how this may have occurred, they completely ignore it. It is too embar-
rassing to evolutionary theory even to discuss in
their anti-creation polemics.[11]

If all of these expert evolutionists, who were writing
specifically to try and discredit creationism, knew of any way
to refute Gish's claims about the huge gap in the ancestry of
fishes, they would certainly have done so. That they were all
silent on this tremendously important point shows their tacit
agreement that the gap is real. In fact, it's such a gaping void
that apparently none of them could imagine how to make up
a "piece of reasoning," or "Darwinian history" of the sort of
"problem-solving strategy" that Philip Kitcher calls "the
heart of Darwinian evolutionary theory."[12]

This one cavernous gap alone should be enough to
absolutely disprove evolutionism.

Fundamental biblical creationists argue that the Cambrian explosion, the sudden appearance of so many different
kinds of life, with no trace of ancestors, is good evidence for
the sort of divine creation described in Genesis; this conclusion is just what the fossil record clearly shows. Yet the
evolutionists say that's just religious nonsense, but their
answer is no clearer, and has almost no evidence to back it up.

FOSSILS SHOW CATASTROPHE

When a plant or animal dies normally, its soft parts are
quickly eaten by scavengers or bacteria, or they decay. Its
bones scatter and slowly decay. When a fish dies, decay
processes cause gas that makes its body tend to float. Never
does a fish body sink to the bottom, to be slowly covered by
sediments.

In order to be fossilized, an animal must be quickly
covered with watery sediment so that it's preserved from
bacteria or scavengers. Then it must lie undisturbed, under
considerable heat and pressure, while minerals percolate
through, allowing silica compounds to replace carbonate

compounds on a molecule-by-molecule basis. In this way, the form is preserved.

When clams die they relax, and their shells open. If a living clam feels an influx of sand around him, he quickly clamps his shell closed. All fossil clam-shells found today are closed, showing they were quickly covered by sediment.

But sudden high-pressure burial under much wet sediment requires some sort of massive catastrophe — it just can't happen under normal conditions. We don't see fossils forming today. But we do find vast graveyards of dinosaurs, swept into huge piles and deeply buried. Surely this is evidence for the Great Flood.

HORSE SERIES FOSSILS

A famous fossil-hunter and professor of vertebrate paleontology, Othniel C. Marsh, during the 1870s found bones and teeth in Wyoming and Nebraska which he put together into what he said were 30 different kinds of fossil horses. He assembled these into a series showing what he called the development of the modern horse; this was displayed at Yale University, and has been copied by numerous other museums. The series includes:

> Eohippus (or "dawn horse") — Eocene epoch,
>   60 MY (million years old)
> Orohippus
> Epihippus
> Miohippus — Oligocene epoch, 40 MY
> Parahippus
> Merychippus — Miocene, 26 MY
> Pliohippus — Pliocene, 7 MY
> Plesippus
> Equus (modern horse)

The earliest of this series, Eohippus, is properly called hyracotherium. Its skeleton is indistinguishable from that of the modern hyrax (sometimes called "daman," an animal the size of a small dog that lives today in Africa). This is not horse-like; it has 4 toes and 18 pairs of ribs, and its feet are padded and dog-like. The next-oldest, orohippus, had 15 pairs of ribs. Pliohippus had 19 pairs, and the modern equus has 18 pairs. Does this sound like a genuine series of transitions? Especially not, when we consider that fossils of eohippus and the modern equus have been found side by side in surface rocks.

Francis Hitching is a very well-known evolutionist, but he criticizes this "horse series." He wrote:

> A complete series of horse fossils is not found in any one place in the world arranged in rock strata in the proper evolutionary order from bottom to top. The sequence depends on arranging Old World and New World fossils side by side, and there is considerable dispute as to what order they should go in.[13]

G. A. Kerkut is also an evolutionist who recognizes that the theory has some faults. His main problem with the horse series is that the original fossils are not available — everything on display is a reproduction, and there's no way of knowing which bones were really found and which were added from imagination. He wrote:

> At present, however, it is a matter of faith that the textbook pictures are true or even that they are the best representations of the truth that are available to us at the present time. . . . It makes quite a difference whether a name on a diagram represents a whole skeleton or just a tooth.[14]

Ian Taylor sums up his discussion of horse evolution in this way:

> When all is said and done, however, a row of look-alike fossils cannot be proof that one species changed into another; we cannot be sure that the

little rock badger of long ago changed into Orohippus, since it is just as likely that they have always been separate species, one still living, one extinct. . . . To put the argument another way, if horses and donkeys were only known by their fossils, they might well be classified as variants within a single species, but the experience of breeders shows that, in fact, they are separate species. Acknowledging all the enormous amount of work that men such as Henry F. Osborn and G.G. Simpson have put into the horse series, the sad fact remains that what has actually been done is to select the fossil data to fit the theory, and this cannot be considered scientific proof. It is little wonder, then, that Raup (1979) makes the comment that the evolution of the horse in North America has to be discarded or modified.[15]

The statement by Raup that Taylor referred to above, is given in "The Fossil Record" section of chapter 3, in this book you are now reading.

Paleontologist Niles Eldredge, curator at the American Museum of Natural History and co-author (with Stephen J. Gould) of the Theory of Punctuated Equilibrium, had this reaction when asked about the horse series:

There have been an awful lot of stories, some more imaginative than others, about what the nature of that history [of life] really is. The most famous example, still on exhibit downstairs, is the exhibit on horse evolution prepared perhaps fifty years ago. That has been presented as the literal truth in textbook after textbook. Now I think that that is lamentable, particularly when the people who propose those kinds of stories may themselves be aware of the speculative nature of some of that stuff.[16]

"ALL THE KNOWLEDGEABLE SCIENTISTS BELIEVE IN EVOLUTION"

This is the most common reason given by lay people who are asked why they believe in evolution. But this is not evidence. Isn't this, instead, more of an unthinking follow-the-leader game or a philosophic cop-out?

And this reason isn't even true; it's simply the acceptance of propaganda. There are many good scientists who believe in God's creation, and many others who realize that macro-evolution is so improbable that it couldn't have occurred. Most of the "founding fathers" of modern science were creationists (see the list in chapter 2). A later section of this book discusses the philosophical reasons why many today do believe in evolution; they have chosen that belief, not because of any scientific evidence, but because it fit their outlook on life.

ADAPTATIONS

Evolutionists often say that biological changes which result from adaptation to environmental changes (the peppered moth, for example) show micro-evolution. But genetics has proven they can't change to anything that wasn't already present in their genes. Horizontal change isn't evolution, because that doesn't show any sort of upward increase in complexity:

> All competent biologists acknowledge the limited nature of the variation breeders can produce, although they do not like to discuss it much when grinding the evolutionary ax.[17]

The peppered moth is a good example of natural selection, because those individual moths that blended smoothly into their environment had a greater chance of survival against predators than those whose color made them more visible. Thus, their proportion tended to increase, changing the relative makeup of their group gene-pool. But the range of genes within that pool did not change. This is definitely not macro-evolution.

MUTATIONS

The only mechanism ever proposed as to how evolution might occur, involves mutations. Yet almost all mutations are harmful, often fatal. There's almost no chance that a long series of favorable mutations could cause higher-order development.

Fruit flies (drosophila) have short reproduction times, and have thus been used for extensive studies on the effects of mutations. Many mutant varieties have been produced, yet they remain fruit flies, and are always damaged by the mutations. A noted authority says:

> A review of known facts about their [mutated fruit flies] ability to survive has led to no other conclusion than that they are always constitutionally weaker than their parent form or species, and in a population with free competition they are eliminated. Therefore they are never found in nature (e.g., not a single one of the several hundreds of drosophila mutations), and therefore they are able to appear only in the favourable environment of the experimental field or laboratory.[18]

THE BAT

Evolutionists speculate that mutations caused the bat to evolve in many tiny steps from a mouse-like shrew, over millions of years. They say the skin behind the forelegs gradually enlarged and formed "wing" surfaces. But if this were so, how could this creature have survived for many generations during the awkward half-developed stages, when the wings were not developed enough to fly well, and yet the legs were encumbered with extra skin that surely would have interfered with running?

Even more difficult for the evolutionist to explain is the very complicated sonar system of the bat. The shrew has nothing of the sort; if bats had evolved from a shrew, that complete system must have developed from nothing, simultaneously with the wings. This is a very complicated apparatus, with transmitter, receiver, and an extremely complex nervous system. But it wouldn't have had any survival value at all until its development was complete enough to work right, yet the bat couldn't fly without this fully functioning capability.

Bats must surely have begun their existence in a fully formed state.

COMPARATIVE ANATOMY, OR HOMOLOGOUS STRUCTURES

One of the favorite "proofs" of evolution theory is the statement that the pentadactyl limb pattern of tetrapods indicates descent through modification from a common ancestor. Before we go further, let's define these words. "Penta-" means "five," "dactyl" means "digits or fingers," "tetra-" means "four," and "pods" means "feet." So we're talking here about four-footed creatures that have five digits on their limbs. This pattern is found in many mammals.

Charles Darwin was curious about why this should occur. In *The Origin of Species* he wrote:

> What can be more curious than that the hand of a man, formed for grasping, that of a mole for digging, the leg of the horse, the paddle of the porpoise, and the wing of the bat, should all be constructed on the same pattern, and should include the same bones, in the same relative positions?"

He went on to speculate that the answer lay in common descent and natural selection.

The explanation is manifest on the theory of

the natural selection of successive slight modifications.

Darwin used this an an argument for homology, that similar structure is an indication of common evolutionary development. He wrote:

> If we suppose that the ancient progenitor, the archetype as it may be called, of all mammals, had its limbs constructed on the existing general pattern, for whatever purpose they served, we can at once perceive the plain signification of the homologous construction of the limbs throughout the whole class.

What he meant by this was that some sort of original ancestor had a five-digit limb structure and, as new generations came along, each descendant had its bone pattern modified slightly. After millions of generations had passed, the result would be the current diversity of characteristics that we see in creatures around us today. That sounded good to scientists in his day, who were looking for an explanation that didn't require a divine creator, and who didn't have the fossil evidences that we have today.

But, as in so many other areas of evolution theory, when the actual facts are examined more closely, they don't fit the prediction. If Darwin had been right, then we should be able to trace back in the fossil record through the ancestry of various creatures and see a pattern of gradual change. The ancestors of a pentadactyl tetrapod should be pentadactyl themselves. This is not what we find in the fossil record. The earliest mammals were not pentadactyl but rather were "polydactylous," that is, of multi-digit structure. They had six, seven, or eight digits.

Several paleontologists have written of this discrepancy between fact and theory. Two of these are M.I. Coates and J.A. Clack.[19]

My favorite evolutionist writer is Harvard's Stephen

Jay Gould, who is a recognized authority, has a way with words, and often shows a refreshing openness about the difference between actual evidences and the commonly-accepted ideas presented in elementary textbooks. As an evolutionist, he believes that tetrapods had a common ancestor, but he wrote:

> The conclusion seems inescapable, and an old "certainty" must be starkly reversed. Only three Devonian tetrapods are known. None has five toes. They bear, respectively, six, seven, and eight digits on their preserved limbs. Five is not a canonical, or archetypal, number of digits for tetrapods — at least not in the primary sense of "present from the beginning."[20]

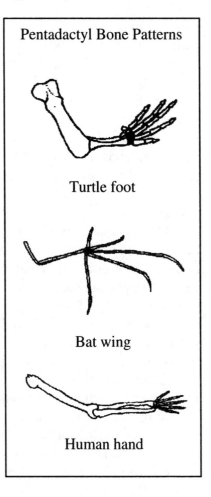

Pentadactyl Bone Patterns

Turtle foot

Bat wing

Human hand

Now, since there's no real evidence of ancestral pentadactylism, how would creationists explain the curious fact that so many mammals have five digits? As with so many other actual facts of nature, we point to the obvious intelligence of the designer. For example, look at the many types of cars that have four wheels. They illustrate the simple fact that, for many applications, four is a good number — it works well. Designers utilize a proven principle. We believe that all the creatures around us were created by a super-intelligent Designer. He utilized whatever design he considered best for each given situation, and in a great many cases we've only begun to recognize the tremendous complexity shown in those designs. Just as the very existence of a fine watch demands a good watchmaker, so the complicated structure of a living creature demands a super-intelligent creator.

Paul Nelson wrote about the broader principle illustrated by this question of pentadactylism. He showed that each time we consider some bit of evidence we put it into a framework of our accumulated knowledge and belief — what we might call our "world view." Our interpretation is determined by that knowledge- system. If a person is committed to a framework of materialistic naturalism, his belief-system forces him to exclude any trace of intelligent design shown by a creator; he must explain everything in purely material ways, even when they don't fit the actual evidence! This is why evolutionists insist that the concept of a God is only religious, and thus outside of the domain of science. Evolution is said to be a "fact" that must be believed even if the evidence doesn't seem to support it.

But the creationist's world view, or knowledge system, includes the belief that there is a divine Creator who has the power and intelligence to make things in the best way, not constrained by the "laws of nature." Nelson wrote that the pentadactyl pattern may be God's "signature," and:

> The creationist system of knowledge, encompassing as it does not only the biological evidence, but the reality of God's mind and His creative activity in history, can allow for that possibility — and the profound zing of truth that may follow.[21]

Homology has been one of the strongest arguments that supposedly bolsters evolution theory — that similar structures evolved from a common ancestor. For this to be true, the genes that control those structures must also have common structure. But Michael Denton said:

> The validity of the evolutionary interpretation of homology would have been greatly strengthened if embryological and genetic research could have shown that homologous structures were specified by homologous genes. . . . But it has become clear that the principle cannot be extended in this way. Homologous structures are often specified by non-homologous genetic systems.[22]

Thus, these new studies of genetic mechanisms by molecular biologists seem to rule out the evolutionist claims that homologous structures show evolutionary descent. They're more likely evidence of intelligent design.

CHEMICAL ORIGIN OF LIFE

In the early 1950s, Stanley Miller's well-publicized laboratory synthesis of several amino acids made it sound as if artificial production of life in the laboratory was just around the corner. However, all of those experimental procedures required complicated filters, traps, alternate heating and cooling, and, most importantly, operator intervention.

Thaxton, Bradley, and Olsen wrote a very comprehensive book devoted solely to examining various aspects of this theory of the chemical origin of life. They described the early work on laboratory synthesis, what is known about conditions on the early earth, and thermodynamic considerations of chemical reactions.

They showed that the probability of destructive reactions in any natural environment is much higher than that for favorable combinations, therefore the probability for a long series of favorable reactions to manufacture any DNA-style complex molecules is practically zero. They said:

> Furthermore, no geological evidence indicates an organic soup, even a small organic pond, ever existed on this planet. It is becoming clear that however life began on earth, the usually conceived notion that life emerged from an oceanic soup of organic chemicals is a most implausible hypothesis. We may therefore with fairness call this scenario "the myth of the prebiotic soup."[23]

VESTIGIAL ORGANS

A century or so ago, before anatomists had learned much about the human body, it was widely believed that many of our organs were "vestigial," that is, a holdover from some previous stage of evolution. Examples that we sometimes still hear are: the appendix (they guessed that it was formerly used for helping to digest grass), the tailbone, the tonsils, etc.

But now that real knowledge has expanded, medical experts have concluded that, of the 150 or so organs once thought to be vestigial, less than a dozen still have no obvious present function. It's no longer a good argument.

> The existence of functionless "vestigial organs" was presented by Darwin, and is often cited by current biology textbooks, as part of the evidence for evolution . . . [but] "vestigial organs" provide no evidence for evolutionary theory.[24]

EMBRYONIC RECAPITULATION

This idea, originally named Haeckel's "law of biogenesis," says that a human fetus re-enacts previous stages of evolution (going through stages of having gill slits, tail, etc.) as it develops. It's been described as "ontogeny recapitulates phylogeny." Over 50 years ago, this was proven to be a deliberate hoax done by Dr. Ernst Haeckel, who was later convicted of forgery at a Jena University court in Germany, and the theory was denounced.[25]

And so it is now a well-known hoax, yet it is still shown in many elementary biology textbooks as a proof for evolution and as a justification for abortion.

Dr. W.R. Thompson, an entomologist, and director of Canada's Biological Control Institute of Ottawa, was chosen to write the Introduction to the centennial republication of Darwin's *The Origin of Species*. In that, he thought it wise to call attention to several faults of evolution theory; one of them was this hoax, so he wrote:

> A natural law can only be established as an induction from facts. Haeckel was of course unable to do this. What he did was to arrange existing forms of animal life in a series proceeding from the simple to the complex, intercalating imaginary entities where discontinuity existed and then giving the embryonic phases names corresponding to the stages in his so-called evolutionary series. Cases in which this parallelism did not exist were dealt with by the simple expedient of saying that the embryological development had been falsified. When the "convergence" of embryos was not entirely satisfactory, Haeckel altered the illustrations to fit his theory. The alterations were slight but significant. The "biogenetic law" as a proof of evolution is valueless.[26]

ARCHAEOPTERYX — REPTILE-TO-BIRD TRANSITION?

The first of these controversial fossils was found in 1820 in "Upper Jurassic" limestone near Solenhofen, Bavaria. A few others were found in the 1860s. This was a very unusual bird, now extinct. It had bird-like wings, beak, sclerotic eye-rings, an opposable hind-claw, and well-de-fined feathers. But it also had reptilian features such as teeth, wing-claws, and a long bony feathered tail.

It's widely claimed that this is today's best example of a transitional fossil. But many experts dispute this.

Feathers are enough to define it as a full-fledged bird. But what about the "reptilian" features? Every one of them can be found in other birds that are not claimed as transitions. The young ostrich, rhea, and touraco have wing-claws, as does the hoatzin, a bird currently living in South America, that looks quite a bit like an archaeopteryx.

The embryos of several of today's birds have more tail vertebrae than archaeopteryx, but these later fuse into one bone called the pygostyle. Today's birds don't have teeth, but a number of fossil birds did have. And, because there are no fossil links either to it (from known reptiles) or from it (to known birds) Stephen J. Gould and Niles Eldredge claim that it shouldn't be called a "missing link."[27]

There are many types of flying creatures that are not birds; these include bats, flying foxes, flying fish, and a number of pterosaurs — extinct members of the archosaur group of reptiles. Yet no one claims that these are transitions, because none has any trace of feathers, which are the distinctive mark of birds.

Several evolutionists have tried to describe how scales might have evolved into feathers. Heilman wrote a long and fanciful story of how a terrestrial running reptile (he called it "pro-avis") began to climb trees and then to leap through the air to catch insects. He said:

> By the friction of the air, the outer edges of the scales become frayed, the frayings gradually changing into still longer horny processes, which in course of time become more and more featherlike, until the perfect feather is produced. From wings, tail, and flanks, the feathering spreads to the whole body.[28]

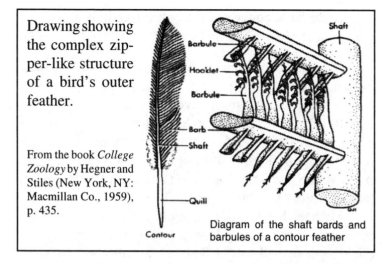

Drawing showing the complex zipper-like structure of a bird's outer feather.

From the book *College Zoology* by Hegner and Stiles (New York, NY: Macmillan Co., 1959), p. 435.

Diagram of the shaft bards and barbules of a contour feather

But Heilman neglects the fact that feathers are not simply "frayed scales." They are made of different material, they are fed from different layers of skin, and, most important, feathers have many thousands of marvelously engineered barbs and hooks that interlock each feather with its neighbors, so that the wing becomes an impervious airfoil. We often see birds "preening" themselves; they're zipping the barbs and hooks back smoothly together. Most birds' wings also have subsidiary airfoils like the "Handley Page slot" of an airplane wing, that increases lift by reducing turbulence.

Another bird expert, John Ostrom, doubts Heilman's story. He came up with his own version that sounds just as farfetched. He proposed that this early transition must have been a good bipedal runner that began to use its front legs to catch insects, and that these then gradually enlarged. He wrote:

> Is it possible that the initial (pre-archaeopteryx) enlargement of feathers on its hand might have been to increase the hand surface area, thereby making it more effective in catching insects? Continued selection for larger feather size

could have converted the entire forelimb into a large, light-weight "insect net."[29]

Ostrom also pointed out the obvious fact that "No fossil evidence exists of any pro-avis. It is a purely hypothetical pre-bird, but one that must have existed."

But the most telling evidence that archaeopteryx, or any other creature, could not have been a transition between reptile and bird doesn't show up in fossils, since they only preserve the hard parts, never the soft fleshy parts, such as the respiratory system.

Michael Denton does a good job of describing the problems of explaining how a bird's respiratory system couldn't have evolved.[30] I'll abbreviate his arguments.

All the vertebrates, except for birds, breathe by means of bringing air into the lungs through a system of branching tubes, which terminate in alveoli. This is a two-cycle system; we breathe in oxygen, it's absorbed into the blood, impurities are transmitted into the air in the lungs, and the bad air is then exhaled through the same tubes and nostrils as those through which the good air came in.

But all birds have a totally different four-cycle system. Air is drawn in and passes through tubes that contain parabronchi; it then flows on through several air-sacs deeper in the bird's body. It flows on through other parabronchi, and finally exits the body through a completely different orifice than that through which it came in. Thus, air moves in the same direction all the way through; it "goes in one hole, and out another."

So we see that the bird's respiratory system is completely different from that of any other creature. It is almost impossible to see how such a system could have evolved, either in tiny steps or in one huge change, and still allowed a creature to stay alive and functional.

The avian respiratory system thus seems to be a perfect answer to Darwin's challenge, when he wrote:

If it could be demonstrated that any complex organ existed which could not possibly have been formed by numerous, successive, slight modifications, my theory would absolutely break down.[31]

I've gone into considerable detail on this "reptile-to-bird transitional fossil" because archaeopteryx is one of the most commonly-quoted "proofs" of evolution, and is surely the closest thing to a transitional fossil that exists. Yet the quotations above should be enough to convince any reasonable reader that it takes a lot of imagination to bridge the gap, and that any sort of factual proof is just not there. This certainly illustrates the faith (not facts) involved in the fairy tale of evolution.

RADIOACTIVE DATING

There are two basically different kinds of radioactive dating methods. One is the Carbon-14 method, used for dating fragments of once-living organisms. It's never used for non-organic samples, and almost never tried if the sample is thought to be much older than about 50,000 years. This method is described in chapter 3 of this book. It furnishes some good evidences that creationists often discuss.

The second broad category is sometimes called "heavy-metal dating," and includes uranium-thorium-lead, rubidium-strontium, and potassium-argon methods. These are the methods that are commonly used on rocks and other non-organic samples, and that often give extremely long ages — millions or billions of years. These are the methods that evolutionists often describe as proving the ancient age of the earth and its strata, and that creationists often criticize as giving totally false results.

All of these dating mechanisms begin with some radioactive isotope such as ^{238}U, ^{235}U, ^{232}Th, ^{40}K, or ^{87}Rb. These are called the "mother" isotopes. These elements are naturally radioactive, that is, they spontaneously emit an alpha or a beta particle and, as a result, are transformed into some different isotope, called the "daughter" isotopes. These systems are briefly described in boxes on the next few pages. Part of the information for the mathematics and principles of dating is taken from the *Impact* article, "Grand Canyon Lava Flows: A Survey of Isotope Dating Methods," by Steven A. Austin, in the Institute for Creation Research *Acts and Facts,* April 1988. Updated descriptions are contained in Austin's beautifully illustrated book *Grand Canyon: Monument to Catastrophe.*[32]

The methods that give ancient ages all give about as many "wrong" answers as "right" ones. The "correct" answer is chosen on the basis of stratigraphic sequences, that is, what fossils are contained nearby. Of course, the fossil dates depend on the assumption of evolution. And, of course, the public doesn't usually hear of these wrong answers.

This statement — that radiometric dates are "corrected" by reference to evolution-based index fossils — is hotly contested, but examination of the technical literature shows that it is true, in spite of what elementary textbooks say. Let's look at a few examples.

The general public has been led to believe that there's a consistency in radiometric results that demonstrates its reliability. But the technical literature shows otherwise. John Woodmorappe did an extensive literature search, looking at 445 technical articles from 54 reputable geochronology and geology journals. These reports listed over 350 dates measured by radiometric methods, that conflicted badly with the ages assigned to fossils found in these same strata. They covered "expected" ages ranging from 1 to >600 million years. In almost every case that had such discrepancies, the fossil dates were accepted as correct; the radiogenic dates were discarded. He quoted one researcher as saying:

> In general, dates in the "correct ball park" are
> assumed to be correct and are published, but those

Principles of Uranium-Thorium-Lead Dating

Uranium-238 (or ^{238}U) is the starting point for a decay series of eight alpha particles and six beta particles, that ends with ^{206}Pb, a stable isotope.

The ^{235}U series involves seven alphas and four betas, to form the stable ^{207}Pb. The ^{232}Th series includes six alphas and four betas, and ends with ^{208}Pb, which is stable.

These were almost the only decay series used for dating for many years.

In each case, the total decay time comes from the first step, since the later isotopes have relatively very short half-lives. For any isotope, half-life and decay constant are related by the following equation:

$T_{half} = \ln (0.5)/^{\lambda} = 0.69315/^{\lambda}$

$$\text{where } \lambda = \quad \text{decay constant}$$
$$\ln (0.5) = \quad \text{the natural logarithm of } 0.5$$
$$\_ = \quad \text{at time of origin}$$
$$p = \quad \text{at present time}$$
$$^{238}U \to T_{half} = 4.55 \times 10^9 \text{ yrs,}^{\lambda} = 1.52 \times 10^{-10}/\text{yr}$$
$$^{235}U \to T_{half} = 0.71 \times 10^9 \text{ yrs,}^{\lambda} = 9.80 \times 10^{-10}/\text{yr}$$
$$^{232}Th \to T_{half} = 13.4 \times 10^9 \text{ yrs,}^{\lambda} = 5.17 \times 10^{-11}/\text{yr}$$

Since it's better to measure ratios than absolute values, it's usual to measure isotope ratios, and the reference isotope is chosen to be ^{204}Pb, which is common stable lead. The three "model age" equations are:

$$(^{206}Pb/^{204}Pb)_p = (^{206}Pb/^{204}Pb)_\_ + (e^{\lambda t} -1) \times (^{238}U/^{204}Pb)_p$$
$$(^{207}Pb/^{204}Pb)_p = (^{207}Pb/^{204}Pb)_\_ + (e^{\lambda t} -1) \times (^{235}U/^{204}Pb)_p$$
$$(^{208}Pb/^{204}Pb)_p = (^{208}Pb/^{204}Pb)_\_ + (e^{\lambda t} -1) \times (^{232}Th/^{204}Pb)_p$$

Rock samples often have mixtures of all three of the "mother" isotopes above, yet these almost never yield the same ages. Lead isotope methods are often preferable, using ^{206}Pb/^{207}Pb. Many seemingly arbitrary "rules of thumb" are involved with each of these methods.

Principles of Rubidium-Strontium Dating (Model Age Method)

Rubidium-87 (^{87}Rb) is commonly found in basaltic volcanic rocks. This is a radioactive isotope that decays to Strontium-87 (^{87}Sr) with a half-life of about 48.8 billion years. If the rock is sealed so that neither isotope escapes or absorbs more, the following equation should hold true:

$$^{87}Sr_p = {}^{87}Sr_- + {}^{87}Rb_p \times (e^{\lambda t} - 1)$$

$\lambda =$ decay constant
$= 1.42 \times 10^{-11}$ per year,
$e = 2.71828$ (natural log base)
$p =$ present value
$_- =$ original value

The laboratory analysis is much improved if isotope ratios are measured, instead of absolute values. For that reason, these isotopes are often measured with respect to the amount of ^{86}Sr in the rock. This is a nonradioactive isotope that's usually present in any rock that has any ^{87}Rb in it.

An equation may have all terms divided by the same value and still remain true. So each term in the above equation is divided by ^{86}Sr to get it into ratio form.

$$(^{87}Sr/^{86}Sr)_p = (^{87}Sr/^{86}Sr)_- + (e^{\lambda t} - 1) \times (^{87}Rb/^{86}Sr)_p$$

But an "educated guess" is needed for the original values, ^{87}Sr and ^{86}Sr. If a single rock is dated by either of these equations it's called a **Model Age**.

Because of the educated guesses required, and because there's no way of telling whether there was leakage in the rock, this is not considered to be a highly reliable age figure. An "Isochron Age" measurement and calculation is thought to be much better. (See the next page.)

Principles of Rubidium-Strontium Dating
(Isochron Method)

If different portions of the same lava rock are analyzed, they are usually found to have different $^{87}Sr/^{86}Sr$ ratios, and also $^{87}Rb/^{86}Sr$ ratios. And it's usually obvious that there was some initial ^{87}Sr in the magma. The problem is how to determine that initial amount.

It seems reasonable that if a rock appears to have come from the same magma flow it should all be the same age. And, if the rock has been a closed system, all regions throughout the rock should show the same age, even if they have different isotope ratios.

Notice that the isotopic ratio equation in the "Model Age" box has the form of the general equation of a straight line, $y = b + mx$, where y and x are the present values of $(^{87}Sr/^{86}Sr)_p$ and $(^{87}Rb/^{86}Sr)_p$, m is the slope of the straight line $(e^{\lambda t}-1)$, and b is the initial ratio $(^{87}Sr/^{86}Sr)$.

If such a graph is constructed, and measurements from different regions of a single rock are plotted, and if they yield a straight line, that's taken as an indication that the rock was a closed system. Then the slope of that line indicates the age. The point where the line intersects the $^{87}Sr/^{86}Sr$ axis shows the initial value. This graph is called a **Rubidium-Strontium Isochron**, and is considered to be the most accurate dating method available, but still not good. The isochron at right was made from lava at western Grand Canyon. The lava had been injected by a volcano onto the top surface of the sedimentary ground, had flowed over the rim and down into the canyon. Obviously, then, it can't be as old as the already-eroded canyon wall, which was carved into the sedimentary rock that had been in place for a long time. It is most likely no older than some 10,000 years. Yet the isochron shows its age to be 1.5 billion years, obviously a totally wrong value.

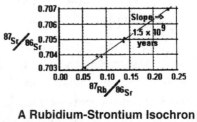

A Rubidium-Strontium Isochron

Principles of Potassium-Argon Dating

Potassium-40 (^{40}K) is a radioactive isotope that decays with a 1.3-billion-year half-life to become Argon-40 (^{40}Ar). Thus, if these isotopes could be formed sealed in a rock that has no leakage, it should be possible to use this decay system as a clock. As was discussed in the Rubidium-Strontium box, ratios are easier to measure than absolute values. For a ^{40}K-^{40}Ar system, Argon-36 is the non-radioactive reference isotope. Thus, in an isochron graph, ^{40}Ar/^{36}Ar is plotted on the y-axis and ^{40}K/^{36}Ar is on the x-axis.

But there are many problems, indicated by the many wildly discordant ^{40}K-^{40}Ar ages that are reported. Known 200-year-old Hawaiian lava was measured to be 22 million years old, for example.

^{40}K decays by electron capture to ^{40}Ar ($\sim$11%) and also by beta emission to ^{40}Ca ($\sim$89%). But ^{40}Ca is the common calcium, and ^{40}Ar is the common argon, so there's much difficulty in determining what's the actual radio-genic ^{40}Ar. In order to make the numbers agree with U-Th-Pb dates, it's normal to choose a branching ratio of about 8%, even though it's known to be wrong; but it's used because it often works!

Argon migrates easily into and out of minerals, and does so at rates that vary according to the depth of burial. Potassium is easily leached from many rocks. These are only a few of the problems in this system. Yet ^{40}K-^{40}Ar dating is the main support for dating of ocean-floor samples in sea-floor spreading studies. No wonder many scientists express doubts about dating of sea-floor spreading.

in disagreement with other data are seldom published nor are discrepancies fully explained.[33]

When these reports did discuss the possible causes of errors, they used many words such as "possibly," "perhaps," "probably," "may have been," etc. Reasons given usually involved detrital intrusion, leakage, or leaching of some of the isotopes in the sample, and sometimes the initial isotopic content of the sample. For K/Ar dates, it's easy to blame argon loss if the reported age is too short, or argon absorption if it's too long. It's well known that argon diffuses easily through rock, and there's no way of knowing whether that may have happened in any given case.

Errors are particularly bad with the K-Ar (potassium-argon) method. Studies have been made of submarine basalt rocks of known recent age near Hawaii. These came from the Kilauea volcano. The results ranged up to 22,000,000 years. Joan Engels wrote:

> It is now well known that K-Ar ages obtained from different minerals in a single rock may be strikingly discordant.[34]

A few pages later in this chapter is a section called "The I.C.R. Grand Canyon Dating Project." This describes a controlled set of measurements of basaltic lava rocks in the Grand Canyon. Two sets of rocks were taken from carefully chosen spots; one of these is obviously foundation rock, dated by most geologists as being close to 2 billion years old. The other is lava from a volcano that is obviously quite recent, since it's on the surface and spilled over the edge of the already-eroded canyon. Geologists usually say this age must be measured in thousands, not millions, of years.

Yet this recent lava, when measured by the "best method," rubidium/strontium isochron, showed an age of 1.5 billion years, obviously badly in error.

Marvin Lubenow documented a sequence of attempts to date a fossil skull that was considered very important in the search for hominid ancestors. This sequence of age measurements is very significant, in that it shows "state of evolution" ideas took precedence over radiogenic dating.

In 1972 Richard Leakey found a skull near Lake Rudolf in Kenya that he said was "virtually indistinguishable" from that of a modern human. Yet it was found beneath a layer of the volcanic KBS Tuff that had an accepted radiometric date of 2.6 MY (millions of years old). Leakey declared that the skull was 2.9 MY, and said that it "fits no previous models of human beginnings." It was named KNM-ER-1470 (for Kenya National Museum, East Rudolf, #1470).

Anthropologist Marvin Lubenow gives a good description of the ten years of controversy surrounding the dating of this skull.

In the first attempt at dating the KBS, Tuff, Fitch and Miller analyzed the raw rocks and got dates ranging from 212 to 230 MY (this is in the Triassic times of dinosaurs!). Because mammal bones had been found below this stratum, they said these dates were obviously in error because of "the possible presence of extraneous argon derived from inclusions of pre-existing rocks." Even though the rock looked good, anything older than 5 MY was obviously wrong in view of their knowledge of the "sequence of evolutionary development."

Meanwhile a UC-Berkeley team led by G.H. Curtis analyzed several KBS pumice rocks and found some that were around 1.6 MY and some that were about 1.8 MY. Other measurements, some as low as 0.5 MY, were said to be anomalously young; these were explained by possible over-printing by an alkaline-rich hot water infusion.

Between 1969 and 1976 several teams made a number of radiometric measurements, and the results clustered around three ages — 1.8 MY, 2.4 MY, and 2.6 MY. Each team criticized the other's techniques of rock sample selection. Most radiometric arguments were said to favor the 2.6 MY date, but the paleontological arguments favored the 1.8 MY date — (that's where the skull would best fit evolution theory). And final agreement came only after paleontologists had agreed on fossil correlations involving two species of extinct pigs! The final accepted date for the skull was 1.9 MY. Lubenow's comment about selecting rock samples for radiometric dating was:

The question arises, "'How does one know

when one has good samples for dating?" The only answer to that question is that "good" samples give dates that are in accord with evolutionary presuppositions. "Bad" samples are the ones that give dates not in conformity with evolution — a classic illustration of circular reasoning.[35]

There are several possible sources for the errors associated with radiometric dating. The main problems (beginning with those of least importance) are:

1. Accuracy of decay rates — most of these are thought to be known within a few percent and, if wrong, would have only a minor effect on dates.

2. Constancy of decay rates — most scientists believe these have been constant through the ages. But one of the early investigators, Prof. John Joly of Trinity College, Dublin, reported evidence showing variation.[36]

Barry Setterfield's report on possible variation of the speed of light also gives historical references to variations in decay rates over the last 300 years.[37] But most scientists have been less than enthusiastic in their acceptance of this concept.

3. Integrity of atoms in the rock — this is certainly a point of much concern, and is the most-cited reason for obvious errors in dating measurements. Uranium salts are water soluble, and most minerals are subject to unequal leaching of chemical components. Argon migrates unpredictably in and out of rocks. Hurley reported that radioactive components of granites lie on the surface of grains, and can easily be leached away. Zircon crystals have been dated by U/Pb methods, but ion microprobe studies have shown that the uranium and lead are embedded in different parts of the crystal structure; this shows that the ^{206}Pb actually could not have come from uranium decay.

4. Neutron activation by unknown source — Professor Melvin Cook examined ores from a Katanga mine and found that it had no ^{204}Pb and no thorium, yet there was appreciable ^{208}Pb! It apparently couldn't have been primordial, and

couldn't have resulted from thorium decay. The only way it could be explained is neutron activation of ^{207}Pb. When he corrected for this, the age was reduced from 600 million years to near modern.[38]

In most ores, it's not possible to see this effect so clearly, but it shows that some neutron flux, possibly from a supernova, must have had a strong effect, and this probably would have been worldwide.

5. By far the most important problem, as far as the creationist is concerned, is the original isotopic makeup of the rock. How can we possibly know what the original material was?

The uniformitarian geologist must assume some initial concentration. If he makes a good guess, and the other error sources can be minimized, he could make an accurate age determination provided his set of assumptions is correct. But his assumptions are always based on the theory of uniformitarianism — that is, that the earth came into existence in a purely materialistic way, a long time ago. If he then tries to use his results to prove the earth is old and was not created, he's using circular logic — he's actually ruling out the possibility of a supernatural six-day creation before the measurement is made.

In his classic geochronology textbook, Henry Faul wrote:

> If one assumes that the solar system condensed from a primordial cloud, it follows that the materials of planets, asteroids, and meteorites have a common origin. Iron meteorites contain some lead but only infinitesimal traces of uranium and thorium, and therefore the lead is uncontaminated by radiogenic lead and can be regarded as a good sample of primordial lead. Table 6-1 [in his book] lists the isotopic composition of lead extracted from some iron meteorites. These data now can be used as ($^{207}Pb/^{204}Pb$) and ($^{206}Pb/^{204}Pb$)

in the Houtermans equation, and all that remains to be found to permit a calculation of the age of the earth is a lead sample from a closed subsystem of well-known age.[39]

Notice his starting-point; a naturalistic earth-origin, over a long period of time.

Faul shows the common belief among almost all evolutionist scientists that the earth and the solar system evolved from a cloud of gas and dust, over a very long time, billions of years ago. From this basic belief, he says that the original makeup of some of earth's chemicals must have been similar to what we can see today in meteorites. This assumption is one of the main evidences about the age of the earth and the composition of primordial rocks. But it is strongly based on belief in uniformitarianism and a naturalistic origin of the earth. Without this foundational belief, long-age dating measurements would be meaningless.

On the other hand, if the earth had been suddenly created (like the Bible says), the Creator could have made it any way He wanted to. He wouldn't be constrained to follow any of man's rules — indeed, He has already demonstrated that. When He made the trees in the Garden of Eden, they already had fruit on them. When He made Adam and Eve, they were in a mature form, not tiny infants. We believe He created these things with an appearance of age. Why couldn't He also have made rocks the same way? Why couldn't they have contained lead-206 and argon-40, so that they appeared mature?

Many schoolteachers, and most of the commercial media, are good spokesmen for the evolutionist position. And too many Christians have too easily accepted these scientists' "long-age-of-the-earth" statements, usually without realizing that these are based on purely materialistic assumptions that completely rule out any sort of intervention by a creator God. They haven't recognized the fallacy of circular reasoning in these statements. In this way, they've needlessly lost the foundation of their faith.

The reader is referred to such books as *In the Minds of Men: Darwin and the New World Order* by Ian Taylor for a longer and more complete discussion of radioactive dating.[40]

I should also note that the four tables describing dating systems, and several paragraphs in this section on radioactive dating, were taken from my article "The Faith of Radiogenic Dating," in *Bible-Science News*.[41]

THE I.C.R. GRAND CANYON DATING PROJECT

Up to now, creationists have criticized many aspects of dating rocks by radioactivity, but have offered little positive proof. The Institute for Creation Research is in the early phases of generating such proof.[42]

Their goal is stated as follows:

> The purpose of this project is to use the "most reliable" radioactive isotope dating method (the "isochron method") with the most accurate analytical measurement technique (the isotope dilution mass spectrograph technique) to establish the "ages" of various Grand Canyon rocks.

They've engaged a licensed commercial geotechnical laboratory to help plan and oversee the project, and to submit rock samples to several qualified laboratories in a manner that will avoid subterfuge.

The Grand Canyon has many different rock strata and types; everyone agrees that the Precambrian metamorphic rocks buried deep below the Canyon have to be the oldest. These include the Trinity Gneiss, Elves Chasm Gneiss, and the Zoroaster Granite.

Everyone also agrees that the Quaternary lava flow on the Uinkaret Plateau are among the youngest igneous types there. This came from a volcano, after all of the beds of sedimentary strata were laid down, and after the canyon was eroded. The lava has flowed over the rim, and down the sides of the canyon.

Most conventional geologists believe that the deep gneisses and granites are more than 600 million years old, probably closer to 2,000 million years, and that the age of the Uinkaret Plateau basaltic lava flows should be measured in just thousands of years. Thus, by comparing the accurately measured ages of a number of samples from these two regions, we should get an idea of the general reliability of radiometric methods. The preliminary results look very interesting. Only the recent lava flow measurements were completed at the time of my last report.

Several "model age" figures were obtained for the same set of recent rocks, and they were quite discordant (that is, they all disagreed with each other). The "more accurate" rubidium-strontium isochron age was reported to be 2.1 billion years, and that is ridiculous! That's many thousands of times older than the actual age! That date alone should be enough to throw strong doubts on heavy-metal radiometric dating methods, but we must wait for project completion before too many conclusions are drawn.

PROBLEMS WITH THE BIG BANG

Since the 1960s, the big bang has been the standard scientific model for the origin of the universe. By now, most people think that it's been proven true, but that's far from correct. Several new evidences don't fit the theory. But recent publicity has used phrases like "the fingerprint of creation" and "it's like looking at God" in connection with announcement of the latest measurements. These are grossly exaggerated, to say the least.

A problem that has troubled the scientific world for several years is this. According to the theory, the universe had its start with all the matter of the universe concentrated at one tiny point, which then exploded in a mighty blast, billions of years ago. Such an explosion in open space should have thrown out debris uniformly in all directions. But our present universe doesn't show that uniformity; everything is extremely "clumpy;" stars are grouped into galaxies, and galaxies are grouped into various structures. There are tremendous regions that are completely devoid of anything at all (like the 100-million-light-year-diameter "Hole in Space"), and others that are relatively dense (like the 1/2- billion-light-year-long "Great Wall").

Arno Penzias and Robert Wilson, in the 1960s, found that the entire universe seems to be filled with faint radiation of about $2.7°K$. This is thought to be cooled-down radiation, left over from the big bang. But it's extremely smooth — everywhere the same. How could such a smooth explosion result in the extremely clumpy universe we see today? For decades, astronomers have tried to solve this riddle.

In 1990 Daniel Lazich, chief engineer for the Kinetic Weapons Project for the U.S. Strategic Defense Command, commented on this problem:

> What troubles scientists the most is the fact that recent advances in quantum cosmology show that the assumptions on which the most cherished theory about the origin of the universe — the big bang — is based are wrong. The big bang theory assumes that the universe was smooth and homogeneous matter at its beginning and predicts that it should be homogeneous on the largest scales today. But the results of the most recent studies directly contradict these assumptions. Our universe is not homogeneous on the large scale, and hence could not have originated from a big bang that yielded a smooth and homogeneous universe. Confounded and dismayed scientists are in total disbelief in the wake of mounting evidence in favor of an intelligent process behind the origin and existence of our universe.

Earth-bound measurements have an accuracy limit of about 1 part in 10,000, but the background radiation is much smoother than this. In order to improve the sensitivity of the measurements, the Cosmic Background Explorer satellite (or COBE) was launched on November 18, 1989. Scientists had hoped that this would provide information about background radiation and details about how the big bang worked. But initial results were discouraging; Lazich describes the situation after the first year:

> Theorists hoped that COBE would provide the information necessary for the rescue of the big bang theory. . . . In order to save [it] . . . COBE would have to discover that this leftover radiation [still reverberating from the big bang] is lumpy, not smooth. . . . But, COBE has created headaches, not a cure. The initial COBE data shows that the early universe was very smooth — the background radiation is the same in all directions and gives no sign of turbulence in the early universe. . . . There is no way to get from a perfectly smooth big bang to the lumpy universe we observe today. . . . Some scientists are reluctantly suggesting that a force external to our universe is responsible for selection of the initial conditions. Some have even been willing to attach the name God to that force.[43]

However, in April 1992, results that sounded spectacular were announced, with a clamor of publicity. "Wiggles in Space" had been found — their problem had been solved! But the eagerness with which this report was accepted may be due to the spirit of pessimism that had settled on the scientific world, as described above. They have begun grasping at straws, and their optimism may be premature.

These new measurements are unimaginably small. The background itself has a temperature of about 2.7°. Earth-bound resolution is about 270 millionths of a degree. COBE's resolution is about 27 millionths, with a noise of about that same amount, yet the variations announced in 1992 are only about 16 millionths — half as big as the random noise background! To reach their conclusions, much data manipulation was used. The results have not been verified by other scientists, and thus are only tentative.

These results have not been universally acclaimed by the scientific world. *Scientific American* has reported:

> Controversy has arisen about whether the COBE measurements have any relation at all to the structure of the universe billions of years ago. . . . Astronomers may wait for years before they resolve the issue.[44]

Russell Ruthen, author of the article, quotes Yale University astronomers Krauss and White as saying, "One should not jump to the conclusion that what COBE is seeing is just density fluctuations. At least some or all of it might be gravitational waves."

Even if COBE's new discovery is verified, one problem may be solved, but others remain. Editor (and astronomer) Don B. DeYoung asks several other questions: Where did all that mass come from, and how did it get compressed into such a tiny volume? What made it explode? What's the source of gravity and other physical laws? What about the problem of "missing mass?" What about the questions still surrounding cosmic red-shifts and an expanding universe? He concludes by saying, "A recent, supernatural creation still remains a credible alternative to the big bang."[45]

George Matzko, in a letter to the September 1992 *Creation Research Society Quarterly*, wondered if the big bang theory survives just because the only alternative is special creation. He referred to Princeton astronomer David Spergel, who lamented the lack of conformance to theory, quoted in science writer Ivars Peterson's, "Seeding the Universe," in *Science News*:

If there were an alternative model that explained the microwave background and the nucleosynthesis abundances observed, and produced galaxies, then people would start thinking about it. But there's no good, viable alternative to the big bang.[46]

In that same article, science writer Ivars Peterson explained more,

The trouble is that no current theoretical model of the evolution of the universe seems to fit all of the observations without at least some inconsistencies. Cosmologists find they must labor to squeeze their pet theories into the steadily tightening straitjacket of observational data.

Astronomers hoped that a few more years of observation might help to alleviate their quandary. It doesn't look as if that's the case. A mid-1996 report showed that, with better techniques and equipment, the clumpiness extends further out than ever. A Cal-Tech team of astronomers, working in Hawaii with the 10-meter Keck telescope, reported:

"By just looking at [the data] in a very cursory way, you can immediately see what we are calling large-scale structures," says [Michael] Pahre; five peaks in the density of galaxies along the line of sight. The team argues that the peaks are likely to indicate structures the size and shape of the Great Wall, but dozens of times farther away.[47]

The problem for big bang cosmology is getting more difficult to explain. It looks like the more that's learned, the more conflicts that are being revealed.

RED SHIFT

Red shift is the term used to describe the apparent reddening of the spectral color of various stars. It's thought to be a measure of the star's recessional velocity, as it moves away from the earth; this is said to be due to the Doppler effect.

At greater distances, cosmological red shift becomes a measure of the star's distance from earth. Astronomers spend much of their energy measuring red shifts and brightnesses of stars and galaxies, and say that gives their distance and recessional velocity. But they've accepted many underlying assumptions that cannot be proven, because of the extreme distances. Most measurements rely on circular reasoning.

William G. Tifft of the University of Arizona has spent 20 years in a careful examination of those red shifts that have been very carefully measured. He's found that their distribution is not continuous, but quantized in intervals of 72 or 36 or 24 km/sec. According to the standard astronomical beliefs, this cannot be. Yet his work has been verified by others, including Guthrie and Napier of the Royal Observatory, Edinburgh. They said that the chance of his being wrong was only 1/3000. This is reported in the August 1992 *Sky and Telescope*.[48]

The December 1991 *Astrophysical Journal* also reports on Tifft's other discoveries showing that red shifts of certain stars are not constant, but have changed in just a few years.

What does quantization of red shifts mean? It's as if police using radar speed-guns found that all cars were traveling at either 40, 50, or 60 mph, but never at any intermediate speed. Obviously this couldn't happen. This is another problem showing that astronomical theory is not really complete, but still has many loopholes.

For years, many astronomers had doubts about these results, thinking they must be errors in measurement. But several teams have carefully extended this work, and the doubts are being squelched. A 1996 report says:

> [John Huchra said] "I'm thinking of writing an observing proposal for checking to see if [the effect] holds up with other galaxies." If it does,

standard cosmology might be turned on its ear: "It would mean abandoning a great deal of present research," says [Mike] Disney.[49]

Carl Wieland, in an article entitled "Hubble, Hubble, Big Bang in Trouble?" wrote this:[50]

There seems little doubt that if these observations did not conflict with the "big bang," they would have been taken much more seriously a long time ago. The problem seems to be, as prominent astronomer Geoffrey Burbidge put it (Burbidge is Professor of Physics at the University of California, San Diego):

Big bang cosmology is probably as widely believed as has been any theory of the universe in the history of Western civilization. It rests, however, on many untested, and [in] many cases, untestable assumptions. Indeed, big bang cosmology has become a bandwagon of thought that reflects faith as much as objective truth.[51]

ADDITIONAL ASTRONOMICAL PROBLEMS

An additional problem is the recent discovery of very distant quasars almost on the edge of the universe. Since it takes time for light to reach us, we're seeing those distant objects as they were near the time of the big bang (according to the theory), yet spectral analysis shows them to look very old. They wouldn't have had time to go through cosmic evolution to form heavier elements, new stars, and galaxy formation. They should look like young gaseous stars if the theories are correct, but they don't.

The general public is led to believe that astronomers have proven the universe to be some 15 billion years old. This is not true. Their theory predicts this, but there's no way it can be proven. All that can be actually measured is the radiation from deep space objects — color and intensity.

The rest comes from computer simulation, and that depends heavily on the assumptions programmed into the simulator. Sir Arthur Eddington, many years ago, wrote of this problem. Since then the tools have improved, but his statement is still true:

> For the reader resolved to eschew theory and admit only definite observational facts, all astronomical books are banned. There are no purely observational facts about the heavenly bodies. Astronomical measurements are, without exception, measurements of phenomena occurring in a terrestrial observatory or station; it is only by theory that they are translated into knowledge of a universe outside.[52]

Most of the objects observed in the study of big bang cosmology are said to be millions or billions of light-years away; our sun is only 8.3 light-minutes away, and our most distant planet, Pluto, is some 5.5 light-hours from the earth. But, at the same time, there are major problems in understanding these relatively nearby objects. Even the origin of our closest neighbor, the moon, is still a mystery. Four different theories compete for acceptance, and there are major problems with each one. If known facts about the nearby solar system don't fit the theories, how can we expect to know much about those extremely distant objects?

One basic problem involves the sun's energy and how it's produced. Most scientists believe that the interior of the sun is a thermonuclear furnace, burning hydrogen and producing helium. However, this reaction should produce a great many neutrinos, and our measurements don't show nearly enough. One textbook understates the importance of this discrepancy:

> A small but troublesome problem remains for scientists trying to understand the internal structure of the Sun. The thermonuclear reactions

that produce the Sun's energy should also release numerous particles called neutrinos, which are extremely elusive and very difficult to detect. Physicists have used huge tanks filled with cleaning fluid (C_2C_{14}) [and buried in deep mine shafts] to trap neutrinos because they convert the chlorine into argon gas which can be collected and measured. However, all such experiments detect only about one-third of the expected number of neutrinos from the Sun. Various explanations have been proposed for this unexpected result but further research is certainly required (bracketed phrase added).[53]

We know that the problem is not in the detection apparatus because when the distant 1987A supernova occurred in the Great Magellanic Cloud galaxy, neutrinos were detected. But the missing solar neutrinos mean that the theories about the sun's reactions don't explain what's really happening. Many other stars are thought to be burning helium and producing carbon and oxygen. Larger stars are said to evolve into different burning processes as they age.

In 1988, I took a course in astronomy at our local college to catch up on current theory. (I got an "A.") In one class, I asked the instructor a series of questions, as follows:

Question: How do we know the temperature in the sun's interior when all we can observe is its surface?

Answer: Because that's the sort of temperature that it takes to maintain a nuclear reaction.

Question: Do we have physical evidence that there is a nuclear reaction there?

Answer: Yes, that's the only kind of thing that could act as a source for the amount of energy we see the sun giving off.

Question: But I've read that the heat caused by gravitational collapse would be sufficient to cause that surface temperature and that amount of solar flux — is that true?

Answer: Well, yes, that's true, but that wouldn't last

very long, and we know the sun is about 5 billion years old.

Question: Am I correct in understanding you to say that the only real reason we know there's a nuclear reaction is that the solar system is billions of years old?

Answer: Yes, that's right.

So we see that the fundamental belief in an ancient universe is the foundation for theories of how the stars produce their heat.

In a later class, I asked other questions.

Question: Has a helium reaction ever actually been observed in a star anywhere?

Answer: No, not really.

Question: Can astronomers tell for sure whether a certain star is actually burning helium?

Answer: No, that's way down in the interior, and they can't see much below the photosphere.

As you can see from these questions and answers, about all that astronomers can tell about a star is determined by its surface temperature and spectral characteristics and its apparent brightness (not its absolute magnitude). The interior of the star, and its burning mechanism, is completely unknown, as far as any direct observation can detect. Eddington's 1958 book is still correct — it's only by theory that we know anything about the universe.

Another major problem in the theory of evolution of our solar system is, "Where did the angular momentum come from?" One of the most important fundamental laws of physics is called "conservation of momentum," and says that it can't just appear, or go away. In describing the evolutionary formation of our solar system, Kaufmann wrote:

> The gravitational pull of the particles on one another caused them to begin a general drift toward the center of the solar nebula. The density and pressure at the center of the solar nebula began to increase, producing a concentration of matter called the protosun. Because of gravita-

tional contraction, temperatures deep inside the solar nebula began to climb. The solar nebula must also have had an overall slight amount of rotation, or angular momentum, as it is properly called. Otherwise, everything would have fallen straight into the protosun, leaving nothing behind to form the planets. As the solar nebula contracted toward its gravitational center, it became transformed from a shapeless cloud into a rotating flattened disk that was warm at the center and cold at its edges.[54]

When I asked the instructor how angular momentum could have simply appeared, she admitted that was a troubling problem that had never been answered.

This same problem, on a larger scale, applies to the theory of galaxy formation. All the galaxies are known to be rotating, and if they weren't, they would all collapse toward their centers. But calculations involving the rate of rotation don't match observations — and a hypothetical "missing mass" concept had to be introduced.

COSMOLOGICAL PROBLEMS FOR CREATIONISTS

To be honest, we must admit that evolutionists are not the only ones who have astronomical problems — creationists have them, too. Although I completely reject the billions-of-years age of the universe, it does seem that some stars must be more than 10,000 light-years away. (NOTE: A light-year is the distance that light can travel in a year. That's about 5.9 million million miles.) The distance to most galaxies should probably be measured in billions of light-years. So, how can their light reach us in the limited time we believe the universe has existed? This is undoubtedly the most difficult question that creationists face.

There have been several proposed answers, but they all have problems. These suggestions include: 1) starlight was created, in situ, distributed along the paths that we see today,

2) the velocity of light may have been higher in the past than it is today, 3) "curved space" or some other esoteric concept may allow light to reach earth more quickly than by a direct straight-line path, and 4) all the distant objects are much closer together than they appear. My own preference leans toward 1), although this opens the door to charges that God is deceiving us by the appearance of events that happened long before the creation — or conceivably may not have actually happened at all!

But creationists do have one advantage in this sort of situation. We are honest enough to admit that we can't know all the details. We simply believe that everything began its existence by a supernatural act of an almighty Creator, who used divine processes that are beyond the understanding of humans, and that didn't follow the present "laws of nature." As the Bible says, in Psalm 33:6, "By the word of the Lord were the heavens made; and all the host of them by the breath of his mouth."

In other words, God simply spoke them into existence. He didn't follow the present "laws of nature" — these were established later. Admittedly, this is a very unsatisfactory explanation to those whose worldview is constrained by materialism.

That's another way of saying that some things are beyond the realm of science. But too often when an evolutionist uses that phrase, he goes on to postulate that anything beyond the realm of science — God's activities, for example — couldn't really have happened.

In such a case, the principle of uniformitarianism says that it must have happened in a completely materialistic way, and all their theories are built on that concept, as if that were the only possibility. This is circular reasoning on a grand scale. In that way, the most foundational basis for their belief system results from their arbitrarily ruling out the possibility of an alternate explanation (God) that could actually be true.

Now having said all that, we must report on another theory that creationists have proposed to solve the problem of "How did light have time to travel from distant galaxies within the time frame that the Bible talks about?" This uses a RELATIVISTIC APPROACH.

Astrophysicist Dr. Russell Humphreys presented two related papers at the Third International Conference on Creationism. The first was entitled "A Biblical Basis for Creationist Cosmology," and the second was "Progress Toward a Young-Earth Relativistic Cosmology." The first was a general description of his theory, based on the Bible. The second was highly technical, filled with equations based on Einstein's Theory of General Relativity (GR).

The key point of Humphreys' theory is that by properly choosing initial conditions to conform to the Bible, the GR equations allow a "white hole" to exist for a certain length of time, during which all the matter (water, in this case) near the starting point rapidly expands outwardly. During this expansion, with the "early earth" near the center, and the rest of the "early cosmos" moving outward, these two regions experience very different gravitational and velocity fields. Gravitational time dilation takes place, meaning that clocks in the two regions tick at radically different rates. As a result, the events near the center (at the earth) take place within six days, while those in the distant cosmos are experiencing billions of years. Humphreys said that God chose "earth standard time" in writing the Bible.

The details of this theory are far beyond the scope of this book (and beyond the mental capabilities of this author), but Humphreys has published a very readable book. The first two-thirds of the book are easily readable by laymen, and describe the biblical basis and a non-technical description of the events of the six days during the formation of the cosmos.[55]

Highly complex theories such as this require a long time to become accepted or rejected by most scientists.

Einstein's theory itself took years for acceptance, as did the big bang idea. Humphreys has requested feedback from those who have a good grasp of General Relativity, and expects several years to pass before his theory can be properly evaluated.

A somewhat similar, but much shorter, paper by Michael A. Maiuzzo, "It's Just a Matter of Time," in the *Creation Research Society Quarterly*, uses an analogical approach to describe the general concept of gravitational time dilation. He bases this on the section entitled "Clock Paradox," in the McGraw Hill Encyclopedia of Science and Technology. Maiuzzo doesn't present a complete new theory of creation, as does Humphreys, but explains how clocks can run at different rates, depending on their motions.[56]

THE DEBATES

Since the fall of 1972, there have been over 200 formal debates between creation scientists and evolution scientists. These have been held in civic auditoriums, college campuses, on nationwide TV, etc. More than 100,000 people have attended. The subject has been scientific evidence concerning origins. The debaters have tried to avoid religious arguments (except in several cases when the evolutionists have ridiculed the Bible.) Most of the creationist debaters have been associated with the Institute for Creation Research in El Cajon, California. Their impact has caused a strong reaction from the mostly evolutionist education lobby.

In almost all of these debates, audience reaction has shown that the creationists have "won." The evolutionists have yet to win a single one of these debates. Most of the audiences have indicated surprise that the creationists came across as more solid in terms of scientific evidence, and the evolutionists have been more vague and philosophical, avoiding specifics. They have offered speculative or unprovable theories, but no proofs.

These debates have clearly demonstrated that the case

for creation is much stronger on technical evidence than is the case for evolution. Evolutionists are strong on a philosophy of materialism, but short on facts. In recent years, the number of these debates has been considerably reduced because qualified evolutionists are becoming very reluctant to take the chance of looking foolish. Not many will accept invitations to debate creationist scientists in a public forum.

THE BOTTOM LINE

The simple facts are these:

1. There is almost no actual scientific evidence showing that evolution ever occurred.

2. Almost all evolutionary teaching is based on unprovable assumptions.

3. There is a lot of scientific evidence favoring a created origin.

It seems clear that belief in evolution is really a philosophy, a type of non-theistic religion — that is, a belief-system that can't be proven, and which affects a person's life-goals and outlook.

Evolutionists say that creationism is religious, and that evolutionism is scientific. But consider the following summary statements, and see if these sound like evolution is really a scientific system.

1. No one has ever seen an actual example of evolution above the "family" level (that is, no new phyla, order, or class).

2. The fossil record shows no trace that macro-evolution has ever happened. Most knowledgeable evolutionists now admit that the fossil record is an embarrassment to them.

3. The idea of evolution violates several well-known and fundamental scientific laws.

4. No one has ever proposed a practical theoretical explanation of how evolution could possibly work. The old Darwinism is dead. Neo-Darwinism is being criticized more

and more by competent scientists. The Theory of Punctuated Equilibrium has been proposed, not because of any sort of proof, but as an attempt to explain all the missing transitional fossils. But this doesn't even try to explain how that may have happened. The simplest way to explain all the missing transitional fossils would be to just acknowledge that "In the beginning, God created the heavens and the earth [and all of its creatures]."

In view of the above, it seems more correct to say that it is evolution that is religious (since it relies on faith without proof) — an unscientific religious philosophy — a religion of atheism.

Endnotes

[1] Arthur Keith, *Evolution and Ethics* (Putnam, NY, 1947), p. 15.

[2] Tom Bethell, "Agnostic Evolutionists," *Harper's Magazine*, February 1985, p. 60.

[3] W.R. Thompson, F.R.S., Introduction to Charles Darwin, *The Origin of Species*, (London: Dent, and New York: Dutton, Everyman's Library, 1928, 1967), p. xxi, xxii.

[4] Fred Barbash, "Missing Link Finally Found in Piltdown Man Whodunit," *Washington Post*, late May 1996.

[5] Ian Taylor, *In The Minds of Men: Darwin and the New World Order* (Toronto: TFE Publishing, 1987), p. 209-215.

[6] Marvin L. Lubenow, *Bones of Contention* (Grand Rapids, MI: Baker Book House, 1992).

[7] Ibid., p. 164.

[8] Phillip Johnson, *Darwin on Trial* (Downers Grove, IL: InterVarsity Press, 1993), p. 54.

[9] Niles Eldredge, *The Monkey Business* (New York, NY: Washington Square Press, 1982), p. 44.

[10] Errol White, Proceedings of the Linnaean Society, (London 177:8, 1966).

[11] Duane T. Gish, *Creation Scientists Answer Their Critics* (El Cajon, CA: Institute for Creation Research, 1993), p. 128-129.

[12] Philip Kitcher, *Abusing Science — The Case Against Creationism* (Cambridge, MA: The MIT Press, 1982), p. 50.

[13] Francis Hitching, *The Neck of the Giraffe — Where Darwin Went Wrong* (New York, NY: Ticknor and Fields, 1982), p. 28-30.

[14]G.A. Kerkut, *The Implications of Evolution* (New York, NY: Pergamon Press, 1960), p. 141-149.

[15]Taylor, *In the Minds of Men: Darwin and the New World Order*, p. 152-153.

[16]*Harper's Magazine*, February 1985, p. 60.

[17]William R. Fix, *The Bone Peddlers: Selling Evolution* (New York, NY: Macmillan, 1984), p. 184-185.

[18]N. Heribert Nilsson (Lund University, Sweden), *Synthetische Artbildung* (Verlag: CWK Gleerup, 1953), p. 1157.

[19]M.I. Coates and J.A. Clack, "Polydactyly in the earliest known tetrapod limbs," *Nature*, 347 (1990), p. 66; and M.I. Coates, "Ancestors and Homology (the origin of the tetrapod limb)," in *Acta Biotheoretica*, 41 (1993), p. 414.

[20]Stephen Jay Gould, "Eight Little Piggies," *Natural History*, January 1991, p. 25.

[21]Paul Nelson, "When An Explanation Fails," *Bible-Science News*, Vol.32:7, October 1994, p. 14-18.

[22]Michael Denton, *Evolution: A Theory in Crisis* (London: Burnett Books, 1985), p. 145.

[23]C.B. Thaxton, W.L. Bradley, and R.L. Olsen, *The Mystery of Life's Origin: Reassessing Current Theories* (New York, NY: Philosophical Library, 1984, p. 66.

[24]S.R. Scadding, "Do 'Vestigial Organs' Provide Evidence for Evolution?" *Evolutionary Theory*, Vol. 5, No. 3, May 1981, p. 173-176.

[25]Michael Pitman, *Adam and Evolution* (London: Rider, 1984), p. 120.

[26]W.R. Thompson, Introduction to *The Origin of Species* by Charles Darwin, Everyman Library No. 811 (New York, NY: E.P. Dutton & Sons, 1956 reprint of 1928 edition), p. 12.

[27]S.J. Gould and N. Eldredge, *Paleobiology*, Vol. 3, 1977, p. 147.

[28]G. Heilman, *The Origin of Birds* (London: Witherby, 1926), p. 200-201.

[29]J.H. Ostrom, Bird Flight: How Did It Begin? *American Scientists*, 67, (1979), p. 45-56.

[30]Denton, *Evolution: A Theory in Crisis*, p. 199-214.

[31]Darwin, *The Origin of Species*, p. 182.

[32]Steven A. Austin, *Grand Canyon: Monument to Catastrophe* (Santee, CA: Institute for Creation Research, 1994).

[33]John Woodmorappe, "Radiometric Geochronology Reappraised," *Creation Research Society Quarterly*, Volume 16, September 1979, p. 102-129, 147.

[34]Joan C. Engels, "Effects of Sample Purity on Discordant Mineral Ages Found in K-Ar Dating," *Journal of Geology*, Vol. 79,

September 1971, p. 609.

[35]Marvin L. Lubenow, *Bones of Contention: A Creationist Assessment of the Human Fossils* (Grand Rapids, MI: Baker Book House, 1992), p. 247-266.

[36]John Joly, Proceedings of the Royal Society, (London, Series A 102, 1923), p. 682.

[37]Trevor Norman and Barry Setterfield, "The Atomic Constants, Light, and Time," Stanford Research Institute Int'l Invited Research Report, August 1987.

[38]Melvin Cook, *Prehistory and Earth Models* (London: Max Parrish and Co. Ltd., 1966), p. 54-55.

[39]Henry Faul, *Ages of Rocks, Planets, and Stars* (New York, NY: McGraw-Hill, Inc., 1966), p. 65, 67.

[40]Taylor, *In the Minds of Men: Darwin and the New World Order.*

[41]Curt Sewell, "The Faith of Radiogenic Dating," *Bible-Science News*, November 1994.

[42]Grand Canyon Dating Project, Institute for Creation Research, 10946 Woodside Avenue North, Santee, CA, 92071.

[43]*Ministry Magazine*, 9/90, p. 24-26.

[44]Russell Ruthen, *Scientific American*, October 1992, p. 30.

[45]Don B. DeYoung, *Creation Research Society Quarterly*, September 1992, p. 102.

[46]Ivars Peterson, "Seeding the Universe," *Science News*, 1990, 137:184-185.

[47]*Science*, Vol.272, 14 June 1996, p. 1590.

[48]*Sky and Telescope*. August 1992, p. 128-129.

[49]*Science*, Vol.271, 9 February 1996, p. 759.

[50]Carl Wieland, "Hubble, Hubble, Big Bang in Trouble?" *Creation ex Nihilo* magazine, Vol.18, No.4, Sept.-Nov. 1996, p. 26-29.

[51]*Scientific American*, February 1992, p. 96.

[52]Sir Arthur Eddington, *The Expanding Universe* (Ann Arbor, MI: University of Michigan Press, 1958), p. 17.

[53]William J. Kaufmann III, *Discovering the Universe* (New York, NY: W.H. Freeman and Company, 1987), p. 225.

[54]Kaufmann, *Discovering the Universe*, p. 93-94.

[55]D. Russell Humphreys, Ph.D., *Starlight and Time: Solving the Puzzle of Distant Starlight in a Young Universe*, (Green Forest, AR, Master Books, Inc., 1994).

[56]Michael A. Maiuzzo, "It's Just a Matter of Time," *Creation Research Society Quarterly*, Vol.33, No.2, September 1996, p. 109-112.

Notes

Notes

Chapter 6

RELIGIOUS AND PHILOSOPHICAL ARGUMENTS

C.S. Lewis said, "What we learn from experience depends upon what kind of philosophy we bring to our experience."

We've mentioned, in a number of spots, that belief in evolution is not driven by overwhelming scientific evidences, but by a philosophic commitment to materialism, rather than a willingness to acknowledge the Creator God. I'll give a few quotations to show that there is a good basis for these statements.

When Thaxton, Bradley, and Olsen wrote their book *The Mystery of Life's Origin: Reassessing Current Theories* (in which they criticized chemical origin of life theories), they asked biology professor Dean Kenyon of San Francisco State University to write the Foreword. Kenyon openly wondered why so many scientists who knew the many inadequacies of that line of thinking still supported it publicly. He wrote:

[The authors] believe, and I now concur, that

there is a fundamental flaw in all current theories of the chemical origins of life. . . . If the author's criticisms are valid, one might ask, why have they not been recognized or stressed by workers in the field? I suspect that part of the answer is that many scientists would hesitate to accept the authors' conclusion that it is fundamentally implausible that unassisted matter and energy organized themselves into living systems. Perhaps these scientists fear that acceptance of this conclusion would open the door to the possibility (or the necessity) of a supernatural origin of life. Faced with this prospect, many investigators would prefer to continue in their search for a naturalistic explanation of the origin of life along the lines marked out over the last few decades, in spite of the many serious difficulties of which we are now aware. Perhaps the fallacy of scientism [the worship of science itself] is more widespread than we like to think.[1]

We should add that the above writer was not a creationist, but was a respected university biology teacher, and author of the evolution textbook *Biochemical Predestination.*

Writer Tom Bethell interviewed evolutionist Dr. Colin Patterson, senior paleontologist at the British Museum of Natural History, and an oft-quoted critic of evolution theory. He wrote:

Patterson told me that he regarded the theory of evolution as "often unnecessary" in biology. "In fact," he said, "they could do perfectly well without it." Nevertheless, he said, it was presented in textbooks as though it were "the unified field theory of biology," holding the whole subject together — and binding the profession to it. "Once something has that status," he said, "it becomes like religion."[2]

Most scientists prefer to continue their belief that evolution is a concept resting on truth and evidence, not materialistic faith. For that reason, not many will risk criticism from their colleagues by making statements to the contrary. But Dr. H.S. Lipson, a professor of physics at the University of Manchester, wrote: "In fact, evolution became, in a sense, a scientific religion; almost all scientists have accepted it and many are prepared to 'bend' their observations to fit in with it."[3]

Dr. George Wald was a biologist and winner of the 1967 Nobel Prize in Science. He was a highly respected scientist, an evolutionist and an outspoken man on several subjects. He said:

> When it comes to the origin of life on this earth, there are only two possibilities: creation or spontaneous generation (evolution). There is no third way. Spontaneous generation was disproved 100 years ago, but that leads us only to one other conclusion: that of supernatural creation. We cannot accept that on philosophical grounds (personal reasons); therefore, we choose to believe the impossible: that life arose spontaneously by chance.[4]

Sir Julian Huxley is known as "Darwin's Bulldog." When asked why he thought Darwinism was widely accepted, he said:

> Darwinism removed the whole idea of God as the creator of organisms from the sphere of rational discussion. Darwin pointed out that no supernatural designer was needed; since natural selection could account for any known form of life, there was no room for a supernatural agency in its evolution. . . . I think we can dismiss entirely all ideas for a supernatural overriding mind being responsible for evolutionary process.[5]

Materialistic scientists often say that evolution is science, while creation is religion. Too many theologians and "ordinary Christians" blindly accept that statement, not realizing the full consequences that are involved.

Phillip Johnson, in examining the Supreme Court's ruling in the 1987 "Louisiana Balanced Treatment" case, wrote:

> As a legal scholar, one point that attracted my attention in the Supreme Court case was the way terms like "science" and "religion" are used to imply conclusions that judges and educators might be unwilling to state explicitly. If we say that naturalistic evolution is science, and supernatural creation is religion, the effect is not very different from saying that the former is true and the latter is fantasy. When the doctrines of science are taught as fact, then whatever those doctrines exclude cannot be true. By the use of labels, objections to naturalistic evolution can be dismissed without a fair hearing.[6]

Johnson's book is the result of his study about the logic and validity of the arguments and evidences used by Darwinian evolutionists. He said (on page 8), "I approach the creation-evolution dispute not as a scientist but as a professor of law [at UC-Berkeley], which means, among other things, that I know something about the ways that words are used in arguments." His conclusion is that much of the "evidence" for evolution is tautological (circular reasoning); it certainly wouldn't stand up in court. He also pointed out in a number of spots the important role that philosophical principles of naturalism play in underlying Darwinist beliefs.

In showing the anti-God religious nature of macroevolution, Johnson wrote:

> A second point that caught my attention was

that the very persons who insist upon keeping religion and science separate are eager to use their science as a basis for pronouncements about religion. The literature of Darwinism is full of antitheistic conclusions, such as that the universe was not designed and has no purpose, and that we humans are the product of blind natural processes that care nothing about us. What is more, these statements are not presented as personal opinions but as the logical implications of evolutionary science.

Another factor that makes evolutionary science seem a lot like religion is the evident zeal of Darwinists to evangelize the world, by insisting that even non-scientists accept the truth of their theory as a matter of moral obligation.

Richard Dawkins, an Oxford zoologist who is one of the most influential figures in evolutionary science, is unabashedly explicit about the religious side of Darwinism. His 1986 book *The Blind Watchmaker* is at one level about biology, but at a more fundamental level it is a sustained argument for atheism. According to Dawkins, "Darwin made it possible to be an intellectually fulfilled atheist."

When he contemplates the perfidy of those who refuse to believe, Dawkins can scarcely restrain his fury. "It is absolutely safe to say that, if you meet somebody who claims not to believe in evolution, that person is ignorant, stupid or insane (or wicked, but I'd rather not consider that)."

Dawkins went on to explain, by the way, that what he dislikes particularly about creationists is that they are intolerant.[7]

Faith in naturalistic uniformitarianism is the driving

force of the evolutionist scientist, in the same way that faith in God is the driving force for the Christian. G.R. Bozarth, writing in the September 1978 *American Atheist* expressed this conflict between Christianity and evolution:

> Christianity has fought, still fights, and will fight science to the desperate end over evolution, because evolution destroys utterly and finally the very reason Jesus' earthly life was supposedly made necessary. Destroy Adam and Eve and the original sin, and in the rubble you will find the sorry remains of the son of God. If Jesus was not the redeemer who died for our sins, and this is what evolution means, then Christianity is nothing.

Finally, this section on the quasi-scientific philosophical basis for evolution wouldn't be complete without quoting the word of God himself:

> But false prophets also arose among the people, just as there will be false teachers among you, who will secretly bring in destructive heresies (2 Pet. 2:1).

> First of all you must understand this, that scoffers will come in the last days with scoffing, following their own passions, and saying, "Where is the promise of His coming? For ever since the fathers fell asleep, all things have continued as they were from the beginning of creation." [Is this a suggestion of the theory of uniformitarianism?] They deliberately ignore this fact, that by the word of God heavens existed long ago, and an earth formed out of water and by means of water, through which the world that then existed was deluged with water and perished [the flood of Noah] (2 Pet. 3:3-6).

In order to grasp the significance of these differences of opinion, let's trace the high spots of philosophical thought, as it developed down through world history.

HISTORICAL ROOTS OF CONTROVERSY

It's informative to give a very brief outline of some of the developments of thought — how different philosophies about the origin of our world have come into being. Of course, the most ancient writings we have access to are in the Bible. We'll show later that the earliest parts of Genesis were probably written by actual eyewitnesses at about the time they happened. We'll also briefly describe several ancient philosophers, in approximately their chronological order.

The Bible tells us that Abraham was the man whom God selected to be the founder of a chosen race. He lived in about 2000 B.C. Some of his descendants became known as Hebrews. But they became slaves in Egypt, and multiplied there. Moses, who led more than a million Hebrews out of Egyptian bondage, lived through the 1400s B.C. It was during Moses's leadership that God gave most of his laws, and melded a disorganized crowd of newly freed slaves into a nation. This was the start of Judaism and of the nation of Israel. The Israeli King Solomon led those people to the peak of their kingdom's glory in about 950 B.C., but after his death that kingdom split into two, which then decayed because of the people's idolatry. The northern portion of their kingdom fell to the Assyrians in 722 B.C., and the southern part was taken into Babylonian captivity in 587 B.C. Some of them finally made their way back into Canaan, but they never regained any kingdom power. During the second century B.C. they were governed by the Maccabbean and Hasmonian dynasties.

This was about the time that the ancient Greek philosophers flourished. Their teachings had a tremendous influence on all educated people. Socrates (470-399 B.C.) believed that the complexity of the world and its living creatures demanded some sort of Divine Spirit who remained active in our affairs, and that this implied some sort of human immortality. His student Plato (428 - 348 B.C.) took Socrates' teachings and applied them to governments. His Republic described an idealized system, that could probably only come true in the immortal realm of that Divine Spirit.

Aristotle (384-322 B.C.) began life as a follower of his teacher Plato, but swung over to a mechanistic set of beliefs, rejecting immortality. He modified the Divine Spirit into a creative force who had originally made everything with a teleological principle (teaching that nature showed strong evidence of design or purpose) but then had left it to run by itself. He viewed life forms as archetypes, created in typological groups but allowing some variations within each type. His many writings were highly organized and logical, appealing to human reason, but rejecting any sort of divine intervention in routine worldly affairs. He wrote on many subjects, but his science was based on intellect, not experiment. Some of his teachings were wrong, and delayed true scientific advances for many centuries. For example, he taught abiogenesis (life coming full-blown from non-life). This was believed until Pasteur's experimental proofs in A.D. 1860.

Ptolemy of Alexandria (A.D. 85-165), no relation to the Egyptian hierarchy of Ptolomies, was a follower of Aristotle. His contribution to scholarship was a view of the cosmos that had everything arranged in a system of celestial spheres, with the earth at the center. The sun, moon, planets, and stars were each set in one of an expansive set of transparent crystalline spheres. As these revolved, their heavenly bodies moved through the sky, always around the geocentric mid-point. This idea was later incorporated into church doctrine, and became solid dogma for almost 1,500 years.

When Alexander the Great conquered the world in the

330s B.C., one of his projects was to spread the Greek civilization over his entire empire. This process was called "Hellenization." The Greek language was a good one, allowing for many gradations of expression. It became almost the official language of the world. Greek philosophy appealed to the intellect, and the works of Aristotle, Ptolemy, and the others became world standards. Alexander died young, and his empire splintered into two major groups, led by dynasties founded by two of his generals, Ptolemy and Seleucus. The concepts of Hellenization were absorbed and strengthened by the Roman Empire when it began its growth in about 100 B.C.

The Roman General Pompey conquered the eastern Mediterranean regions, including the land called Canaan or Israel in 63 B.C., and set up a short dynasty of Herods to rule that land that came to be known as Palestine.

The exact dates of Jesus' birth and death are not known, but He was probably born in about 4 or 6 B.C. and died on a Roman cross in about A.D. 30 or 33. His resurrection from the dead has been widely debated, but those who had the best opportunity to know the true facts were eloquent in proclaiming it as truth. Those opposed to his teachings never gave any substantive denial of that resurrection, but simply persecuted those who proclaimed it. Early Christianity mushroomed, and quickly spread over most of the then-known world.

Jesus' followers came to be known as Christians in about A.D. 50, and for several decades were all Jewish. But soon other nationalities joined, and it wasn't long before those early Christians were persecuted by both the Jewish leaders (who resented Jesus' claim of being part of the Godhead) and also by the Roman government (who called them atheists because they refused to worship the Roman polytheistic system of pagan gods). The Jewish rabbi-turned-missionary Paul was killed by the Roman Emperor Nero in about A.D. 67.

Then, in A.D. 312, Emperor Constantine accepted Christianity and declared it to be the official religion of the Roman Empire. He merged the church into the government, and it wasn't long before secular power brought corruption. As the Roman Empire decayed from onslaughts of barbarians and various internal problems, ecclesiastical control grew, and the only educated people were the priests. The Dark Ages took over the world from about A.D. 400 to 1000.

The early Greek philosophers, notably Plato and Aristotle, disbursed their teachings by means of informal "universities," or public discussion groups. This format remained popular for many centuries. But the Christianized Roman Empire objected to this uncontrolled spread of ideas foreign to its dogma, and Emperor Justinian I closed these universities in A.D. 529. Intellectual studies retreated behind monastery walls, and most "ordinary people" mindlessly followed the rituals of the established church. Thus began the Dark Ages, which lasted until sometime after A.D. 1000.

Mohammed was born in Mecca in about A.D. 570. He wrote the Koran and founded the religion of Islam. His followers, the Moslems, soon swept over the Middle East and much of Europe. They took Jerusalem in 638, and soon built the fabulously beautiful "Dome of the Rock" mosque on the Temple Square on Mount Moriah, where Solomon had built his famous temple some 1,600 years before. For many centuries these Arabs were the custodians of the world's culture. They absorbed and amplified the philosophies of the old Greeks, which had been spread into those regions by the Hellenization of Alexander the Great. Their art and architecture is outstanding. And it's to these early Moslems that we owe our system of arithmetic.

Some light began to shine into the "Dark Ages" of Europe in about A.D. 1000, with the beginning of the movement called "Scholasticism." At that time, the world's intellectual culture was found among the Arabs, with their adaptation of the old Greek philosophers. Aristotle's *Metaphysics* was translated in A.D. 1167.

The best-known Scholastic was St. Thomas Aquinas, (A.D. 1225-1274). He succeeded in rationalizing Christian doctrine with Aristotelian logic, and this syncretism (fusion of two different beliefs into one) changed both ecclesiastical and secular life forever. The *Encyclopaedia Britannica* wrote:

> Scholasticism opens with a discussion of certain points in the Aristotelian logic; it speedily begins to apply its logical distinctions to the doctrines of the church; and when it attains its full stature in St. Thomas [Aquinas] it has, with the exception of certain mysteries, rationalized or Aristotelianized the whole churchly system. Or we might say with equal truth that the philosophy of St. Thomas is Aristotle Christianized.[8]

In the 15th century, opposition to ecclesiastical authority over intellectual activity led to the school of thought called "Humanism." This movement rejected the concept of divine intervention and revelation, emphasizing instead human thought and logic. Francis Bacon (1561-1626) formalized the humanist ideas as "Every truth can only be found inductively," (the opposite of divine revelation) and totally separated the realm of reason and science from that of faith and religion. This was the foundation of what was called the "Age of Enlightenment," which featured the philosophies of Descartes (1596-1650), Spinoza (1632-1677), and Immanuel Kant (1724-1804).

Kant's concept of "Religion Within the Bounds of Reason," in the late 1700s, set the stage for the rise of the philosophies that still dominate western European and most major American universities. These combine Aristotelian logic, humanistic ideals, and rejection of God's intervention and revelation of himself. This is the environment of the great theological centers of biblical criticism which began in several German universities. We can't be surprised that most of these Bible critics come out sounding like atheists — that's how they were trained.

DEVELOPMENTS WITHIN CHRISTIANITY

Thomas Aquinas didn't start the Scholastic movement, but he is known as its greatest expositor. His philosophy changed the thinking of much of Europe and the western world. In the biography, *The Philosophy of St. Thomas Aquinas,* the publisher's cover note says:

> St. Thomas Aquinas (1225-1274) is the medieval mind at its finest. . . . Thomism is first and foremost a theology, but it is a theology that could not have come into being without an underlying philosophy. . . . Drawing from pagan, Mohammedan, and Jewish sources in addition to Christian writers and the Bible, his broad vision combines in one synthesis the metaphysical principles of reality. . . . Before Thomism, the framework of Medieval Western thought demanded a choice between Christianity and Aristotelian Humanism. In choosing not one, but both sides, and in uniting them in an unbreakable bond, Aquinas promises the perfect development of natural man and of reason both by means of both the supernatural and of Revelation.[9]

This summary was intended to be complimentary to Aquinas, but we can see here how, by combining pagan thought with biblical truth, Aquinas drove the opening wedge between the truth of the Bible and what would become the beliefs and practices of established Christianity. Aquinas' philosophical ideas became known as "Thomism," and were accepted by the Church on an equal basis with

Holy Scripture. We'll see that they led to a couple of monumental conflicts — Luther's Reformation movement, and the controversy between science and religion.

But Aquinas's teachings were far too radical for immediate acceptance; they opened the door of divine revelation to admit human reasoning also. It took some three centuries for Aquinas to be officially adopted by the Council of Trent (1545-1563), and it was not until 1879 that Pope Leo XIII declared his theology to be eternally valid.

For many centuries Bibles had only been available in Latin, and thus were not accessible to most people; only the priests could read them. John Wyclif (1324-1384), an English scholar, recognized that this had led to all sorts of mistaken ideas about what the Bible did or didn't say. He translated the Latin Bible into English, and laboriously hand-copied his new text. Popular availability of these readable scriptures had to wait until 1447, when Johann Gutenberg introduced his newly invented printing press.

Martin Luther (1483-1546) became a priest in 1507, and a doctor of theology and professor of biblical literature at the University of Erfurt, Germany, in 1512. A turning point in his life is described in Luther's biography in the *Encyclopaedia Britannica*:

> Towards the end of 1510 he had paid a short visit to Rome on business connected with his order, and though his visit was that of the devout pilgrim, he appears to have been painfully impressed by the secularized ecclesiasticism and the low moral standard of the Holy City.[10]

Then, in 1512-13, after pondering on Romans 1:16-17, he was impressed with the "gospel of Christ . . . the power of God unto salvation," and "the just shall live by faith." After considerable spiritual ordeal, he prayed for this salvation, and became a "born again" Christian. The mental transformation brought about by this spiritual rebirth led to his realization of the inadequacy of church practices, which had degenerated into rituals. He began to attack the Scholastic theology of Thomas Aquinas and the Aristotelian philosophy on which it was based. Luther was also bothered by obvious abuses in the practices of penitential indulgences as a means of raising money. This led to his posting the famous "95 Theses Against the Abuse of Indulgences" on the door of the Castle Church at Wittenberg on October 31, 1517. Church authorities accused him of heresy and schism; conflicts with Pope Leo X simmered for several years.

In a famous debate against John Maier of Eck, Luther championed the supreme authority of Scripture as opposed to the "divine right of the papacy" in July 1519. This led to his excommunication in April 1521. He spent his remaining years in Bible study and translation, preaching, writing, and attempting to continue his Reformation of the Catholic Church. His goal was to change those practices where he saw obvious differences from the doctrines of Holy Scripture. He didn't intend to start a new church; his later followers were the ones who actually founded the Lutheran Church. But the Reformation was born. In the next few centuries several other Protestant denominations were begun — most with the initial goal of "going back to the Bible," of being "like the New Testament church."

One very influential movement of this type was led by John Wesley (1703-1791) in England. He preached a powerful message that began a nationwide revival that lasted for many years, and changed the course of history. It is said that Wesley's work prevented the French Revolution from spilling across the channel into England.

THE CHURCH'S CONFLICT WITH SCIENCE

Thomas Aquinas had incorporated Ptolemy's geocentric universe (part of the system of Aristotelian logic) into church philosophy, even though the Bible doesn't teach anything suggesting this. We read in his biography:

This Universe, as conceived by St. Thomas, is essentially that of Aristotle: viz. a series of seven concentric planetary spheres, contained within an eighth sphere, that of the fixed stars, and containing in their turn the Earth as their centre. (Summa Theologica, I. 68, 4, ad Resp.) . . . To each sphere a moving Intelligence is assigned which maintains and directs its circular motion. . . . Below the lowest sphere, that of the Moon, are arranged the spheres of the four elements: fire, air, water, and earth. . . . All this cosmology lies within a framework well-known from other sources.[11]

The established church had accepted Thomism, including the Ptolemaic geocentric idea, into its set of doctrines. These beliefs had become on a par with the Bible. But soon scientists began to learn some of the actual facts about the universe and its motions. Nicolaus Copernicus (1473-1543) first proposed that the earth and other planets revolved around the sun. Johannes Kepler (1571-1630) found that they moved in elliptical paths. Galileo Galilei (1564-1642) used telescopic observations to prove that these ideas were true. He published them in 1610, and in so doing he stirred a storm of controversy.

The church considered Galileo's heliocentric proposal (that the earth moves around the sun) as heretical, because it violated the Ptolemaic system that Thomas Aquinas had incorporated into their doctrines. Galileo was persecuted for years, then in 1633 he was placed under house arrest, until his death in 1642.

Of course, Galileo was correct, and became a well-known martyr to scientific truth "at the hands of a biased church." It became a political issue for scientists who have never yet tired of pointing out the folly of belief in religious doctrine. They've made a whipping-boy of Christianity because of Aquinas's merging of human philosophy into Bible doctrine. But we seldom hear the real truth of the matter. It was not the Bible that was at fault; the fault lay with the church's acceptance of man-made doctrines.

Many main-line churches have, since then, bent over backward to avoid another such disgrace. These churches have adopted the so-called "scientific method" of biblical historical criticism, so that they can't be accused of persecuting science. Several have openly admitted that they don't accept the historicity or literal accuracy of the Bible; in that way, they can't be accused of religious absolutism. But, in so doing, haven't they lost their godly perspective?

HISTORICAL-CRITICAL THEOLOGY

This almost universal method of theological study in major universities and seminaries is described by Kummel as follows:

> In the second half of the eighteenth century, in connection with the intellectual movement of the Enlightenment, within Protestant theology the insight began to prevail that the Bible is a book written by men, which, like any product of the human mind, can properly be made understandable only from the times in which it appeared and therefore only with the methods of historical science.[12]

The age of Enlightenment recognized as truth only that which could be arrived at inductively — by man's own reason. When this principle was applied to biblical truth, what had been God's Word became, not a revelation, but only a source of humanly reasonable wisdom. Kummel continued his discussion:

> One simply could not stop halfway; if the Bible must be historically investigated as the work of human authors in order to understand its actual meaning, then one may not and cannot cling to the assumption that the Old Testament

and New Testament form, each in itself, a conceptual unity, and then one must also heed the differences within the two Testaments and also take into consideration a possible development and adulteration of the ideas. Consequently the concern about a theology of the New Testament found itself from the outset confronted with the problem of diversity and unity in the New Testament.

TESTIMONY OF AN EX-CRITIC

Dr. Eta Linnemann was formerly one of the leading professors in this humanistic study of the Bible from the historical-critical viewpoint. She achieved broad acclaim as a critical scholar, then she became a Christian, and renounced her previous career. In telling of her previous life, she said, in the "Introduction" to her book:

> I had the best professors which historical-critical theology could offer to me. . . . My first book turned out to be a best seller. I became professor of theology and religious education at Braunschweig Technical University, West Germany. . . . I was awarded the title of honorary professor of New Testament in the theology faculty of Philipps University, Marburg, West Germany. I was inducted into the Society for New Testament Studies. I had the satisfaction of an increasing degree of recognition from my colleagues. . . . I was deeply convinced that I was rendering a service to God with my theological work, and contributing to the proclamation of the gospel.

But despite this worldly acclaim she felt "profound disillusionment," which led to a crisis that was finally solved by God's saving grace. She continued:

Finally God himself spoke to my heart by means of a Christian brother's words. By God's grace and love I entrusted my life to Jesus. He immediately took my life into his saving grasp and began to transform it radically.

After describing a little of how that transformation worked, she made this surprising statement, asking readers to destroy all of her older writings:

That is why I say "No!" to historical-critical theology. I regard everything that I taught and wrote before I entrusted my life to Jesus as refuse. I wish to use this opportunity to mention that I have pitched my two books, *Gleichnisse Jesu* and *Studien zur Passionsgeschichte*, along with contributions to journals, anthologies, and Festschriften. Whatever of these writings I had in my possession I threw into the trash with my own hands in 1978. I ask you sincerely to do the same thing with any of them you may have on your own bookshelf.[13]

Her book, *Historical Criticism of the Bible: Methodology or Ideology?* is almost like an "expose." It's devoted to explaining how this atheistic criticism works, where its roots lie, and the devastating effect it has on faith in God and His Word. Linnemann said the fundamental starting point for critical analysis is to assume the Bible to be a human book that can be understood only by applying human reasoning.

The one who takes up study is required to approach theological study "without presuppositions," to seek the truth "radically and without holding back." All that has previously been learned from God's Word and experienced in faith is to be laid aside in favor of that which must be learned in studies.[14]

In other words, the student (or the critic) must begin by assuming that the Bible is not inspired inerrantly by God, and its truths can be learned only by applying human logic.

DOCUMENTS OR TABLETS?

One of the best examples of how historical criticism of the Bible has affected the creation-vs-evolution controversy concerns the JEDP Documentary Hypothesis. Still in active use by liberal seminaries, it teaches that the Book of Genesis wasn't written for several thousand years after the events it describes. Thus, the accounts of God's creation and the worldwide flood of Noah were simply stories, passed down for many centuries by word of mouth, and therefore must have been embroidered with a great deal of imaginative details. Let's look at this idea, and then describe a better explanation of Genesis authorship, called the Tablet Theory. A more complete comparison is in my article "Documents, Tablets, and the Historicity of Genesis."[15] We'll see how undercutting the historical accuracy affects the reader's understanding and beliefs.

THE JEDP DOCUMENTARY HYPOTHESIS

G.W.F. Hegel (1770-1831) was a German philosopher and historian who taught that civilization had developed gradually, and that writing wasn't common until about 1000 B.C. He said that primitive "cavemen" began a polytheistic worship of the things around them. Later, he said, higher concepts such as a supreme God evolved in people's minds and then modern religion had slowly developed.

Hegel built on an idea first proposed by Jean Astruc (1684-1766) and suggested that parts of Genesis began as documents from unknown writers sometime after 1000 B.C. and then were merged into the present form, maybe by Ezra. Hegel's student, K.H. Graf (1815-1868), and his student, Julius Wellhausen (1844-1918), refined this theory. Essentially it refers to four portions of the early Bible, each distinguished by the name used for God.

The J-Document is supposed to have used the name "Jehovah," while the E-Document used the name "Elohim." The D and P parts were named for Deuteronomic and Priestly. There's never been any kind of proof for this idea, and no one has ever claimed to find the evidence of those so-called documents; they're merely derived from reading the text of Genesis. The original basis for this theory was Hegel's teaching that writing didn't develop until about 1000 B.C. Of course, that is now known to be completely wrong — archaeologists have uncovered and translated entire libraries from Abraham's day, and some tablets from earlier than that. But once an idea gets accepted, it's hard to displace it.

THE TABLET THEORY

During his duty in Mesopotamia, where the early parts of the Bible were written, British Air Commodore P.J. Wiseman studied the archaeology of the area, and was struck by the format of many clay tablets found there. He recognized strong similarities to Genesis, and published a book in 1936. Later his son, Professor of Assyriology D.J. Wiseman, updated and revised his father's book. This describes the Tablet Theory of Genesis Authorship, which adds tremendously to the believability of those early portions of the Bible. He says:

> The book of Genesis was originally written on tablets in the ancient script of the time by the patriarchs who were intimately concerned with the events related, and whose names are clearly stated. Moreover, Moses, the compiler and editor of the book, as we now have it, plainly directs attention to the source of his information.[16]

Wiseman noticed that most of the ancient tablets ended with a "colophon phrase," which named the writer or owner of the tablet and gave some brief description of the subject matter. Many of these tablets concerned family history, while others were records of various commercial activities.

He noticed that these colophons bore striking resemblance to the Genesis phrases "These are the generations of. . . ." Here the word in the Hebrew text that's translated "generations" is toledoth, which means "history, especially family history . . . the story of their origin."[17]

He saw that if one realizes that these phrases mark the end of a Genesis portion that had originally been written as a clay tablet, the portion just prior to that phrase is a description of events that occurred within the lifetime of the man named in that phrase — events that he would be familiar with and probably wrote down for posterity. Most modern scholars have recognized that toledoth phrases were important, but have incorrectly assumed that they marked the beginning of a section. With this in mind, the tablet sections are shown in the table below. Each section ends with a toledoth phrase, "These are the generations of. . . ."

As an example of how the Tablet Theory can assist our understanding, consider the common accusation that a conflict exists between Genesis 1 and Genesis 2, in terms of the sequence of creative actions. This criticism is not valid, since Chapter 2 does not attempt to say "This happened and then that happened." This apparent conflict is partly because of peculiarities in words; it only shows up in some languages. The English language has definite past, present, and future tenses for its verbs, but Hebrew (the language of Genesis) does not. In Hebrew, the relative timing must be taken from the context, not the actual words themselves. In chapter 1, the timing is definitely stated — these events (creation of mammals and humans) took place on the sixth day, and in the order stated (animals, then man and woman). This chapter is written from the Creator's viewpoint (on His tablet), and outlines the exact things He did. His timing sequence is clearly stated.

Tablet Divisions

Tablet No.	Verses	Owner or Writer
1.	Gen. 1:1 through Gen. 2:4a	God?
2.	Gen. 2:4b through Gen. 5:1a	Adam
3.	Gen. 5:1b through Gen. 6:9a	Noah
4.	Gen. 6:9b through Gen. 10:1a	Shem & Ham & Japheth
5.	Gen. 10:1b through Gen. 11:10a	Shem
6.	Gen. 11:10b through Gen. 11:27a	Terah
7.	Gen. 11:27b through Gen. 25:19a	Isaac
8.	Gen. 25:12 through Gen. 25:18	Ishmael, through Isaac
9.	Gen. 25:19b through Gen. 37:2a	Jacob
10.	Gen. 36:1 through Gen. 36:43	Esau, through Jacob
11.	Gen. 37:2b through Exod. 1:6	Jacob's 12 sons

But there are no timing statements in chapter 2. This chapter is written from a different viewpoint (probably by Adam himself), and describes events as he saw them. He first told of the huge task that he had been given by God (naming all the animals) and how he did that. These verses show that Adam was a very intelligent person and a knowledgeable biologist, not the ignorant "caveman" that some people imagine.

The Hebrew words in Genesis 2:19 could have been translated, "And out of the ground the Lord God had formed every beast...." It seems to this writer that Adam simply put verses 19 and 20 (naming the animals) at this spot for his own convenience, not for indicating sequential action, so that he could then move on to the more pressing matter of the establishment of the human home, family, and population growth. He went on to describe the creation of his wife (which had happened previously), and then moved smoothly into their activities together.

JEDP OR TABLETS?

Since it's not possible for us to positively know just how the Book of Genesis was written, let's briefly compare, in an oversimplified way, the basis and effects of these two leading theories of biblical authorship.

THE JEDP THEORY was originated by people who were agnostics and did not believe in the Bible's authenticity.

It has been used in modern times to cast the Bible into the role of a collection of folk-tales.

It has been used to cast doubt on the validity of many biblical incidents. Many liberal Bible scholars openly doubt the truth of early Genesis.

But Jesus spoke as if early Genesis was true history. He referred more to events in Genesis than to any other part of the Old Testament.

The JEDP theory is not upheld by any sort of physical evidence, such as archaeological artifacts. No one has ever found the remains of a "document," and critics can't even agree on which portions of the Bible form one document.

THE TABLET THEORY, on the other hand, was originated by those who believed the Bible to be true.

It is based on real archaeological evidences — many ancient clay tablets (non-biblical) dug from the ruins of libraries used thousands of years ago.

It provides reasonable explanations for previously inexplicable stories and phrases, especially the "Toledoth" phrases, whose importance was recognized but not understood.

It leads to a belief in the Bible's historicity and authenticity, since it suggests that Genesis was written by eyewitnesses, and thus leads to a greater confidence in His Word.

Which of these theories of biblical authorship should I choose to believe? In the absence of overpowering proof as to which is more correct, it seems to this writer that the one leading toward God is better than the one leading away from

Him; the one leading to a stronger belief in His word is better than the one that often leads toward doubt. I'll go along with Joshua's basic line of reasoning — I'll choose to believe the Tablet Theory.

> Choose ye this day whom ye will serve . . .
> but as for me and my house, I will serve the Lord
> (Josh. 24:15).

RELIGIOUS ARGUMENTS AGAINST THEISTIC EVOLUTION

This next section is not intended to be a scientific argument; it's intended for those compromisers who have some religious appreciation, and may even be active church members, but who have been led to believe in theories such as theistic evolution, progressive creation, the gap theory, etc. It's also for the millions of good people who haven't studied the actual evidences, but who naturally accept the materialist explanations they've been exposed to by the secular majority.

This writer knows by personal experience the frustration that beliefs of this sort can cause, and now realizes that the only good starting point for knowing God is the Book that He gave us — the Bible.

Some say that belief in God's sudden miraculous creation, as described in Genesis, isn't all that important. I agree that creationism isn't the most vital doctrine of God's teachings; it's true that belief in creation can't save anyone; only a personal faith in Jesus' atoning sacrifice can do that. But just as His blood is like a scarlet thread tracing its way through the entire Bible, God's creation is like a multi-colored strand, giving a foundation for it all. If we take away that foundation, the rest of Christianity is on shaky ground — we must depend on human reason to decide which parts of the Bible to believe. Many people have had their faith badly damaged by attempting to compromise on this basic issue of God's miraculous recent creation.

IN THE BEGINNING GOD CREATED...

Genesis 1 and 2 describe how God, in just six days, created all of the wonderful things we see around us — earth, sky, light, stars, plants, trees, fish, birds, animals, and humans. There are dozens of references in all parts of the Bible that refer to creation. It never mentions any sort of evolutionary development. He spoke it into being, and immediately He saw that it was good.

Colossians 1:13-20 goes further, and shows that Jesus was the creative power in the Godhead. Paul wrote: "For by him [that is, Jesus] were all things created, that are in heaven, and that are in earth, visible and invisible . . . and by him all things consist (or hold together)."

Scholars all agree that if we take the simple primary meaning of all the Bible's words, the intention seems to show a sudden quick creation, in six real days, less than about 15,000 years ago. For example, Biology Professor P.P.T. Pun of Wheaton College (who does not accept sudden recent creation) said:

> It is apparent that the most straightforward understanding of the Genesis record, without regard to all the hermeneutical considerations suggested by science is that God created heaven and earth in six solar days. . . . However, the recent creationist position . . . has denied and belittled the vast amount of scientific evidence amassed to support the theory of natural selection and the antiquity of the earth.[18]

Many professors who are Christians, teaching in Christian schools, have fallen into the trap of supporting the so-called "truth" of science over the truth of Scripture. But they seem to neglect the fact that many Scriptures have to be twisted completely out of context to get an evolutionary meaning. And it seems to this writer, at least, that Pun's statement about the "vast amount of scientific evidence" neglects the vast amount of circular logic involved in arriving at this so-called evidence.

OTHER BIBLICAL REFERENCES

Jesus referred to events in the early parts of Genesis more than to those in any other part of the Old Testament. For example, Jesus said:

> Verily I say unto you, It shall be more tolerable for the land of Sodom and Gomorrah in the day of judgment, than for that city (Matt. 10:15).

He seems to say clearly that Sodom's destruction for its sin was a real fact of history, just as the Judgment Day will be real. Would he choose a folk legend to illustrate a coming event?

In Mark 10:6-9, Jesus was asked about divorce; He replied, "But from the beginning of the creation God made them male and female."

Notice that he said that the creation of male and female occurred at the beginning, not billions of years later.

In teaching about the end times of the world, Jesus compared the surprise that will overtake most people then to the surprise that overtook the people of Noah's day, in Luke 17:26,27:

> And as it was in the days of Noe, so shall it be also in the days of the Son of man. They did eat, they drank, they married wives, they were given in marriage, until the day that Noe entered into the ark, and the flood came, and destroyed them all (Luke 17:26-27).

Does that sound as if Jesus considered the Great Flood to have been just a local heavy rain? Wouldn't he have chosen a real fact of history to illustrate a real coming event? If we try to say that He simply spoke in the idiom of His day, we're changing the obvious meaning of His statements and denying the authority of Scripture. There are many other spots in the Bible that refer to early events of creation, or to Adam and his original sin, or to the Great Flood in Noah's day. These all refer to them as real, not figurative. Many of the vital truths of Christianity are directly connected to these early events; for example:

> Sin came into the world through one man and death through sin. . . . death reigned from Adam to Moses. . . . abundance of grace and the free gift of righteousness . . . through the one man Jesus Christ (Rom. 5:12-19).

If there was no recent creation, then there must have been millions of years of life and death for billions of creatures, and the man Adam must have been just a fable, and the fall of man (in Gen. 3) didn't really happen. Removing that explanation of the original entry of sin into the world would have terrible theological implications. And notice that Paul spoke as if both Adam and Jesus were real; if Adam was just a fable, was Jesus also a fable? God Forbid!

If we try to take away the truth of a six-day literal creation and the worldwide flood, then we are robbing the entire Bible of its truth and reliability.

CREATION EX NIHILO (out of nothing)

When God created this universe and all of its marvelously complex creatures, He didn't shape them from previously existing materials; He brought into being things that had never existed before — He spoke, and "a nothing became a something." The writer of Hebrews expressed it like this, in the opening of his famous chapter on faith:

> Now the just shall live by faith: but if any man draw back, my soul shall have no pleasure in him. . . . Now faith is the substance of things hoped for, the evidence of things not seen. . . . Through faith we understand that the worlds were framed

by the word of God, so that things which are seen were not made of things which do appear (Heb. 10:38-11:3).

The psalmist expressed it this way:

By the word of the Lord were the heavens made; and all the host of them by the breath of his mouth. . . . For he spake, and it was done; he commanded, and it stood fast (Ps. 33:6-9).

These are referring back to God's initial creation, where Genesis says over and over that "And God said . . . and it was so."

Genesis 1:3 — creation of light.
Genesis 1:6,7 — creation of the firmament.
Genesis 1:9 — separation of land mass and ocean.
Genesis 1:11 — creation of vegetation.
Genesis 1:14,15 — creation of the heavenly lights.
Genesis 1:20,21 — creation of aerial and aquatic animals.
Genesis 1:24 — creation of land animals.
Genesis 1:26 — creation of humans.

Nowhere is there a biblical suggestion that God somehow made these things by modifying things that were already there, as the theory of evolution demands. Nowhere does it suggest a gradual materialist origin, instead "He spoke, and it was done."

NATURE SHOWS GOD'S CREATION

The biblical Book of Romans is sometimes described as Paul's textbook of the mechanics of salvation. He shows that we all are guilty and that God provided a way to atone for that guilt. He contrasts law and grace, faith and works, and how to achieve that new life in Jesus Christ. He opens that textbook with the charge that nature itself gives us all an instinctive knowledge that God created everything we see around us. The Living Bible expresses this most clearly:

> But God shows his anger from heaven against all sinful, evil men who push away the truth from them. For the truth about God is known to them instinctively. God has put this knowledge in their hearts. Since earliest times men have seen the earth and sky and all God made, and have known of his existence and great eternal power. So they will have no excuse [when they stand before God at Judgment Day]. Yes, they knew about him all right, but they wouldn't admit it or worship him or even thank him for all his daily care. And after awhile they began to think up silly ideas of what God was like and what he wanted them to do. The result was that their foolish minds became dark and confused (Rom. 1:18-22).

This text then goes on to say that people wouldn't acknowledge God, but began to made their own idols and worship material things. Three times in the remainder of the chapter, it says that

"God gave them up . . ." to more and more degrading practices, and they began to suffer the penalties of their own actions.

The Old Testament's main accusation against the people was their idolatry — they substituted material "gods" for the living God of heaven. Isn't our praise of scientific materialism, that takes the place of praise of God's creative power, in that same category? Aren't we making idols of the material things around us, while saying that the creative power of God is outside of the realm of reality?

SIX LITERAL DAYS

Each of the days of creation is described as "the evening and the morning." This was obviously written to describe just one night/day period, not some indeterminately long age. If Day #3 lasted for millions of years, how could the plants have survived without sunlight (that didn't come until Day #4) or insects (those didn't come until Day #6)?

In Exodus 20:8-11 God instructs man to keep the Sabbath day, so as to commemorate the seventh day of creation week, when God rested after the creation. This is the fourth of the Ten Commandments. Verse 11 says: "For in six days the Lord made heaven and earth, the sea, and all that in them is, and rested the seventh day: wherefore the Lord blessed the sabbath day, and hallowed it."

The same word "day" is used in both spots, making it obvious that these two days were of the same sort.

True, there are many cases where "day" is used in the Bible to denote a general period of time, but never when there is a number associated with it, such as "the third day." The context is always clear if an indeterminate meaning is intended.

Some people mistakenly quote "one day is with the Lord as a thousand years," to try to say that the six days of creation might have been six long periods of time. But when they do that, they're picking that phrase out of context, thus changing the meaning. But read the entire passage in 2 Peter 3:3-13. He begins with a denunciation of scoffers, and seems to refer to the theory of uniformitarianism (in verse 4). He says that they "deliberately ignore . . . that by the word of God. . . ." He goes on to mention the Great Flood of Noah, refers to God's judgment, and then describes God's patience with man before final destruction. We must consider the full context of "one day is as a thousand years" — it refers to God's patience, not to His creation.

Finally, what natural phenomenon accounts for our six-day week? All other time measurements are related in some way to the movements of heavenly bodies. A day is the time required for one rotation of the earth, an hour is 1/24 of a day, a month is the approximate time for one orbit of the moon, and a year is the time for an earth orbit around the sun. But what about the week? No one has come up with an explanation for that, other than the one suggested in the Bible — the six days of creation plus the one day of rest. Many commands of God about rules of conduct and worship referred to specific days of the week. Henry Morris tells us that:

> Leaders of the French Revolution of 1789 and the Russian Revolution of 1917 both tried to lengthen the work week, hoping thereby to get rid of the theological implications of the seven-day week. Both had to abandon their experiment after a few years because human nature and physiology couldn't cope with it. Thus, they inadvertently confirmed both the importance of the fourth commandment and the truth of the biblical account of creation.[19]

THE TIME SCALE

Look at the fifth chapter of Genesis. This relates the exact number of years from Adam's creation until the birth of Noah. In each generation, there is an arithmetic cross-check. For example, Seth lived 105 years before Enosh was born, then he lived 807 years, and died at the age of 912 years. This kind of sequence is continuous, and shows a total of 1,656 years, according to the Masoretic text. If God was so careful with numbers, doesn't that show their importance?

Now look at Genesis 11:10-12:4. A very similar description of the timing between the flood and Abraham is given. It shows that Abraham was born just over 300 years after the flood. Some critics speak of gaps, but the text of the Bible does not contain gaps. There's no question but that a simple reading of the Bible clearly describes a creation less than 8,000 years ago, and a worldwide flood less than 2,000 years later.

It's true that Bible scholars don't agree on the exact numbers for this ancient history. There are several factors that enter into those differences. A number of these factors are discussed in my article "Biblical Chronologies Compared" in the Winter 1995 issue of *Bible and Spade*.

But there's no way that the million- and billion-year dates used by secular science can fit the Bible, except by completely disregarding the clear biblical teaching.

BIBLICAL DINOSAURS

Many people have asked, "Well, if dinosaurs lived at the same time as people, why aren't they mentioned in the Bible?" One answer is that the word "dinosaur" wasn't invented until 1841, so obviously that word can't be in the Bible. That word means "terrible lizard." But dinosaurs are mentioned by other names.

For example, Genesis 1:21 says that God made "great sea monsters." And Job 40 and 41 give descriptions of a couple of monsters. In Job 40:15-24 we read about "behemoth" — a very large vegetarian that lived both on land and in water:

> Behold, behemoth, which I made as I made you; he eats grass like an ox. Behold, his strength in his loins, and his power in the muscles of his belly. He makes his tail stiff like a cedar; the sinews of his thighs are knit together. His bones are tubes of bronze, his limbs like bars of iron. . . . Behold, if the river is turbulent he is not frightened; he is confident though Jordan rushes against his mouth. Can one take him with hooks, or pierce his nose with a snare? (RSV).

Many scholars have said this section must refer to the hippopotamus, but does that large animal have a tail like a cedar? No, this must be describing a huge creature, perhaps a sauropod of some sort.

Let's look at the description of leviathan. This one is more fearsome than behemoth — it sounds like a fire-breathing dragon!

> Can you draw out leviathan with a fishhook, or press down his tongue with a cord? Can you put a rope in his nose, or pierce his jaw with a hook? ... Can you fill his skin with harpoons, or his head with fishing spears? Lay hands on him; think of the battle; you will not do it again! ... Who can strip off his outer garment? Who can penetrate his double coat of mail? Who can open the doors of his face? Round about his teeth is terror. His back is made of rows of shields, shut up closely as with a seal. One is so near to another that no air can come between them. ... His sneezings flash forth light, and his eyes are like the eyelids of the dawn. Out of his mouth go flaming torches, sparks of fire leap forth. Out of his nostrils comes forth smoke, as from a boiling pot and burning rushes. His breath kindles coals, and a flame comes forth from his mouth. ... When he raises himself up the mighty are afraid; at the crashing they are beside themselves. ... Upon earth there is not his like, a creature without fear. He beholds everything that is high; he is king over all the sons of pride (Job 41:1-34;RSV).

Some scholars say this must be talking about crocodiles, but that would be a poor description; do crocodiles breathe smoke and fire? This sounds much more like some huge carnivorous dinosaur — possibly a tyrannosaur.

What about the fire-breathing part? Is that possible? It's interesting to note that many stories from ancient history (such as those involving Sir Lancelot and the knights of the Round Table) involve fire-breathing dragons; this doesn't prove the point, but most legends do have some basis in fact.

And there is at least one insect today that could qualify — the bombardier beetle, brachinus. Its body contains reservoirs for hydroquinone and hydrogen peroxide, together with an inhibitor and two special enzymes, that it uses to squirt at its enemies; when these unite, a very hot and smoky reaction takes place, and the enemies are burned. The full story on these marvelous beetles can be read in a wonderful book that children can enjoy by Duane T. Gish, entitled *The Amazing Story of Creation from Science and the Bible*.[20] This book is highly recommended for every family to read; it uses accurate scientific terminology in an easily readable format.

Several dinosaurs such as corythosaurus had reservoirs in the top of their heads; these had passages connected to their mouths. Their function is completely unknown, because none of the fleshy parts are preserved, but it's quite possible that they were chemical chambers to serve a function similar to that used by the bombardier beetle. They may well be examples of "fire- breathing dragons," and it's quite possible that some of their members may have still been around in King Arthur's day.

It's interesting to note that many creatures once thought to have been extinct for millions of years have been discovered, alive and flourishing, in little-known parts of the world. For example, the horse-sized paleotragus was thought to have disappeared some 30,000 years ago, but in 1901 whole herds were discovered living in central Africa. Also, within recent decades, a number of people have told of large strange creatures in Africa. They've identified drawings of the apatosaurus dinosaur as being most similar to what they've seen.

In 1977, Japanese fishermen netted the corpse of a Plesiosaurus (not a true dinosaur, but a "sea dragon" that lived during those same times) in the South Pacific. The body was photographed, identified by biologists, and samples of its flesh were taken and later identified as reptilian. The

U.S. news media (which is dominated by the evolutionist establishment) has largely ignored this, but other publications the world over gave it much publicity; the Japanese postal service even issued a special plesiosaurus stamp in 1977, commemorating the "discovery of the year." It does seem quite reasonable to say that the dinosaurs may not have become completely extinct, after all.

Endnotes

[1]Thaxton, Bradley and Olsen, *The Mystery of Life's Origin: Reassessing Current Theories* (New York, NY: Philosophical Library, 1984).

[2]Tom Bethell, "Agnostic Evolutionists," *Harper's Magazine*, February 1985, p. 52.

[3]Dr. H.S. Lipson, "A Physicist Looks at Evolution," *Physics Bulletin*, Vol. 31, 1980.

[4]Dr. George Wald, quoted by Dennis Lindsay, *The Dinosaur Dilemma*, 1982, p. 4-14.

[5]Sir Julian Huxley, quoted in "Evolution and Genetics," edited by J.R. Newman, *What Is Science?* (New York, NY: Simon and Schuster, 1955).

[6]Phillip E. Johnson, *Darwin on Trial* (Washington, D.C: Regnery Gateway, 1991), p. 7.

[7]Ibid., p. 8-9.

[8]*Encyclopaedia Britannica*, 1949 edition, Volume 20, page 81-d, "Scholasticism."

[9]Etienne Gilson, *The Philosophy of St. Thomas Aquinas* (New York, NY: Dorset Press, 1929).

[10]*Encyclopaedia Brittanica*, "Luther, Martin," 1949 Edition, Volume 14, p. 492-b.

[11]Gilson, *Philosophy of St. Thomas Aquinas*, p. 187.

[12]Werner Georg Kummel, *The Theology of the New Testament* (Nashville, TN: Abingdon, 1973), p. 14.

[13]Eta Linnemann, *Historical Criticism of the Bible: Methodology or Ideology?* (Grand Rapids, MI: Baker Book House, 1991), p. 17-20

[14]Ibid., p. 107.

[15]Curt Sewell, "Documents, Tablets, and the Historicity of Genesis," *Bible and Spade*, Vol.7, No.1, Winter 1994.

[16]P.J. Wiseman, *Ancient Records and the Structure of Genesis* (Nashville, TN: Thomas Nelson, Inc., 1985), p. 20.

[17]Ibid., p. 62.

[18]*Journal of the American Scientific Affiliation*, March 1987, p. 14, cited by Henry M. Morris in "Christ and the Time of Creation," in the Institute for Creation Research's *Acts and Facts*, October 1994, p. c.

[19]Henry M. Morris, *The Bible, Science & Creation* (Santee, CA: Institute for Creation Research, 1991), p. 21.

[20]Duane T. Gish, *The Amazing Story of Creation from Science and the Bible* (El Cajon, CA: Institute for Creation Research, 1990), p. 96-101.

Notes

Notes

EPILOGUE

WHAT DOES GOD EXPECT OF US?

HOW DO WE FIND HIS PEACE?

Discussion of scientific evidences and biblical references may be interesting, but they don't do us any long-term personal good unless we each apply them to our own lives. God created us, so He owns us; thus we're responsible to Him, and the Bible says that one day He will judge us. What does He expect from us?

1. God loves you and has a great plan for you.

> For God so loved the world, that He gave His only begotten Son, that whoever believes in Him should not perish, but have eternal life (John 3:16).

> [Jesus said] "I came that they might have life, and might have it more abundantly" (John 10:10).

2. But why doesn't everyone experience that more abundant life? Because we all have a sin-nature, and that separates us from God. We're all egocentric — our natural tendency is to put ourselves ahead of God, and the end result will be eternal hell.

For all have sinned and fall short of the glory of God (Rom. 3:23).

For the wages of sin is death (Rom. 6:23).

3. The only way to bridge that separation is through God's Son, Jesus Christ. He gave himself as a sacrifice to pay the penalty for our sins.

Jesus said to him, "I am the way, and the truth, and the life; no one comes to the Father, but through Me"(John 14:6).

But God demonstrates His love toward us, in that, while we were yet sinners, Christ died for us (Rom. 5:8).

4. This is not an automatic process that God arranged for everyone; it's a personal choice — we must each deliberately choose to receive Jesus as Saviour and Lord so as to make this effective in our own lives.

[Jesus said] "Behold, I stand at the door and knock; if any one hears My voice and opens the door, I will come in to him" (Rev. 3:20).

But as many as received Him [that is, Jesus], to them He gave the right to become children of God, even to those who believe in His name (John 1:12).

5. Receiving Jesus means that we must turn from our ego-centered life, repent of our sins (including the sin of rejecting His creation), accept Jesus' sacrifice as applying to us, and pray something like this:

Oh God, I need You. Please forgive me. Thank You for Jesus' death on the cross so as to pay the penalty for my sins. I open the door of my life to You, and receive You as my Lord and

Saviour. Thank You for saving me, and for giving me eternal life. Please take control of me, and make me the sort of person You want me to be.

In Jesus' name, Amen.

6. When you sincerely pray this, God will answer that prayer "Yes." You will be "born again" into His family; you'll be a new creation. That's what it means to be a Christian.

After you do that, you should maintain your fellowship with God by daily prayer and Bible study. Find other Christians so you can grow together. Begin attending a Bible-believing Church. You'll be amazed at how much richer and happier your life will be, with Jesus beside you and helping you.

BOOKS FOR FURTHER READING

This is not at all a complete list — just some that I've read and recommend. Some of these criticize the theory of evolution; some recommend the theory of creation. Some are by Christians; some are by non-Christians. None of them are what you could call impartial (actually, almost all books push some viewpoint). These are arranged alphabetically by author. Most of these are in my home library and thus the publication data given here are not necessarily the latest versions.

• Ackerman, Paul D., *It's a Young World After All: Exciting Evidences for Recent Creation* (Grand Rapids, MI: Baker Book House, 1986). The author has a Ph.D. in psychology and teaches at Wichita State University. He's a Christian and a scientific creationist. His book is easily read, well-arranged, and presents many technical evidences that the earth is not actually millions of years old.

• Austin, Steven A., *Grand Canyon: Monument to Catastrophe* (Santee, CA: Institute for Creation Research, 1994). Dr. Austin has a Ph.D. in geology and is chairman of the geology department at the Institute for Creation Research Graduate School. He has made a number of significant contributions to creationist geology. This book is beautifully illustrated, and explains a lot about the geology of the Grand Canyon area, the strata exposed, and how it was probably carved. He explains conventional beliefs, and why the creationist view is better.

• Bergman, Jerry, *The Criterion: Religious Discrimination in America* (Richfield, MN: Onesimus Publishing, 1984). Dr. Bergman was a professor at Bowling Green State University, was considered to be an excellent teacher and authored a number of published papers. He was never accused of teaching religion in classes, but was terminated because of his religious (creationist) views. He documents the cases of dozens of others, mostly teachers, who have received similar treatment within the last few years. I've read it; it makes you think.

• Brown, Walter T., Jr., *In the Beginning* (Phoenix, AZ: Center for Scientific Creation, 1989). This book is used as the framework for seminars the author has presented. It's well organized, listing over a hundred evidences that favor the concept of God's creation and the worldwide flood as a better explanation of our world than is evolution. The book is valuable for its large number of quotations from scientific books and journals. There is also a well-thought-out explanation of a possible meaning of the phrase "the fountains of the deep," and how these operated as a trigger for Noah's flood, with its devastation of the world of that time.

• Chittick, Donald E., *The Controversy: Roots of the Creation-Evolution Conflict* (Portland, OR: Multnomah Press, 1984). The author has a Ph.D. in physical chemistry, and is a university professor, writer, and lecturer on creation/evolution. He describes the religious and philosophical background of this controversy, and discusses a number of evidences.

• Davis, Kenyon, and Thaxton, *Of Pandas and People: The Central Question of Biological Origins* (Dallas, TX: Haughton Publishing Co., 1989). This is intended as a supplementary biology textbook. It presents evidence unfavorable to evolution theory, but has no religious content. It covers six areas: 1) Origin of Life, 2) Genetics, 3) Origin of Species, 4) Fossil Record, 5) Homology, and 6) Biochemical Similarities. Each of these subjects is presented in separate chapters in "overview" style and also in "in-depth" style, so that instructors can tailor reading assignments to fit the class.

• Denton, Michael, *Evolution: A Theory in Crisis* (London: Burnett Books, 1985). Dr. Denton is an Australian medical researcher, a religious agnostic, not a creationist. This book contains his criticisms of evolution theory from a technical viewpoint. It has been widely acclaimed as a devastating blow against the possibility that life may have developed by evolution.

• DeYoung, Donald, *Astronomy and the Bible* (Grand Rapids, MI: Baker Book House, 1988). Dr. DeYoung teaches physics and astronomy at Grace College, Winona Lake, Indiana. He's also adjunct professor at Institute for Creation Research, and is a past editor of the *Creation Research Society Quarterly*. This book is arranged as 100 questions and answers. His approach is a good compromise between technical detail and easy reading.

• DeYoung, Donald, *Astronomy and Creation: An Introduction* (Ashland, OH: Creation Research Society Books, 1995). This short, easy-to-read book describes answers to five common questions about the universe, written from the creationist viewpoint. These include Origins, Order, Structure, Time Scale, and Change. Three short essays include some suggestions for research.

• Faid, Robert W., *A Scientific Approach to Biblical Mysteries* (Green Forest, AR: New Leaf Press, 1993). An interesting and easy-to-read book, this is not primarily a study of the creation vs. evolution controversy, but shows the truth of many biblical incidents that scoffers have used to cause doubts in many people's minds. A number of new scientific studies are included, and verify the biblical account.

• Gentry, Robert V., *Creation's Tiny Mystery* (Knoxville, TN: Earth Science Assoc., 1986). This book describes the author's research, mostly at Oak Ridge National Lab, and discusses pleochroic halos — tiny spherical discolorations found in micas and granites. These are caused by radiation damage from alpha particles emanating from grains of radioactive material in the rock. Most of these come from uranium, but in many cases there is no uranium present. These "mystery" halos were proven to be caused by polonium, which has an extremely short half-life. Since rock must be hard to form halos, this is a very strong evidence that the rock did not slowly cool from magma, but must have been formed in situ in an already-hardened form. I consider this book to give the most convincing evidence that the earth was suddenly created, not formed by a slow evolutionary process. This book also documents a number of cases of bias against those scientists who, like Gentry, hold views that are contrary to those of the "establishment." His testimony as an expert witness at the Arkansas creation/evolution textbook trial led to the loss of his research grant.

• Gish, Duane, *Creation Scientists Answer Their Critics* (El Cajon, CA: Institute for Creation Research. 1993). Dr. Gish is the leading spokesman for scientific creationism, and has therefore been the person most widely criticized by evolutionists. This book is his response to those criticisms. He discusses scientific evidences such as thermodynamics and the fossil record. As such, it is a valuable sourcebook for the details of those evidences. He also addresses specific books written by scientists who have shown much animosity in their criticism of him personally. He quotes rather extensively from their writings, showing either that they have misquoted him or that their arguments lack validity. It makes interesting reading, although some of the discussions get rather technical.

• Gish, Duane, *Evolution: Challenge of the Fossil Record* (Green Forest, AR: Master Books). Dr. Gish is a well-known biochemist and creationist debater, associated with the Institute for Creation Research. This book describes many fossil evidences that indicate creation is a better explanation for life as we know it. I consider this to be an excellent sourcebook. This is a revision of his popular *Evolution? The Fossils Say No!*

• Gish, Duane, *Teaching Creation Science in Public Schools* (El Cajon, CA: Institute for Creation Research, 1995). This provides semi-technical descriptions of the evidences in the creation vs. evolution controversy, and tells

270

the legal aspects of teaching creationism in public schools.

• Ham, Ken, *The Lie: Evolution and Genesis and the Decay of the Nations,* (Green Forest, AR: Master Books, 1987 and 1991). Mr. Ham was the organizer of the Back-to-Genesis Seminars sponsored by the Institute for Creation Research. He's a popular speaker and writer. These two books are easily read, and present the need for belief in the literal truth of the Bible. Most of his arguments use religious logic, not technical.

• Ham, Ken, Andrew Snelling, and Carl Wieland, *The Answers Book* (Sunnybank, Queensland, Australia: Creation Science Foundation Ltd., 1990). Discusses 12 basic questions, related to both biblical and scientific aspects of belief in literal creationism.

• Ham, Ken and Paul Taylor, *The Genesis Solution* (Green Forest, AR: Master Books, 1988). Mr. Ham was formerly active in the Australian creationist movement, but is now associated with Answers in Genesis in Florence, Kentucky. He is a good writer, and his books are illustrated with interesting cartoon-style drawings. This book is meant to accompany a video of the same name.

• Helfinstine, Robert, and Jerry Roth, *Texas Tracks and Artifacts* (Anoka, MN, and Zimmerman, MN: Helfinstine and Roth, 1994). This book is a report, commissioned by the Bible-Science Association, on evidences and controversies surrounding the many dinosaur tracks and human-like tracks found in the same strata of the Paluxy River. They both look real.

• Hitching, Francis, *The Neck of the Giraffe: Where Darwin Went Wrong* (New Haven, CT: Ticknor and Fields, 1982). Also (London: Pan Books, 1982). Dr. Hitching is a scientist at the Royal Institute of Archaeology in England. My understanding is that he is not a creationist, but that this book describes a number of evidences showing evolution to be a poor explanation for life development. I haven't read this book, but have seen it referred to in a number of other places.

271

• Humphreys, D. Russell, *Starlight and Time* (Green Forest, AR: Master Books, 1994). Dr. Humphreys holds a Ph.D. in physics. This important book describes his new theory, first presented at the Third International Conference on Creationism, using the laws of General Relativity and its *gravitational time dilation*. It shows that it's possible that the six days of creation, measured on earth, could be equivalent to billions of years in the distant cosmos. This could take place, given special initial conditions that were first noticed in a careful study of the Bible, then applied to General Relativity.

• Huse, Scott M., *The Collapse of Evolution* (Grand Rapids, MI: Baker Book House, 1993). This introductory book is simple to read, and presents many evidences intended to persuade those who are not familiar with the facts. It makes a fairly strong case in favor of creation instead of the more commonly-believed evolution theory. It would probably be good for high school students, but is lacking in detailed technical discussion and some parts are not well explained.

• Johnson, Phillip E., *Darwin on Trial* (Washington, DC: Regnery Gateway, 1991). Johnson is Professor of Law at the University of California at Berkeley. He examines the evidences and the logic involved in various segments of Darwinist theory and application, and concludes that it wouldn't stand up in a court of law. He shows the religious basis for macro-evolution theory, and how its naturalistic materialism tends to rule out the existence of God.

• Lubenow, Marvin L., *Bones of Contention* (Grand Rapids, MI: Baker Book House, 1992). Lubenow, a theologian and anthropologist, spent 25 years in the study of paleoanthropology. This book contains probably the most complete listings of the 4,000 hominid fossils, as well as descriptions of where and how they were found, and the controversies involved in their dating and classification. His conclusion is that humans did not descend from an ape-like ancestor. This book is a valuable resource, that should be read by everyone interested in paleoanthropology.

• Macbeth, Norman, *Darwin Retried: An Appeal to Reason* (Ipswich, MA: Gambit Publishers, 1971). Macbeth, an attorney, took an interest in the logical aspects of evolution science. Not a scientist, he read several well-known science textbooks and concluded that the reasoning used to support belief in evolution was faulty. He refers to evolution as a "tautology," or as "circular reasoning." I enjoyed this book; it's well-written, well-documented, and very informative.

• McDowell, Josh, *More Than A Carpenter* (Wheaton, IL: Tyndale House Publishers, 1973). This book doesn't touch the creation/evolution question, but I've included it because I enjoyed his logical description of why we can believe the Bible is true, and how Jesus, the Son of God, really did come to earth to die for our sins.

• Morris, Henry, *Men of Science, Men of God* (Green Forest, AR: Master Books, 1982). This book refutes the common idea that "all the good scientists believed in evolution." To show that fallacy, it gives brief (1/3 to 1 page) biographies of about a hundred scientists and educators, all of whom were devout godly men. Many of these actively opposed Darwinism and were young-earth creationists, and most are known as founding fathers of branches of scientific knowledge. These include Newton, Linnaeus, Faraday, Babbage, Herschel, Morse, Joule, Agassiz, Mendel, Pasteur, Lord Kelvin, Maxwell, and many others.

• Morris, Henry M., *Scientific Creationism* (Green Forest, AR: Master Books) This book argues the case for creation from both a religious and a scientific viewpoint. It is a good summary of the various evidences on both sides. Dr. Morris is president of the Institute for Creation Research, and has been active in the cause of creationism since its modern beginnings.

• Morris, Henry M. and John C. Whitcomb, *The Genesis*

Flood (Green Forest, AR: Master Books, 1970). This is the book that is credited with starting the modern scientific creationist movement. Dr. Morris was head of the Department of Civil Engineering at Virginia Polytechnic Institute and Dr. Whitcomb was professor of Old Testament at Grace Theological Seminary. The book discusses both geological and biblical aspects for and against the possibility of the worldwide flood of Noah, and concludes that it was not only possible, but probable.

• Morris, Henry M., *The Genesis Record* (Grand Rapids, MI: Baker Book House; and San Diego, CA: Creation-Life Publishers, 1976). This comprehensive verse-by-verse commentary on the Book of Genesis is written from the position of belief in the literal truth and inspiration of this biblical book of beginnings. Many inspirational and devotional explanations are included. Over 700 pages, it includes maps, appendices, and several comprehensive indexes.

• Morris, Henry M., *The Long War Against God* (Grand Rapids, MI: Baker Books, 1989). This well-documented book shows how Satan, from the earliest historical times, has waged a war against God, trying to lead people away from God by using evolution and other materialist philosophies. Much of this warfare has been conducted from within the ranks of the Christian Church.

• Morris, John D., *Noah's Ark and the Lost World* (Green Forest, AR: Master Books, 1988). This hard-cover large-page book is beautifully illustrated with both photos and paintings. It is intended primarily for children, but I found it fascinating. Using both biblical and scientific language, it explains a number of questions about the pre-flood earth, the great flood of Noah, dinosaurs and other animals, the ark, and modern sightings of the ark. The book includes color photos which the author himself took during his trips to Mount Ararat. He briefly describes some of his experiences in climbing that dangerous mountain.

• Morris, John D., *Adventure on Ararat* (San Diego,

CA: Institute for Creation Research, 1973). This is a fascinating account of Dr. Morris' climb of Mount Ararat, in eastern Turkey, in search of the remains of Noah's ark. He vividly describes storms, wild animal attacks, and being almost killed by rock slides and lightning. He also documents a number of the recent sightings of the ark, and describes why it is believed that the ark is now frozen into a glacier near the top of the mountain.

• Morris, John D., *Tracking Those Incredible Dinosaurs and the People Who Knew Them*, (San Diego, CA: CLP Publishers, 1980). This describes the history and modern status (as of 1980) of the dinosaur and human footprints that are found in the same strata in the rocks of the Paluxy riverbed in Texas. There has been continued controversy as to the genuineness of the human tracks, but many people believe that this area furnishes proof of the co-existence of humans and dinosaurs.

• Petersen, Dennis R., *Unlocking the Mysteries of Creation* (El Dorado, CA: Creation Resource Foundation, 1990). This is a beautiful book, lavishly illustrated with photos and drawings. It's divided into four basic sections, Early Earth, Evolution, Original Man and Missing Links, and Ancient Civilizations. Each section has many subsections, each designed to show that the biblical account is more reasonable than the secular beliefs that oppose them. Most of the arguments are based on scientific evidences, and are written in an easy-to-understand manner. It's ideal for use in a family discussion or in Christian schools.

• Pitman, Michael, *Adam and Evolution* (London: Rider, 1984; and Grand Rapids, MI: Baker Book House, 1987). Pitman was instructor in biology at Cambridge. The book discusses life forms, mostly from the biologist's point of view. He finds many reasons to explain how evolutionary changes from one form to another are so unlikely as to be virtually impossible. He uses similar arguments to show that life couldn't have originated from chemical evolution. He doesn't sound like a typical fundamentalist Christian creationist (but he doesn't say). One sentence is interesting, "I started as devil's advocate for the creationist view and came, in principle, though not according to any particular creed, to prefer it."

• Sunderland, Luther D., *Darwin's Enigma: Fossils and Other Problems* (Green Forest, AR: Master Books, 1988). This book is based on interviews that Sunderland conducted with five leading scientists — Colin Patterson, Niles Eldredge, David Raup, David Pilbeam, and Donald Fisher — all acknowledged experts and officials of natural history museums. The general subject was fossils and how they support (or don't support) the theory of evolution. Dr. Michael Denton said, about this book: "This book does more than any other publication that I am aware of to highlight the fact that leading scientific authorities in evolutionary biology express considerable skepticism over many aspects of evolution, while school texts present the theory as proven beyond reasonable doubt."

• Taylor, Ian T., *In the Minds of Men: Darwin and the New World Order* (Toronto, Canada: TFE Publishing, 1987). I consider this to be one of the best books I've ever read on this subject. He gives a very good historical and philosophical background for the growth of scientific thought, and the differences between the creation and evolution viewpoints. It also includes good descriptions of many scientific evidences favoring the creationist position.

• Taylor, Paul S., *The Great Dinosaur Mystery and the Bible* (Denver, CO: Accent Books, 1989). This is a beautifully illustrated children's book. It tells a lot about dinosaurs, and how the biblical explanation fits the facts better than does the popular evolutionist story that students learn in school.

• Thaxton, C.B., W.L. Bradley, and R.L. Olsen, *The Mystery of Life's Origin: Reassessing Current Theories* (New York, NY: Philosophical Library, 1984). This is a very important book. It discusses the theory of biochemical evolution (that life supposedly originated from chemicals in a "primordial soup" ocean). It describes current "origin of life" experiments and shows major shortcomings. It also discusses evidences of the early atmosphere of earth, and shows how unsuitable it was for life to have evolved. One of the chapters is titled "The Myth of the Prebiotic Soup." At least one of the authors is a creationist, but they hide that so well that I had to learn it from other sources.

• Van Bebber, Mark and Paul Taylor, *Creation and Time: A Report on the Progressive Creationist Book by Hugh Ross* (Mesa, AZ: Eden Communications, 1994). This is an unusual book, in that it was written specifically to debunk another book, and the teaching of "progressive creation" that that book espouses. That teaching has been popularized as a compromise between secular science and biblical Christianity. It claims to follow the Bible, but actually introduces many distortions into the biblical account. Van Bebber and Taylor document 46 claims made by Ross in his book, and show that these claims are not true, or that they violate scriptural integrity.

• Whitcomb, John and Donald DeYoung, *The Moon: Its Creation, Form and Significance* (Winona Lake, IN: BMH Books, 1978). I learned a lot from this book. It describes the physical and astronomical makeup of the moon, its geology, surface features, and exploration history. Many of the results of the Apollo moon landings are discussed. It tells of various secular theories of its formation, and how they all fail to explain important aspects. It discusses the biblical account of its formation, and shows that this is most reasonable.

• Wilder-Smith, A.E., *Man's Origin, Man's Destiny* (Wheaton, IL: H. Smith Publishers, 1984). Dr. Wilder-Smith has a worldwide reputation as a philosopher, scientist, and creationist writer. He is said to hold five earned Ph.D. degrees.

• Wilder-Smith, A.E., *He Who Thinks Has To Believe* (Minneapolis, MN: Bethany House Publishers, 1981). If you can get through the first three chapters, a lengthy allegorical-philosophical story, the rest of this little book gives a good philosophical argument that establishes the logic of the Christian religion. It begins by showing how design in nature demands a Creator. From there, it shows that such a Creator must be personal, must require that man be reconciled to himself before fellowship can be established, and must have become man himself to accomplish that.

Modern Creation Trilogy

Volume I - Scripture and Creation
Volume II - Science and Creation
Volume III - Society and Creation

Dr. Henry M. Morris
and Dr. John D. Morris

The definitive work on the study of origins, from a creationist perspective, *The Modern Creation Trilogy* examines the evidences for both evolution and special creation. Authored by the prolific father-son research team of Henry and John Morris, this three-volume gift set is a "must-have" for those who believe the Bible is God's plain-spoken Word.

Volume I looks at what the Bible says about origins — man, animal, planet, and universe. Volume II studies the scientific evidences for evolution and creation, contending that the evidence favors creation, since none of us were there in the beginning. Volume III sheds light on the fruits of each worldview — which stance produces better results for all creation? Interest level: Adult.. CD Rom included.

ISBN: 0-89051-216-7
Gift-boxed set of three • Paperback • 5-1/4 x 8-1/2 • $44.95